Cultural Worlds of Early Childhood

Edited by Martin Woodhead,
Dorothy Faulkner and
Karen Littleton

Routledge
Taylor & Francis Group

LONDON AND NEW YORK

in association with The Open University

First published 1998
by Routledge
11 New Fetter Lane, London EC4P 4EE

Reprinted 2003

Routledge is an imprint of the Taylor & Francis Group

© 1998 The Open University
Compilation, original and editorial matter

Typeset in Garamond by RefineCatch Limited, Bungay, Suffolk
Printed and bound in Great Britain by
TJ International Ltd, Padstow, Cornwall

British Library Cataloguing in Publication Data
A catalogue record for this book is available from the British Library

Library of Congress Cataloguing in Publication Data
Cultural worlds of early childhood / edited by Martin Woodhead,
    Dorothy Faulkner, and Karen Littleton.
        p.   cm.
    Includes bibliographical references and index.
    1. Child development.   2. Early childhood education.
I. Woodhead, Martin.   II. Faulkner, Dorothy.   III. Littleton, Karen.
HQ772.C85   1998
305.231 – dc21   98–14104
                                                              CIP

ISBN 0–415–17372–8

Cultural Worlds of Early Childhood

Child Development in Families, Schools and Society I

The companion volumes in this series are:

Learning Relationships in the Classroom
Edited by Dorothy Faulkner, Karen Littleton and Martin Woodhead

Making Sense of Social Development
Edited by Martin Woodhead, Dorothy Faulkner and Karen Littleton

These three readers are the core study material for students taking the course ED840 Child Development in Families, Schools and Society. This course may be taken as part of the Open University MA in Education programme. The course may also be taken as part of the Open University MSc in Psychology.

The Open University MA in Education

The Open University MA in Education is now firmly established as the most popular postgraduate degree for education professionals in Europe, with over 3500 students registering each year. The MA in Education is designed particularly for those with experience of teaching, the advisory service, educational administration or allied fields.

Structure of the MA

The MA is a modular degree and students are therefore free to select from a range of options the programme that best fits in with their interests and professional goals. Study in the Open University's Advanced Diploma and Certificate in Continuing Professional Development programmes may also be counted towards the MA. Successful completion of the MA in Education entitles students to apply for entry into the Open University Doctorate in Education (EdD) programme.

OU supported open learning

The MA in Education programme provides great flexibility. Students study at their own pace, in their own time, anywhere in the European Union. They receive specially prepared study materials, are supported by tutorials, and have opportunities to work with other students.

How to apply

The Professional Development in Education prospectus contains further information and application forms. To request your copy please write to the Course Reservations and Sales Centre, The Open University, PO Box 625, Walton Hall, Milton Keynes MK7 6AA.

Contents

Illustrations

Figures

Tables

Acknowledgements

We would like to thank the authors who contributed their chapters, as well as colleagues within and outside The Open University who gave advice on the contents. Special thanks are due to Helen Boyce (Course Manager), Bronwen Sharp and Christine Golding (Course Secretaries) and Jenny Monk (Copublishing) for their assistance in the production of this book.

The Open University would like to thank all those who have granted permission to reproduce copyright material in this volume. The publishers have made every effort to contact copyright holders with regard to permission to reproduce articles and will be happy to handle any queries relating to these.

Introduction

Chapters in this selection are united by the view that child development is a cultural process, in two senses. Firstly, children's development is cultural, in so far as they inhabit an environment constructed through centuries of human endeavour, and they are encouraged to participate in culturally defined ways of talking, behaving, thinking and feeling, mediated through their relationships with other, generally more experienced cultural actors. Secondly, 'Child Development' is itself culturally constructed. As a body of theoretical knowledge and research descriptions, Child Development reflects a minority of world childhoods, based mainly on North American and European children as studied from the perspective of North American and European researchers. In this selection, we aim to offer a more balanced account, setting dominant images of the goals and processes of early development within a broader cultural framework.

Studying child development in social and cultural contexts cuts through the conventional demarcation between cognitive, social and emotional development. Relationships provide the foundation of emotional security, the context for early learning and the mediating process of cultural influence. Even quite young children are skilful in negotiating a diverse repertoire of relationships, from imaginative, playful encounters with their peers to didactic exchanges with their preschool teachers. For the most part, authors of these chapters see children not as passive products of socialization, but as actively contributing to the process of their own development, at the same time recognizing that their status and power as social actors varies between contexts and between cultures.

The case for a more cultural approach to developmental psychology is set out in Chapter 1. Cole summarizes some conventional ways of theorizing about the question 'What are the major influences on a child's development?' He rejects dichotomies between nature and nurture, heredity and environment, maturation and learning, by adding in a further, fundamental ingredient – culture. The environment for child development is a social environment, peopled by others, mediated by cultural beliefs, values and practices and amplified by the cultural tools and artefacts into which children are initiated –

everything from eating with a spoon, reading and writing, to accessing the Internet. Cole argues that psychologists have neglected culture because the discipline is founded on a belief in human 'psychic unity' that can be revealed by empirical research. Cross-cultural studies have held marginal status, mainly applying Western concepts and experimental paradigms to test for universality. A more fully Cultural Psychology challenges what he calls the 'culture-as-difference model', asserting that 'the capacity to inhabit a culturally organized environment is the universal, species-specific characteristic of homo sapiens' (pages 11–12). Recognizing that culture using is a feature of human biology forces a re-examination of taken-for-granted developmental processes. Developing emotional attachments, learning language and acquiring reasoning skills may be universal, but that doesn't make these human activities any less cultural, in so far as they take place within culturally regulated social relationships, and they are mediated by cultural practices. These practices are in turn shaped by knowledge and beliefs about what is normal and desirable, including the knowledge offered by developmental psychology itself. Chapter 1 is a short extract from a much longer chapter, and concentrates on two examples only: the place of attachment in early emotional development, and language acquisition.

The first example is taken up by Super and Harkness (Chapter 2). They emphasize the universal regularities in early emotional development that are linked to the biological substrate of maturational processes – for example, the emergence of smiling around four months and separation distress towards the end of the first year – but they go on to describe the equally universal cultural shaping of these emergent infant competences. The concept of 'niche' is introduced to characterize the way in which infant development is differentially patterned according to the structural arrangements for care and the cultural beliefs and practices of caregivers. Super and Harkness's description of early childhood in a rural Kenyan community during the 1970s, where older siblings had major child-care responsibilities, draws attention to the insularity of much psychological theorizing, especially about the exclusivity of the mother–child relationship.

The same point is vividly conveyed in Schieffelin and Ochs's study of language acquisition amongst the Kaluli of Papua New Guinea (Chapter 3). They argue that most academic researchers have a Western cultural orientation, and they mostly study children growing up in cultural niches similar to their own. The literature is replete with studies of mothers as caregivers, responding to their children's initiative, adapting and simplifying their speech, adopting the children's perspective, scaffolding their learning to diminish the competence and status differential, etc. Because these caregiving patterns appear so pervasive, at least amongst middle-class Western society, they are all too easily idealized and assumed to be a universal characteristic. In Kaluli, by contrast, the status differential between adult and child is maintained, and there is little evidence of baby-talk, or reciprocal, dyadic mother–infant exchanges. Juxtaposing Kaluli alongside Euro-American developmental stories draws attention to the possibility that textbook child development is a particular cultural description, an idealization of childhood based on the shared cultural experience of researchers and the children they study.

This theme is taken up by Singer in Chapter 4. Her starting point is the growing demand for day care outside the family. She traces the history of Western theories about the role of mothers in child care, from the eighteenth century through to contemporary debates that focus on controversial measures of 'attachment security'. Like Cole, Super and Harkness, and Schieffelin and Ochs, Singer emphasizes the importance of cultural context, but she expands 'context' to include psychologists themselves, as producers of cultural knowledge. Adopting a 'social constructionist' perspective, Singer urges psychologists to become more aware of the 'pedagogies' of childhood implicit in their theorizing, and to recognize that issues about quality in child care are not reducible to scientific inquiry alone, since they are framed within cultural values that can best be addressed within more local, context-bound, collaborative research, in which the researcher's own position is made explicit.

Conventional accounts of early childhood in terms of attachment theory and sensitive caregiving have shaped cultural practices both in family and in day-care settings. A feature of these accounts is the relative passivity accorded to young children themselves, and their failure to recognize the sense in which quite young children are 'thinking about' as well as acting in social relationships. In Chapter 5, Trevarthen offers a very different account of early childhood in which human infants are active culture users from the start, strongly attuned to features of their social world, striving to comprehend their environment by sharing experience with others and negotiating in joint action. Trevarthen reinterprets the 'milestones' of early development, offering evidence that infants monitor their caregivers' behaviour and emotional expressions as a forerunner to their earliest efforts to joke with and tease their siblings or peers. He goes on to describe the way in which early communicative skills are transformed through growing capacities for speech and fantasy play, as young children gradually become more competent as interdependent contributors to a shared world of feelings, beliefs and actions.

The next three chapters elaborate on specific issues introduced by Trevarthen, about children's empathy and perspective-taking abilities, their capacities for imaginative pretend play and for integrating in social groups governed by shared goals and rules.

Dunn (Chapter 6) has pioneered the use of systematic naturalistic observations to reveal the way in which children acquire social understanding of family settings. She begins by drawing attention to the discrepancy between observed evidence of social sensitivity even amongst young infants and experimental evidence with older children that suggests they lack awareness of other minds. Much of this research has involved simple story scenarios, in which children are asked to judge how another child will act, based on their understanding of what the other child wants and believes. This so-called 'theory of mind' paradigm demonstrates that children do not acquire 'mind-reading' abilities until they are at least four years old. These findings are in sharp contrast with Dunn's account of 1- and 2-year-old children negotiating disputes, teasing and joking with parents and siblings, attributing intentions and blame, joining in pretend play and talking about inner feelings. Dunn speculates whether it is the emotional power of early relationships that drives children to social understanding. She also draws attention to the influence of family conversations about interpersonal relationships in supporting children's capacities to make sense of their social world.

Pretend play is one of the most distinctive features of early childhood, simultaneously revealing and extending children's sophisticated capacities for social perspective taking, their exploration of a repertoire of possibilities for social relationship and social action, and their construction of a sense of personal identity. This is the focus of Chapter 7, in which Göncü offers a theoretical analysis of the intersubjective skills that enable children to participate effectively. He offers the concept of 'prolepsis' to describe the shared presuppositions that make play participation possible, the mutual trust that underlies a play partnership, and the shared implicit knowledge that makes co-operation productive. Close analysis of young children's play sequences reveals the ease with which they negotiate moment by moment and simultaneously at several different representational levels: to do with whether or not they are 'pretending'; to do with the symbols or roles they are adopting; and to do with the particular narrative of the play. Rapid transformations of time and place, role exchanges and reversals are hallmarks of the creative imaginings of preschool-age children.

Chapter 8 is also about children's play, with the focus on interpreting individual differences in children's success in joining in the ongoing themes of the group. Using ethnographic methods, Kantor and colleagues show how play in a preschool group in the USA became the context for children to establish friendship groups, based on a stable culture of roles, play themes and objects. They concentrate on just three children, the group leader, the sole girl within the group and a boy who tries unsuccessfully to be accepted by the group. Each child brings a distinctive personality to the group, but, the authors argue, more important is the children's ability to 'read' the dominant themes of the group and to apply a repertoire of interaction strategies with flexibility. They conclude that social competence should be seen not as a static set of abilities possessed in varying degrees by children, but rather as a dynamic, local and contextualized relationship amongst children within a group, in which the children's roles, including whether they are deemed worthy of group membership or not, become part of the shared culture of the group's expectations.

The chapters in Part II emphasize the fact that children play an active role

in understanding the social world of family and preschool life, skilfully negotiating their self-interest, taking other perspectives through their play and
through their conversations about others. In Part III we turn to processes of
teaching and learning in which children also become skilled participants. In
Chapter 9, Wood begins by making clear that the context for teaching and
learning that dominates Western thinking about these issues – schooling – is
a relatively recent cultural invention, which has quite distinctive characteristics and appears to promote particular forms of abstract reasoning valued in
modern industrial societies. He describes experimental studies carried out
with colleagues in the mid-1970s, linking analysis of contingency, control
and scaffolding to a key Vygotskian concept – the 'zone of proximal development'. Wood explores the relevance of these concepts to the everyday cultural
contexts in which young children's learning is embedded, in the family, at
nursery or at school. He notes distinctive features of these settings as contexts
for learning, the particular kinds of learning exchange that they seem to
promote, or inhibit, and the way in which children learn to manage their role
in both home and school.

The research paradigm of studying parents scaffolding children's performance has been enormously influential for more than twenty years, but it has
limitations, as Hoogsteder and colleagues point out in Chapter 10. By concentrating on the behaviour of 'teachers' within a restricted set of teaching
contexts (often laboratory-based), they all too easily convey the process as
unidirectional, neglecting the skills that 'learners' bring to the process, in
terms of substantial knowledge about the task and in terms of their skills in
using the support of their teacher. They also risk conveying the impression
that particular ways of teaching are universal, rather than a culturally constructed set of practices into which Western children are initiated from
infancy. Hoogsteder and colleagues report a series of studies of mothers at
home with their 3- to 5-year-old children. Even within this specific caregiving context, they observe that both partners are adept in negotiating
their respective roles on a moment-by-moment basis, adopting any number
of interaction repertoires, of which the didactic role is but one.

Brownell and Carriger (Chapter 11) take the argument one step further,
pointing out that teaching–learning relationships are not always asymmetrical – about a competent adult and less competent child. At the same
time as children are learning how to participate in such asymmetrical relationships, they are also learning how to co-operate in more symmetrical and
co-operative relationships. Brownell and Carriger describe a study of collaborative problem solving amongst 12–30-month-olds, highlighting the
gradual emergence of young children's collaborative strategies, and their
increasing ability to co-ordinate with the other partner's strategies. By the
time most children are 3 or 4 they will have become accomplished collaborators with siblings or peers as well as adults. They will also have become
adept in switching between the roles of learner, play partner and increasingly

of 'teacher' as well. Each of these roles or interaction repertoires is a culturally constructed form of relationship that shapes and enhances possibilities for communication, thinking and behaviour.

For many 3- and 4-year-olds, these socio-cognitive skills are not just practised within family contexts. Nurseries and reception classes are a distinctive context in which children encounter new agendas for play, for social relationships and for learning. Chapter 12 elaborates on a theme introduced in Chapter 9 about styles of interaction with teachers compared with other adults in the early school environment. Hughes and Westgate analyse audio-recordings of adult–child interaction in terms of the roles children play, the discourse functions served and the cognitive skills expressed. They note that the teachers in their study offered a distinctive style of interaction with children, linked to their role and purposes – a style in which children's initiatives are largely eliminated and talk is dominated by teacher questions with little opportunity for exploratory talk, making connections or recalling related experiences.

Part IV extends the discussion about how children are initiated into particular ways of interacting, communicating, thinking, behaving, learning and teaching by revisiting the central question of Part I. Young children in Western contexts experience a range of patterns of social interaction, play and cognition, in both home and preschool contexts. How do these experiences relate to a wider range of cultural niches experienced by the world's children? Rogoff and colleagues (Chapter 13) argue that the concepts Western researchers use to analyse early development have become associated with heavily language-based interactions oriented to schooling contexts that serve mainly literate, academic goals. By adopting the concept of 'guided participation', Rogoff et al. seek to enlarge the study of how children become competent cultural actors to encompass a much broader range of learning experiences. At the same time, 'guided participation' emphasizes that learning is about active engagement in cultural activity, not about passive individual internalization of valued knowledge. Chapter 13 summarizes findings from a cross-cultural comparison between Mayan communities in Guatemala and American communities in Salt Lake City. Rogoff et al. note several points of difference, notably between contexts in which caregivers adapt to children and contexts in which children are expected to learn through monitoring and imitating mature models of competence.

Rogoff et al.'s quasi-experimental comparison of caregiver–child interactions offers a powerful illustration of both the universal character and the culture-specific features of guided participation. One disadvantage is that the play activities on which the observations were based may themselves have different cultural salience in the two settings. This possibility is highlighted in Chapter 14. Nsamenang and Lamb describe socialization amongst Nso communities in Northwest Cameroon, where siblings play a central role in child socialization and where toys or other artefacts have a much diminished status. To make the point, Nsamenang and Lamb contrast two orientations to child socialization. Academic, cognitive orientations individualize children, encouraging their personal mastery of physical and, later, symbolic environments, supported by toys, books and computers. By contrast, socio-affective orientations emphasize collective solidarity, role- and status-appropriate behaviour and functional mastery of specific valued skills. Nsamenang and Lamb argue that deference and obedience to elders is a fundamental feature of Nso socialization, where childhood stages are marked not according to developmental criteria in the Western sense, but according to children's ability to perform tasks and roles. Parental expectations are closely related to the necessity that children contribute to a subsistence economy by taking on domestic chores and learning to cultivate the land from an early age. Whilst hard work and honesty are seen as desirable traits, playfulness, disobedience and inquisitiveness are seen as highly undesirable. Bearing in mind the accounts in Part II of assertive toddlers challenging parents and engaging in elaborate pretend play, Nsamenang and Lamb's account raises the question of how far these forms of self–other understanding and social relationship may be adaptive to the socio-historical context of individualistic, child-centred childhoods. At the same time, Nsamenang and Lamb recognize that the ecology of Nso childhood is undergoing rapid social change, challenging traditional expectations of childhood and encouraging convergence towards a more 'modern' global child development model.

One feature of modern early childhood is the professionalization of care through nurseries, kindergartens and pre-school programmes. Chapter 15 is a case study of the way in which cultural and professional expectations for childhood impact on child-care practices. It is taken from a book comparing children's experience of preschool education and care in China, Japan and the United States. Tobin and colleagues video-recorded the daily lives of these preschool groups, and then asked teachers from all three settings to comment on each other's practice. Not surprisingly, there were marked contrasts in terms of physical setting, teacher–child ratios, material resources and daily regime. In this extract, the authors describe children's daily life in a Japanese preschool, concentrating on the way in which the teacher worked with a boy called Hiroki, who (from the observers' point of view) appeared to be misbehaving. Intercultural discussions about how to interpret this boy's behaviour, explanations for why he might be behaving in this way and the appropriate strategies for working with him lead into a wider exploration of cultural differences in views of intelligence, dependency, self-control, individualism, personal and group identity. Arguably, recognizing the multiplicity of these cultural perspectives is a first step towards reconstructing the study of early child development in ways that are relevant to all the world's children.

Part I

Development as a socio-cultural process

Chapter 1

Culture in development*

Michael Cole

Introduction

Although it is generally agreed that the distinctive characteristic of human beings as a species is their ability to inhabit a culturally organized environment, it is a curious fact that the topic of culture and human nature is little represented in basic texts of either general or developmental psychology. To appreciate just how markedly absent culture is, all one has to do is to scan the indices of leading texts and journals. In a great many cases there will be no citation for culture at all. In some cases there will be references to cross-cultural research in a few, restricted, domains: IQ testing, Piagetian conservation tasks, Kohlbergian moral dilemmas, and perhaps the question of the origins of emotion or aggression. (Lonner took the trouble to collect systematic data to prove the point, as reported in Segall, Dasen, Berry, and Poortinga, 1990, p. 372.)

Implicit in even the limited treatment of culture available in the psychological literature is the notion that culture is synonymous with cultural differences. This assumption is embodied in the contents of various handbook chapters on cultural psychology (e.g., De Vos and Hippler, 1969; Kluckhohn, 1954; Price-Williams, 1985), whose authors promise to consider culture and behavior or cultural psychology but whose presentations are restricted to cross-cultural studies. The assumption that culture refers to cultural difference is made explicitly by Hinde (1987), who argued that culture is "better regarded as a convenient label for many of the diverse ways in which human practices and beliefs *differ between groups*" (pp. 3–4).

This emphasis on culture-as-difference overlooks the fact that the capacity to inhabit a culturally organized environment is the universal, species-specific characteristic of *homo sapiens*, of which particular cultures represent special cases. A full understanding of culture in human development requires both a

* This is an edited version of a chapter that appeared in *Developmental Psychology: An Advanced Textbook*, Hillsdale, NJ: Lawrence Erlbaum Associates, 1992.

specification of its universal mechanisms and the specific forms that it assumes in particular historical circumstances. [. . .]

Three dualistic theories and a cultural alternative

Figure 1.1 contains a schematic representation of the three positions that have dominated theorizing about development in this century, along with a fourth approach in which the category of culture has been added as third force. The uppermost line in the figure represents the view articulated in the first half of this century by Arnold Gesell, according to whom endogenous factors dominate development, which goes through a series of invariant

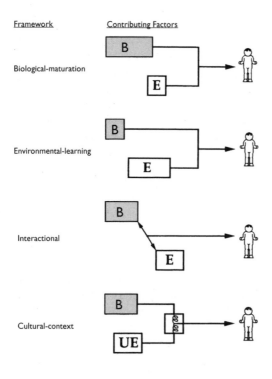

B = Biological
E = Environmental
UE = Universal features of environment
ℓℓℓ = Culture (historically specific features of environment)

Figure 1.1 Four theoretical frameworks for interpreting the sources of development and the major ways in which they interact. In the first three frameworks, development is seen as the interaction of two factors; the theories differ in the weight they give to each and the mode of their interaction. The fourth approach assumes that the two factors included in the first three frameworks interact indirectly through the medium of culture.

stages, characterized by qualitatively different structures of the organism and qualitatively different patterns of interaction between organism and environment. Gesell wrote, for example,

> Environment . . . determines the occasion, the intensity, and the correlation of many aspects of behavior, but it does not engender the basic progressions of behavior development. These are determined by inherent, maturational mechanisms.
>
> (Gesell, 1940, p. 13)

Elsewhere he added,

> Neither physical nor cultural environment contains any architechtonic arrangements like the mechanisms of growth. Culture accumulates; it does not grow. The glove goes on the hand; the hand determines the glove.
>
> (Gesell, 1945, p. 358)

Gesell's ideas went out of fashion in the 1950s, but in recent years there has been a significant revival of interest in innate biological constraints on development (Carey, 1985; Gelman, 1990; Plomin, 1986).

The view that the environment provides the major impetus for developmental change is represented in row two of Figure 1.1. An extreme version of this view was put forward by B. F. Skinner, whose views are summarized in the following striking paragraph:

> Operant conditioning shapes behavior as a sculptor shapes a lump of clay. Although at some point the sculptor seems to have produced an entirely novel object, we can always follow the process back to the original undifferentiated lump, and we can make the successive stages by which we return to this condition as small as we wish. At no point does anything emerge which is very different from what preceded it. The final product seems to have a special unity or integrity of design, but we cannot find a point at which this suddenly appears. In the same sense, an operant is not something which appears full grown in the behavior of the organism. It is the result of a continuous shaping process.
>
> (Skinner, 1953, p. 91)

In this view, it is not the past, coded in the genetic makeup, that is the active agent in development; rather it is the environment, the sculptor, that is the source not only of the minute changes that gradually modify the lump of clay, but of the new forms that emerge from this process in a continuous fashion. Contemporary psychologists sympathetic to an environmentalist perspective may consider Skinner's position somewhat exaggerated. The analogy between the organism and a lump of clay is especially unfortunate, because it implies a totally passive organism (contrary to Skinner's own principles!), but his emphasis on the dominant role of the environment in shaping development continues to have many adherents (e.g., Bandura, 1986; Zimmerman, 1983).

Jean Piaget, perhaps the most influential developmental theorist of the twentieth century, argued forcefully for the equal weight of endogenous and exogenous factors in development. On the one hand, he asserted that "Mental growth is inseparable from physical growth; maturation of the nervous and endocrine systems, in particular, continues until the age of sixteen" (Piaget and Inhelder, 1969, p. viii).

At the same time, Piaget, like those who adopt an environment-shaping perspective, argued that the role of environmental input goes well beyond determining the occasioning, intensity, and correlation of behavioral aspects.

> The human being is immersed right from birth in a social environment which affects him just as much as his physical environment. Society, even more, in a sense, than the physical environment, changes the very structure of the individual. . . . Every relation between individuals (from two onwards) literally modifies them.

> (Piaget, 1973, p. 156)

Piaget's view is often contrasted with the maturational and environmental shaping views by his emphasis on the crucial role of the active organism, who constructs her or his own development through attempts to adapt to the environment.

Although they differ in the weights that they assign to phylogenetic constraints or ontogenetic experiences and the importance of children's active modifications of their environments, the adherents of all three positions conceive of development as an interaction between two juxtaposed forces. Although Gesell, Skinner, and Piaget all implicitly or explicitly suggest that the environmental side of the equation can be partitioned into culture or social factors versus the physical environment, these distinctions are not well developed in their writings.

The fourth row of Figure 1.1 explicitly includes culture as a separable constituent of development. According to this cultural context view, the two factors labeled *biology* and *the environment* or *the individual* and *society* in the previously described approaches do not interact directly. Rather, their interaction is mediated through a third factor, culture. In order to develop this fourth perspective more fully, it is necessary to pause briefly to consider the concept of culture in more detail.

Conceptions of culture

In thinking about culture as it relates to development, I have found it useful to begin with the intuitive notion underlying this word, as it has evolved since entering English from Latin many centuries ago. As Williams noted, the core features that coalesce in modern conceptions of culture originate in terms that refer to the process of helping things to grow. "Culture," Williams wrote, "in all of its early uses was a noun of process: the tending of something, basically crops or animals" (1973, p. 87). From earliest times, the notion of culture included a general theory for how to promote development: create an artificial environment in which young organisms could be provided optimal conditions for growth. Such tending required tools, perfected over generations and designed for the special tasks to which they were put.

Although it would be foolish to overinterpret the metaphorical parallels between the theory and practice of growing next generations of crops and next generations of children, the exercise has considerable heuristic value. To begin with, the properties that one associates with gardens bear an obvious affinity to one broad class of definitions of culture offered by anthropologists. For example, E. B. Tylor, in his classic book *Primitive Culture* (1874), defined culture as "that complex whole which includes knowledge, belief, art, morals, law, custom, and any other capabilities and habits acquired by man as a member of society" (p. 1). A garden as an artificial-environment-for-growing-things is also a "complex whole," and gardening requires knowledge, beliefs, and the like, as an integral part of the process. The root English conception fits just as well with Herskovitz's (1948) definition of culture as "the man made part of the environment" (p. 17).

The garden metaphor for culture also reminds us that gardeners must attend not only to a specialized form of environment created inside the garden but also to the ecological circumstances surrounding the garden. These two classes of concern often seem to be addressable independently of each other, but in reality are interdependent. Inside the garden one must consider the quality of the soil, the best way to till the soil, the right kinds of nutrients to use, the proper amount of moisture, as well as the best time to plant and nurture the seeds, and the need to protect the growing plants against predators, disease, and so forth. Each of these tasks has its own material needs, associated tools, beliefs, and knowledge. The theory and practice of development at this level focuses on finding exactly the right combination of factors to promote development within the garden walls.

In thinking about development it is necessary to consider the conditions outside of the garden or culture as well as those within it. It is possible to raise any plant anywhere in the world, given the opportunity first to arrange the appropriate set of conditions, but it is not always possible to create the right conditions, even for a short while. If one is interested in the creation of conditions that sustain and even enhance the needed properties of the artificial environment, then it is as important to attend to the ways in which the system in which the garden is embedded shapes the properties of the garden itself. This common sense understanding fits well with ecocultural approaches to the study of culture and development (Berry, 1976; Whiting, 1980), which trace relations among physical ecology, economic activities and institutions, and the organization of children's experience.

Humanizing the garden metaphor

Although the garden metaphor is useful for thinking about culture and development because it emphasizes the fact that human beings live in an artificial environment, and that cultures exist within, are shaped by, and in turn shape their ecological settings, it fails to capture several aspects of modern conceptions of culture that need to be elaborated in the study of development. One point of elaboration occurred in the sixteenth century when the word "culture" began to apply to the rearing of children. When this occurred, both the gardener and the plants were now seen to be from the same species, and, therefore, we are pushed to ask the question, "What is the general property of an organism that can inhabit an artificial environment in the process of creating and recreating both itself and its environment?" That is, "What are the specifically human characteristics of both culture and human development?"

To deal with these questions, it is helpful to think of the garden in which human beings live as an environment transformed by the artifacts of prior generations, extending back to the beginning of the species (Geertz, 1973; Leontiev, 1981; Luria, 1979; Sahlins, 1976). The basic function of these artifacts is to coordinate human beings with the physical world and each other; in the aggregate, culture is then seen as the species-specific medium of human development.

Because artifact mediation was present hundreds of thousands of years prior to the emergence of *homo sapiens*, it is not appropriate to juxtapose human biology and human culture. The human brain and body co-evolved over a long period of time with our species' increasingly complex cultural environment. The implications of the co-evolution of human culture and human biology have been succinctly summarized by Washburn.

> Selection is based on successful behavior, and in man-apes the beginnings of the human way of life depended on the learned skills of tool-using. The success of the new way of life based on the use of tools changed the selection pressures on many parts of the body, notably the teeth, hands and brain, as well as on the pelvis.
>
> (Washburn, 1960, p. 69)

Geertz points out that, as a result of their tangled relations in the course of human phylogeny, culture and biology are equally tangled in the course of human ontogeny:

> Rather than culture acting only to supplement, develop, and extend organically based capacities logically and genetically prior to it, it would seem to be ingredient to those capacities themselves. A cultureless human being would probably turn out to be not an intrinsically talented though unfulfilled ape, but a wholly mindless and consequently unworkable monstrosity.
>
> (Geertz, 1973, p. 68)

This long-term, phylogenetic perspective is important to keep in mind when considering the ontogeny of children, for it reminds us that causal influences do not run unidirectionally from biology to culture. [. . .]

Infancy

It has long been recognized that there is an intimate link between the relative immaturity of the human newborn, which will require years of nurturing before it can approach something akin to self-sufficiency, and the fact that human beings inhabit a culturally mediated environment. Both facts are distinctive characteristics of our species. Infancy (from a Latin word meaning one who does not speak) is widely, if not universally, considered a distinctive period of development that extends from birth until approximately the age of 2½.

Getting on a schedule

The earliest essential condition for continued development following birth is that the child and those who care for him or her must become coordinated in such a manner that the adults are able to accumulate enough resources to accommodate the newcomer. In this process, there is an intricate interplay between the initial characteristics of children and the cultural environment into which they are born, resulting in what Super and Harkness (1982, 1986) refer to as the developmental niche.

A clear-cut example of a cultural influence on the way in which the process of coordination is achieved is afforded by the contrasting patterns of sleep in the months following birth by American urban dwelling and rural Kenyan (Kipsigis) children (Super and Harkness, 1982). Among children in the United States, there is a marked shift toward the adult day/night cycle a few weeks after birth; by the end of the second week, they are averaging about 8½ hours of sleep between the hours of 7 p.m. and 7 a.m. Between 4 and 8 months, the longest sleep episode increases from about 4 to 8 hours a night. The pressures toward sleeping through the night are not difficult to identify.

American urban dwellers live by the clock. In an era in which a very large proportion of mothers as well as fathers have jobs outside the home, they must leave the house at a specified time, and the child must be ready at that time. As a consequence of the child's need for sleep, the adults' needs to get to work, and the adults' desires to spend some leisure time without the child to worry about, they are likely to push as hard as possible for the child to eat and sleep when it is convenient for them.

Among the Kipsigis infants, the course of getting on a schedule is very different. At night they sleep with their mothers and are permitted to nurse on demand. During the day they are strapped to their mothers' backs, accompanying them on their daily rounds of farming, household chores, and social activities. They do a lot of napping while their mothers go about their work. At one month, the longest period of sleep reported for babies in the Kipsigis sample was 3 hours, and their longest sleep episode increases little during the first 8 months of postnatal life.

At one level, these observations are banal. They show only that children fit into the community into which they are born. A seemingly simple case can, however, be useful when it comes to analyzing more complex cases, and even this simple case contains some important lessons. First, the shaping process that produces different patterns of sleeping is indicative of more than a temporary convenience. As adults, assuming there is little change in Kipsigis life circumstances, the children socialized into a flexible sleep schedule will themselves be more flexible than their American counterparts. Second, the rather rigid schedule imposed by modern industrialized lifestyles may be pushing the limits of what the immature human brain can sustain; hence, while the length of a longest sleep period may be a good indicator of physical maturity, pushing those limits may be a source of stress, with negative consequences for children who cannot measure up to parental expectations (Konner and Super, 1987).

From sucking to nursing

In the 1940s, Margaret Mead and Frances Macgregor (1951) set out to test Gesell's ideas about the relation between growth (maturation) and learning through cross-cultural research. They argued that basic principles of the way in which cultures interweave learning and maturation can be seen in the way in which the change from reflex sucking to nursing is organized and in the long-term behavioral implications of this organization.

Some cultures, they noted, take advantage of the sucking reflex by putting the baby to the mother's breast immediately to stimulate the flow of milk, although the baby remains hungry; others provide a wet nurse; others will give the baby a bottle, and so on. In an immediate sense, all of these routes to mature nursing are equally adequate. However, they have various different implications in the short, and even the long run. Mead and Macgregor point to one potential short-run effect: babies who are bottle fed until their mothers' milk comes in may elaborate nursing behaviors that interfere with breast-feeding, changing both short-run nutritional and social-interactional experiences.

Longer term effects arise from the interconnection of the adults' choice of feeding method and larger life patterns. For example, if a mother who stays at home gives her baby a bottle because she believes that bottled milk is more nutritious, the use of a bottle rather than breast-feeding may have no differential impact on the development of social relations between mother and child (although it may produce a tendency to obesity, which can have other long-term effects). However, if the baby is bottle fed because the mother works at a factory and must return to work in a week and knows that the baby will be placed in infant day care, the bottle feeding at birth will become part of a life pattern in which the mother and baby have a less intimate relationship and the baby becomes accustomed at an early age to social interactions with peers and several caretakers.

The future in the present: a cross-cultural example

To elaborate mechanisms of cultural mediation, I have selected an example from work by Bornstein and his colleagues on the interactions between American and Japanese mothers with their 5-month-old offspring (Bornstein, Toda, Azuma, Tamis-LeMonda, and Ogino, 1990; Bornstein, Tal, and Tamis-LeMonda, 1991; see Nugent, Lester, and Brazelton, 1989, for another set of articles).

The focus of this work was the way in which mothers living in New York and in Tokyo respond to their infants' orientations to events in the environment or to the mothers themselves. Using a variety of measures of infant behaviors (level of activity, the rate at which they habituate to the sight of their mothers' faces or objects in the environment, the level of vocalization of various kinds), Bornstein and his colleagues established the fact that infants in the two cultures behaved in similar manners and, in this important sense, provided similar starting points for their mothers' responses to them. Of particular importance in light of maternal behaviors, infants from the two societies displayed equal levels of orientation to their mothers and to physical objects in the environment.

Despite the fact that these infants represented equivalent stimuli in the objective sense provided by the researchers' behavioral measurements, there was a distinctive difference in the way in which the mothers responded to their infants. American mothers were more responsive when their children oriented to physical objects in the environment; Japanese mothers were more responsive when their infants oriented to them. Moreover, the mothers made overt attempts to change the locus of their infants' orientation when it did not fit their preference: American mothers diverted children's attention from themselves to objects, while Japanese mothers showed the opposite pattern.

Once again we see a pervasive feature of cultural influences on development. Japanese maternal behavior is part of a system that highly values a strong dependence of the child on the mother, while American maternal behavior is part of a system that values independence. These different value orientations make little difference to the welfare of the children at 5 months of age; both forms of interaction are caring and supportive. They are however, part of a system of constraints on the children that do make a difference as the child grows older. Bornstein and his colleagues note that, as toddlers, Japanese and American children do not differ in their global language and play skills, but they do differ in the kinds of language and the kinds of play they are best at in ways that correspond to the differences evident in their mothers' behaviors at the age of 5 months. We see other ways in which they differ in the following sections.

A shift in socio-emotional and cognitive development at 6 to 9 months

The period from 6 to 9 months of age is strategically useful for illustrating several points about culture and development, for several reasons. First, there is a good deal of evidence pointing to a universal and distinctive reorganization of the overall way in which children interact with their environments at this time, illustrating the stage-transformation process that we refer to as a bio-social-behavioral shift (Cole and Cole, 1989, Chap. 6). Second, there is a good deal of cross-cultural data that allow us to address both general and culture-specific ways in which this change occurs. The cross-cultural data are also interesting as much for the general methodological problems of cross-cultural research that they raise as for their substantive contributions to understanding the role of culture in development.

The universal changes occurring at 6 to 9 months of age are apparent in all parts of the bio-social-behavioral shift. With respect to the biological strand, we find that new patterns of electrical activity, associated with increased levels of myelinization, arise in several parts of the brain (Dreyfus-Brisac, 1978; Goldman-Rakic, 1987). The affected areas include the frontal lobes (which play a crucial role in deliberate action and planning), the cerebellum (which is important in controlling movement and balance), and the hippocampus (important in memory). In addition, the muscles have become stronger and the bones harder than they were at birth, providing support for increasingly vigorous movement.

[. . .]

Once children begin to crawl and walk, caretakers can no longer directly prevent mishaps, no matter how carefully they arrange the environment. Newly mobile babies keep a watchful eye on their caretakers for feedback about how they are doing – called *social referencing* (Campos and Stenberg,

1981). At the same time, children become wary of strangers and become upset when their primary caretakers leave them. This complex of apparently related social behaviors has led a number of psychologists to hypothesize that a new quality of emotional relationship between caretaker and child emerges, called attachment.

Attachment

Although various aspects of the complex of changes that occur between 6 and 9 months of age have been investigated cross-culturally (e.g., Kagan, 1977, reported data supporting the hypothesis of cross-cultural universals with respect to various aspects of remembering and object permanence), by far the greatest amount of data has been collected on cultural contributions to attachment, so it is on this issue that I focus in attempting to specify the role of culture in overall behavior at this time. Despite the fact that there are competing theories to account for how and why children form special emotional bonds with their caretakers (see Cole and Cole, 1989, for a summary), current research appears to be motivated primarily by ideas put forth by Bowlby (1969). The starting point for Bowlby's work on attachment was his attempt to explain why extended periods of separation from parents were so upsetting to small children, even though they were maintained in perfectly adequate circumstances from a purely physical point of view. His explanation, briefly stated, was that one has to interpret contemporary forms of behavior in terms of the environment of evolutionary adaptedness into which our species evolved. Behaviors that might seem irrational today were once crucial to survival, becoming a part of the human biological repertoire through natural selection.

Bowlby based his ideas about the environment of evolutionary adaptedness of attachment behaviors in part on what is known about mother–infant interactions among currently existing large, ground-living apes. These presumed phylogenetic cousins share their environment with predators from whom they protect themselves by banding together. Owing to their relatively long immaturity, the offspring of these apes must remain close to their mothers to survive. This need for proximity and safety is counterbalanced by the equally strong need to explore and play, which separates offspring and parent. Bowlby hypothesized that attachment arises during the first year of life as a way of maintaining a dynamic equilibrium between safety and exploration controlled by the mother–child dyad. When the distance between mother and child is too great, one or the other gets upset and seeks the other out. When there is too much proximity, one of the partners gets bored or annoyed, resulting in increased distance.

Described in this way, the development of attachment would seem to be a necessary, universal biological requirement to be found in all cultures under normal circumstances, because it is a species-specific consequence of our phylogenetic heritage. However, the fact of universality (should it be demonstrated) would in no way contradict the principle of cultural mediation. Rather, it forces a closer look at precisely how the formation of attachment is mediated and how that pattern of mediation fits into the overall life course of human beings reared in varying cultural–historical circumstances. During the past two decades, there has been an increasingly heated dispute on precisely this point. This dispute is worth examining in some detail because it is typical of difficulties facing the use of cross-cultural approaches to culture and development in a great many other cases.

Appropriately, the studies that began the modern debate on culture and attachment arose from comparison of the behaviors of mother–child pairs observed in their homes in the United States and Uganda by Mary Ainsworth (Ainsworth, 1967; Ainsworth, Blehar, Waters, and Wall, 1978). Ainsworth was struck by the fact that children in both cultural groups exhibited similar patterns of attachment-related behavior (distress during brief, everyday, separation from their mothers, fear of strangers, and use of the mother as a secure base from which to explore). However, the Ugandan children seemed to express these behavior patterns more readily and intensely than did the American children Ainsworth studied. As a means of provoking attachment-related behaviors in American children, Ainsworth devised the Strange Situation, a sequence of interactional episodes acted out by the mother in a specially designed laboratory environment that typically resembles a doctor's waiting room. It is important to note that she assumed that this artificial situation would evoke levels of anxiety in American children roughly comparable to those evoked among Ugandan children in the everyday settings she had observed, so that she could have comparable phenomena to study.

The standardized Strange Situation consists of eight phases, each of which lasts 3 minutes or less: After giving instructions (Phase 1), the experimenter leaves the child and caregiver alone (Phase 2). Then the experimenter returns (Phase 3), the caregiver leaves (Phase 4), the caregiver returns (Phase 5), and then leaves the child alone (Phase 6), after which the experimenter returns (Phase 7), and finally the caregiver returns (Phase 8).

During the 1970s and continuing to the present time, there has been a great deal of research on the behavior produced in this situation, its antecedents, and its sequelae (see Bretherton and Waters, 1985, or the entire issue of *Human Development*, 1990, No. 1, for reviews and references to additional primary sources of information). Slowly at first, and with increasing frequency in the past 5 years, the Strange Situation has been used in cross-cultural research. This time (ironically, in light of the reasons why Ainsworth introduced it in the first place) it was used as a standardized research instrument, to be administered to all subjects in all cultures in precisely the same way, instead of as a procedure for creating slightly discrepant series of events designed to model and assess development in relation to its cultural origins.

As a way to establish the antecedents and consequences of different qualities of attachment, Ainsworth and her colleagues constructed three categories, based heavily on how the infant reacts when the caretaker returns after an absence:

- Type A (anxious–avoidant) children turn away or look away when their caregivers return, instead of seeking closeness and comfort.
- Type B (securely attached) children go to their caregivers, calm down quickly after their early upset, and soon resume playing.
- Type C (anxious–resistant) children are often upset while their mothers are with them just as a result of being in the strange environment. They become very upset when their caregivers leave, and they simultaneously seek closeness and resist contact when the caregivers return.

Use of these categories in cross-cultural research is significant because the distribution of children among categories is used to underpin the claim that it is possible to identify precursors of habitual socioemotional characteristics of children and their relationships to their caregivers that have developmental consequences that last for months, and perhaps years (see, e.g., the articles by Grossmann and Grossmann, 1990; Main, 1990). The primary antecedent to varying degrees of attachment has been assumed to be maternal sensitiveness, the degree to which the caretaker responds reliably and satisfactorily to the infant's behavior; the main consequence has been thought of as increased sociocognitive competence.

Grossmann and Grossmann's summary of the research literature captures well one view of the results of this work:

> Caretakers' responsiveness to infants' signals of insecurity seems to be the main determinant of secure versus avoidantly or ambivalently insecure infant behaviors to mothers or fathers at 1 year of age. An individual's "inner working model," resulting from differential dyadic attachment history, may determine how inner emotional conflicts are resolved. On the basis of existing longitudinal data, the following emotional response styles appear to be prevalent: Individuals with secure attachment histories pay attention to the full range of external causes for conflicting emotions and they tolerate contradictory emotions. Individuals with insecure attachment histories, in contrast, pay attention only to selected fractions of their emotional reactions at any given time, and they tend to lose sight of the full range of external causes for potentially conflicting emotions. These developmental sequences appear to be universal. Cultural differences may exist in terms of frequency and difficulty of potentially conflicting challenges.
>
> (Grossman and Grossman, 1990, p. 31)

Clearly, if this summary is taken at face value, secure attachment, especially secure attachment as manifested in the Strange Situation, is important to the future well-being of the child, and populations in which secure attachment occurs infrequently ought to be concerned. Because rather wide cross-national variations in the proportion of children assigned to the three major attachment categories have been reported in the literature, it should come as no surprise that the Grossmanns' view is somewhat controversial.

To begin with, consider the data in Table 1.1 which are taken from four widely cited studies of attachment using the Strange Situation (from van IJzendoorn and Kroonenberg, 1988). The top line is from an early study by Ainsworth and colleagues that has often been taken as a standard of comparison. Roughly two-thirds of the children are assessed as securely attached. In contrast, only one-third of children tested in northern Germany are assessed as secure, with fully half assessed as anxious–avoidant. In Israel and Japan, the proportions of securely attached children are roughly equivalent to that in the US sample, but there are almost three times as many children assessed as anxious–resistant as in the other two samples.

What are we to make of such variation? When interpretation is based on the distribution of types of attachment behaviors manifested in the Strange Situation alone, two lines of explanation are offered. The first assumes that the Strange Situation is a valid index of a universal form of emotional reaction that is distributed differently in different cultures. The second assumes that, although standardized, the Strange Situation is really a different situation in different cultural circumstances, in that it takes on different meanings for the participants.

As LeVine and Miller (1990) point out, the assumption that the meaning of the Strange Situation is a culture-neutral and valid indicator of a universal form of relationship called *attachment* leads to the further assumption that the American pattern is a universal norm, and the conclusion (for example) that, in northern Germany, a high proportion of the children will display various forms of incompetence owing to deficient attachment formation in early childhood. Precisely such interpretations have been given in the case of American subpopulations, such as families in which there are high levels of

Table 1.1 Patterns of attachment from four cultural samples

Country	Anxious–Avoidant	Secure	Anxious–Resistant
USA (n = 105)[a]	21	67	12
Germany (n = 46)[b]	52	35	13
Israel (n = 82)[c]	7	57	34
Japan (n = 60)[d]	0	68	32

Sources:
a From Ainsworth, Blehar, Waters, and Wall, 1978
b From Grossmann, Grossmann, Huber, and Wartner, 1981
c From Sagi et al., 1985
d From Takahashi, 1986

conflict and child abuse (Vaughn, Egeland, Sroufe, and Waters, 1979). An alternative strategy of explanation, which retains the notion that the Strange Situation is a valid indicator of attachment, retains the categories and measuring criteria, but redefines the meaning of the categories according to the local culture. This is what the Grossmanns and their colleagues did (Grossmann, Grossmann, Spangler, Suess, and Unzner, 1985; Grossmann and Grossmann, 1990) when they suggested that, *vis-à-vis* the American standard, northern German parents emphasize autonomy at an early age, which induces their children to show autonomy in this situation (perhaps a slight, but certainly a significant, reinterpretation of anxious–avoidant).

The other choice is to assume, as does Takahashi (1990) for example, that, although standardized, the Strange Situation is really a different situation in different cultural circumstances, in that it has different meanings for the participants. For example, in Japan, children are almost never away from their mothers during the first year of life, so the Strange Situation is indeed very strange, and the resulting stress pushes children from the secure to the anxious–resistant category. In Israel, the children are often away from their parents, but always with one of a small set of familiar caretakers, so they, like the Japanese, are especially stressed by the Strange Situation because it exposes them, perhaps for the first time in their lives, to separation from their major attachment figure(s). These explanations have one thing in common: they assume that the fit between the Strange Situation and children's prior experience differs systematically from culture to culture, and that differences in Strange Situation behaviors are a function of this difference. The only way to obtain functional equivalence of Strange Situations in different cultures, it would seem, would be to create a different assessment instrument for each culture; this is, in effect, what Ainsworth did when she took her appearance in a village as the criterial situation of Ugandan infants and the artificially created Strange Situation as the functionally equivalent situation for the American children with whom she worked. However, using a different observational setting for each cultural group would immediately undermine the equivalence of procedures which is the foundation of standardization needed by those who seek to establish the universal validity of the Strange Situation.

As Grossmann and Grossmann (1990) and LeVine and Miller (1990) point out, the dilemma of standardization (literal equivalence of the test environment) versus culture-contingent standardization (functional equivalence of the test environment; see Frijda and Jahoda, 1966) cannot be solved using the Strange Situation alone. Detailed analyses of the cultures under study are required to determine the normative life courses of members that shape the everyday interactions of child–caregiver relationships. This line of action also requires psychologists to study individuals in a way that not only includes their behaviors in the Strange Situation, but that traces back to their earlier life experiences and follows them forward to later behaviors in a variety of culturally common circumstances for each culture involved. In the work of the Grossmanns and Main, a variety of ingenious techniques, including ratings of the quality of mother–child interaction in later years, the quality of children's communication with other children in different settings, and even adult memories of their own childhoods, has been used to establish the longitudinal predictiveness of different qualities of behavior in the Strange Situation in some cultures. However, in other cases, such as that reported by Takahashi (1990) for Japanese children, it appears that while behavior in the Strange Situation is predictive of such characteristics as curiosity toward unfamiliar objects and social competence for about one year, the behavioral difference between babies categorized as securely and insecurely attached disappeared by the time the children were 3 years of age. These findings indicate that it will require culturally sensitive longitudinal research to tease apart the universal and culture-specific aspects of the socioemotional development presumably indexed by the Strange Situation.

It should also be pointed out that recent culturally sensitive longitudinal research using the Strange Situation has yet to be extended to non-industrial societies in which very different values relating to desirable infant behaviors may exist. For example, Greenfield and colleagues (1989) report that among Zinacantecans there is a strong emphasis on socializing children to maintain old traditions; exploration, experimentation, and novelty are negatively valued. In line with this value system, infants are breast-fed at the slightest hint of any activity on their part as a way of quieting, and, Greenfield and colleagues speculate, as a way to teach them to allow their elders to take the initiative. There is no doubt that this is sensitive responding on the part of the mother, but its effects on infant behavior can be expected to be quite different from any of the societies in which the ontogenetic implications of attachment have thus far been studied.

Language

No area of culture and human development has attracted as much scholarly attention as the interrelation among culture, language, and development. Two major, and related, questions have organized discussion in the field. First, the acquisition of language has been one of the major battlefields on which the nature–nurture controversy has been fought: must language be acquired through a process of culturally mediated learning or constructive interaction like any other human cognitive capacity, or is language a specialized, bounded domain (module) that needs only to be triggered to spring into action? (See Bruner, 1983; Piatelli-Palmerini, 1980; Wanner and Gleitman, 1982, for excellent discussions of the contending viewpoints.) Second, what role does the acquisition of language play in the development of thought? If language is a structurally distinct module, then there should be no particular relation between language and thought. On the other hand, in so far as culturally organized experience is seen to be essential to the acquisition of language, then language, thought, and development are likely to be intimately connected.

In contrast with the research on attachment, but like the research on the earliest adaptations of infants to the culturally scripted schedules into which they must fit, the research on language depends more on the study of natural variations in cultural circumstances, and less on standardized test procedures.

Hardly anyone believes that language can be acquired in the total absence of interaction with other human beings who speak a language. Rather, the position of those who adopt a nativist position with respect to language assumes that its development proceeds akin to the development of any bodily organ. Thus any environment that sustains the life of the social group is considered adequate to produce the development of language without any special attention needing to be paid to the process.

With respect to human beings, the environment that sustains life is one that exists in the medium of culture, which leads one to attempt to specify more carefully what minimum conditions of culturally mediated interaction between children and adults are sufficient to support development of the language organ.

Two categories of cases in which children are reared in conditions that systematically reduce their immersion in culture help to specify the universal lower limits of cultural support needed to sustain language development. The first is the well-known case of Genie, studied by Susan Curtiss (1977). Genie was locked in a room by herself sometime before her second birthday. She lived chained by day to a potty and trussed up in a sleeping bag at night for 11 years, during which time she had virtually no normal linguistic input and only a minimum of social interactions that could be considered culturally normal in any culture.

When she was liberated from these horrible circumstances at the age of 13, she was in pitiful shape. She was emaciated and very short. She could not walk normally, rarely made a sound, and was not toilet trained. Although on testing she showed remarkable skills for spatial analysis, she had failed to acquire language. Nor did she recover from her many years of severely deprived existence; she acquired a small vocabulary and some forms of appropriate social interaction, but her behavior remained abnormal, despite attempts at therapeutic intervention.

There are several intermediate cases between the extreme deprivation resulting in development without language or culture (the case of Genie) and the situation of the vast majority of children. One particularly instructive situation arises among children born deaf to hearing parents who do not believe that it is useful for their children to sign, insisting instead that they learn to interact through oral language (Goldin-Meadow, 1985). These children are reared in an environment that is rich in culturally mediated social interactions (including linguistic mediation), which include the child and proceed very much as they would if the child could hear; people eat meals together, the children are given baths and put to bed, they go to the store, and are toilet trained. Thus, they live in a world suffused with meaning; it is only the linguistic behavior that fills the gaps between movements and provides accounts of the rationale and prior history of those actions that they are missing.

Under these circumstances, children are known spontaneously to begin to employ *home sign*, a kind of communication through pantomime. Goldin-Meadow showed that home sign acquired in these circumstances exhibits a number of properties also found in the early stages of natural language acquisition. Children who start signing in the absence of adult sign language knowers begin to make two, three, and longer sign sequences around their second birthdays, at about the same time that hearing children create multi-word sentences. Most significantly, Goldin-Meadow reported that these deaf children were able to embed sign sentences within each other ("You/Susan give me/Abe cookie round"). This kind of behavior reveals that the children could engage in recursion, a form of communicative behavior that is characteristic of all human languages and absent from the communicative system of chimpanzees or other creatures, even following extensive training.

However, their language development comes to a halt at this point. The cultural medium is simply too thin to support the development of fully mature language. It appears that unless such children are provided access to some form of language as a part of the culturally organized environments they participate in, they will not develop the more subtle features of language on which sustainable cultural formations depend.

It is important to add that at the other extreme, where children have access to language, but not to culturally organized activity, language development also fails to take place. Children who have been left alone for a long time with a television set broadcasting in a foreign language do not acquire that language (Snow *et al.*, 1976).

It seems an inescapable conclusion from this kind of evidence that in order for children to acquire more than the barest rudiments of language, they must not only hear (or see) language but they must also participate in the activities that that language is helping to create. In everyday activity, words are essential material—ideal artifacts, by means of which people establish and maintain coordination, filling in the gaps between gestures and other actions, and making possible the fine tuning of expectations and interpretations.

Bruner (1982) referred to the social interactional constraints of ongoing everyday activities as *formats*. The format, he wrote,

> is a rule-bound microcosm in which the adult and child *do* things to and with each other. In its most general sense, it is the instrument of patterned human interaction. Since formats pattern communicative interaction between infant and caretaker before lexico-grammatical speech

begins, they are crucial vehicles in the passage from communication to language.

Later he added that once they become conventionalized, formats seem to have a kind of exteriority that allows them to act as constraints on the actions that occur within them. In this respect, Bruner's notion of format is very similar to Nelson's (1981, 1986) concept of generalized event schemas called *scripts*: "sequentially organized structures of causally and temporally linked acts with the actors and objects specified in the most general way" (Nelson, 1981, p. 101). In effect, these event-level cultural artifacts, embodied in the vocabulary and habitual actions of adults, act as structured media within which children can experience the covariation of language and action while remaining coordinated in a general way with culturally organized forms of behavior. In the process of negotiating such events with enculturated care-givers, children discover the vast range of meanings encoded in their language at the same time as they find new ways to carry out their own intentions.

Bruner captured the cultural view of language development when he wrote that language acquisition cannot be reduced to

> either the virtuoso cracking of a linguistic code, or the spinoff of ordinary cognitive development, or the gradual takeover of adults' speech by the child through some impossible inductive *tour de force*. It is, rather, a subtle process by which adults artificially arrange the world so that the child can succeed culturally by doing what comes naturally, and with others similarly inclined.
>
> (Bruner, 1982, p. 15)

Cross-cultural research on language interaction supplements intracultural studies by laying bare the incredible diversity of cultural modes of involving children in adult-run activities, such that they come to acquire language.

Arguments over the importance of the environment in language acquisition gave rise to a large literature on the different ways in which parents structure children's activities (see, e.g., de Villiers and de Villiers, 1978). Parents in many societies adopt something akin to a baby-talk mode when speaking to their children, before and while the children are acquiring language. Evidence available at the time led Ferguson (1977) to speculate that a special *baby talk register* (using higher pitch and intonation, simplified vocabulary, grammatically less complex sentences, and utterances designed to highlight important aspects of the situation) is a universal, acquisition-enhancing form of adult language socialization behavior. Cross-cultural data have shown that although adults everywhere speak to young children differently than they speak to older children and adults, the particular form of baby talk involving simplified grammar and vocabulary characteristic of middle-class

American parents is not universal. There is some evidence that other features of baby talk, such as the use of distinctive pitch and intonation, may be universal, but the data on cultural variation remain sparse (Fernald, 1989).

In many societies, adults deliberately teach vocabulary, styles of address, and other linguistic features. The Kaluli of Papua New Guinea, for example, are reported to hold their small infants facing away from them and toward other people while the mothers speak for them. There are also subcultures within the United States (e.g., working-class people in Baltimore, Maryland; Miller, 1982) in which it is firmly believed that children must be explicitly taught vocabulary, using quite rigid frames of the sort "How do you call this?" (See Schieffelin and Ochs, 1986, for a wide range of examples.) However, although the adults involved in such practices may believe that such special tailoring is helpful to their children's language acquisition, the data indicate that significant benefits associated with variations in cultural patterns of mother–infant interactions involving language are found rather rarely and in restricted domains (Snow and Ferguson, 1977).

The most secure overall generalization at this point is that culturally organized joint activity that incorporates the child into the scene as a novice participant is one necessary ingredient in language acquisition. As children in such activities struggle to understand objects and social relations in order to gain control over their environments and themselves, they recreate the culture into which they are born, even as they reinvent the language of their forbears.

[. . .]

References

Ainsworth, M. D. (1967). *Infancy in Uganda: Infant care and the growth of love.* Baltimore, MD: Johns Hopkins Press.

Ainsworth, M. D., Blehar, M. C., Waters, E., and Wall, S. (1978). *Patterns of attachment.* Hillsdale, NJ: Lawrence Erlbaum Associates.

Bandura, A. (1986). *Social foundations of thought and action: A social cognitive theory.* Englewood Cliffs, NJ: Prentice-Hall.

Berry, J. (1976). *Human ecology and cultural style.* New York: Sage-Halstead.

Bornstein, M. H., Tal, J., and Tamis-LeMonda, C. S. (1991). Parenting in cross-cultural perspective: The United States, France, and Japan. In M. H. Bornstein (Ed.), *Cultural approaches to parenting.* Hillsdale, NJ: Lawrence Erlbaum Associates.

Bornstein, M. H., Toda, S., Azuma, H., Tamis-LeMonda, C. S., and Ogino, M. (1990). Mother and infant activity and interaction in Japan and in the United States: II. A comparative microanalysis of naturalistic exchanges focused on the organization of infant attention. *International Journal of Behavioral Development, 13,* 289–308.

Bowlby, J. (1969). *Attachment and loss: Vol. 1. Attachment.* New York: Basic.

Bretherton, I., and Waters, E. (Eds). (1985). Growing points in attachment theory. *Monographs of the Society for Research in Child Development, 50,* (1–2, Serial No. 209).

Bruner, J. S. (1982). The formats of language acquisition. *American Journal of Semiotics*, *1*, 1–16.

Bruner, J. S. (1983). *Child's talk*. New York: Norton.

Campos, J. J., and Stenberg, C. R. (1981). Perception, appraisal, and emotion: The onset of social referencing. In M. E. Lamb and L. R. Sherrod (Eds), *Infants' social cognition: Empirical and social considerations*. Hillsdale, NJ: Lawrence Erlbaum Associates.

Carey, S. (1985). *Conceptual change in childhood*. Cambridge, MA: MIT Press.

Cole, M., and Cole, S. (1989). *The development of children*. New York: Scientific American Books.

Curtiss, S. (1977). *Genie: A psychological study of a modern-day wild child*. New York: Academic Press.

de Villiers, J. G., and de Villiers, P. A. (1978). *Language acquisition*. Cambridge, MA: Harvard University Press.

DeVos, G. A., and Hippler, A. E. (1969). Cultural psychology: Comparative studies of human behavior. In G. Lindzey and E. Aronson, (Eds), *The handbook of social psychology* (Vol. 4, 2nd ed.). Reading, MA: Addison-Wesley.

Dreyfus-Brisac, C. (1978). Ontogenesis of brain bioelectrical activity and sleep organization in neonates and infants. In F. Falkner and J. M. Tanner (Eds), *Human growth: Vol. 3. Neurobiology and nutrition*. New York: Plenum.

Ferguson, C. A. (1977). Baby talk as a simplified register. In C. E. Snow and C. A. Ferguson (Eds), *Talking to children*. Cambridge: Cambridge University Press.

Fernald, A. (1989). Intonation and communicative intent in mothers' speech to infants: Is the melody the message? *Child Development*, *60*, 1497–1510.

Frijda, N., and Jahoda, G. (1966). On the scope and methods of cross-cultural research. *International Journal of Psychology*, *1*, 110–127.

Geertz, C. (1973). *The interpretation of cultures*. New York: Basic.

Gelman, R. (1990). First principles affect learning and transfer in children. *Cognitive Science*, *14*, 79–107.

Gesell, A. (1940). *The first five years of life* (9th ed.). New York: Harper & Row.

Gesell, A. (1945). *The embryology of behavior*. New York: Harper & Row.

Goldin-Meadow, S. (1985). Language development under atypical learning conditions. In K. E. Nelson (Ed.), *Children's language* (Vol. 5). Hillsdale, NJ: Lawrence Erlbaum Associates.

Goldman-Rakic, P. S. (1987). Development of cortical circuitry and cognitive function. *Child Development*, *58*, 601–622.

Greenfield, P. M., Brazelton, T. B., and Childs, C. P. (1989). From birth to maturity in Zinacantan: Ontogenesis in cultural context. In V. Bricker and G. Gossen (Eds), *Ethnographic encounters in southern Mesoamerica: Celebratory essays in honor of Evon Z. Vogt*. Albany: Institute of Mesoamerican Studies, State University of New York.

Grossmann, K. E., and Grossmann, K. (1990). The wider concept of attachment in cross-cultural research. *Human Development*, *33*, 31–47.

Grossman, K. E., Grossman, K., Huber, F., and Wartner, U. (1981). Children's behavior towards their mothers at 12 months and their fathers at 18 months in Ainsworth's Strange Situation. *International Journal of Behavioral Development*, *4*, 157–181.

Grossmann, K., Grossmann, K. E., Spangler, S., Suess, G., and Unzner, L. (1985). Maternal sensitivity and newborn orientation responses as related to quality of attachment in northern Germany. In I. Bretherton and E. Waters (Eds), *Growing points of attachment theory. Monographs of the Society for Research in Child Development, 50* (1–2, Serial No. 209).

Herskovitz, M. J. (1948). *Man and his works: The science of cultural anthropology.* New York: Knopf.

Hinde, R. (1987). *Individuals, relationships, and culture.* Cambridge: Cambridge University Press.

Kagan, J. (1977). The uses of cross-cultural research in early development. In P. H. Liederman, S. Tulkin, and A. Rosenfeld (Eds), *Culture and infancy: Variations in the human experience.* New York: Academic Press.

Kluckhohn, C. (1954). Culture and behavior. In G. Lindzey (Ed.), *Handbook of social psychology* (Vol. 2). Cambridge: Addison-Wesley.

Konner, M. J., and Super, C. (1987). Sudden infant death syndrome: An anthropological hypothesis. In C. Super (Ed.), *The role of culture in developmental disorder.* New York: Academic Press.

Leontiev, A. N. (1981). *Problems of the development of the mind.* Moscow: Progress Publishers.

LeVine, R. A., and Miller, P. M. (1990). Commentary. *Human Development, 33,* 73–80.

Luria, A. R. (1979). *The making of mind.* Cambridge, MA: Harvard University Press.

Main, M. (1990). Cross-cultural studies of attachment organization: Recent studies, changing methodologies, and the concept of conditional strategies. *Human Development, 33,* 48–61.

Mead, M., and Macgregor, F. C. (1951). *Growth and culture.* New York: Putnam.

Miller, P. (1982). *Amy, Wendy and Beth: Learning language in south Baltimore.* Austin, TX: University of Texas Press.

Nelson, K. (1981). Social cognition in a script framework. In J. H. Flavell and L. Ross (Eds), *Social cognitive development.* Cambridge: Cambridge University Press.

Nelson, K. (1986). *Event knowledge: Structure and function in development.* Hillsdale, NJ: Lawrence Erlbaum Associates.

Nugent, J. K., Lester, B. M., and Brazelton, T. B. (1989). *The cultural context of infancy: Vol. 1. Biology, culture, and infant development.* Norwood, NJ: Ablex.

Piaget, J. (1973). *The psychology of intelligence.* Totowa, NJ: Littlefield & Adams.

Piaget, J., and Inhelder, B. (1969). *The psychology of the child.* New York: Basic.

Piatelli-Palmerini, M. (1980). *Language and learning.* Cambridge, MA: Harvard University Press.

Plomin, R. (1986). *Development, genetics, and psychology.* Hillsdale, NJ: Lawrence Erlbaum Associates.

Price-Williams, D. (1985). Cultural psychology. In G. Lindzey and E. Aronson (Eds), *Handbook of social psychology* (Vol. 2, 3rd ed.). New York: Random House.

Sagi, A., Lamb, M. E., Lewkowicz, K. S., Shoham, K. R., Dvir, R., and Estes, D. (1985). Security of infant–mother, father, metapelet, attachments among kibbutz-raised Israeli children. In I. Bretherton and K. Waters (Eds), Growing points of attachment theory. *Monographs of the Society for Research in Child Development, 50* (1–2, Serial No. 209), 257–275.

Sahlins, M. (1976). *Culture and practical reason.* Chicago: University of Chicago Press.

Schieffelin, B., and Ochs, E. (1986). *Language socialization across cultures.* New York: Cambridge University Press.

Segall, M. H., Dasen, P. R., Berry, J. W., and Poortinga, Y. (1990). *Human behavior in global perspective.* New York: Pergamon.

Skinner, B. F. (1953). *Science and human behavior.* New York: Macmillan.

Snow, C. E., Arlman-Rupp, A., Hassing, Y., Jobse, J., Joosken, J., and Vorster, J. (1976). Mother's speech in three social classes. *Journal of Psycholinguistic Research,* 5, 1–20.

Snow, C. E., and Ferguson, C. A. (Eds) (1977). *Talking to children.* Cambridge: Cambridge University Press.

Super, C. M., and Harkness, S. (1982). The infant's niche in rural Kenya and metropolitan America. In L. Adler (Ed.), *Issues in cross-cultural research.* New York: Academic Press.

Super, C. M., and Harkness, S. (1986). The development niche: A conceptualization at the interface of child and culture. *International Journal of Behavioral Development,* 9, 545–569.

Takahashi, H. (1986). Examining the Strange Situation procedure with Japanese mothers and 12-month-old infants. *Developmental Psychology,* 19, 184–191.

Takahashi, K. (1990). Are the key assumptions of the "Strange Situation" procedure universal? *Human Development,* 33, 23–30.

Tylor, E. B. (1874). *Primitive culture: Researches into the development of mythology, philosophy, religion, language, art, and custom.* London: John Murray.

van IJzendoorn, M. H., and Kroonenberg, P. M. (1988). Cross-cultural patterns of attachment: A meta-analysis of the strange situation. *Child Development,* 59, 147–156.

Vaughn, B., Egeland, B., Sroufe, L. A., and Waters, E. (1979). Individual differences in infant–mother attachment at twelve and eighteen months: Stability and change in families under stress. *Child Development,* 50, 971–975.

Wanner, E., and Gleitman, L. R. (Eds). (1982). *Language acquisition: State of the art.* Cambridge: Cambridge University Press.

Washburn, S. L. (1960). Tools and human evolution. *Scientific American,* 203, 63–73.

Whiting, B. B. (1980). Culture and social behavior: A model for development of social behaviors. *Ethos,* 8, 95–116.

Zimmerman, B. J. (1983). Social learning theory: A contextualist account of cognitive functioning. In C. Brainard (Ed.), *Recent advances in cognitive developmental theory.* New York: Springer-Verlag.

Chapter 2

The development of affect in infancy and early childhood*

Charles M. Super and Sara Harkness

[. . .]

In our view, a satisfactory theory of social and affective development must eventually incorporate three elements: (1) a statement of the thrust of growth universal to our species, (2) a recognition of the expressive behavioral patterns encouraged by culturally regulated socialization for particular situations, and (3) an appreciation of the sequences of developmental events as they occur in the context of the full span of life.

In this chapter we consider aspects of these three points from a comparative perspective. First, we present evidence of the universal emergence of some basic emotional displays, namely happy social play with caretakers and distress at their departure. Second, we illustrate the shaping of these universals into patterns of particular cultural significance. Third, we discuss the importance of the sequences of emotional learning within a culture in understanding the consequences of early affective socialization. Our examples are drawn from a variety of sources and locales, but in the second and third sections we describe in more detail the affective development of children in Kokwet, a Kipsigis community in rural Kenya.

The emergence of emotional displays

The display of any behavior, or integrated complex of behaviors, rests on neuromotor competence. Mature, appropriate displays of emotional behavior involve not only the overt acts (such as smiling), but also associated internal feeling states and the cognitively influenced connections among a particular environmental circumstance (such as a greeting from a friend), a feeling state, and a behavioral display. While the socialization of affect is a psychological and cultural process, it occurs only in coordination with a biological substrate that is unique to, and generalized across, our species. In short, there are neurological and hormonal universals in the way in which humans work; these univer-

---

* This is an edited version of a chapter that first appeared in *Cultural Perspectives on Child Development*, Oxford: W. H. Freeman, 1982.

sals contribute to the mechanisms of emotional socialization and also limit the possible range of variation. Since infants do not enter the world with these or any other biological mechanisms fully mature, observations on the maturationally guided emergence of particular kinds of behavior provide a useful technique for understanding possible universals. Knowing some of the universal elements, the process of tracing environmental influences is much easier.

One of the most dramatic early changes in emotional behavior occurs when a baby is 3 or 4 months old. To the American parent, the baby begins to seem more "like a real person." The third month, it is occasionally said, makes the first two worthwhile. The baby becomes not only less incessantly demanding – often sleeping through the night, for example, and fussing less – but also more reliably rewarding. Many American parents find a qualitative change in the baby's social responsiveness and expressiveness that brings real joy. A similar reaction by Kipsigis mothers in rural Kenya may be reflected in the fact that they begin to refer to their babies as "children" at this time, and no longer as "monkeys."

There is a parallel change at this point in the mothers' behavior in the two cultures: they are more likely to be found holding their babies than they were in the previous month, even though the general trend over the first year is to decrease physical contact (Super, 1980). The kinds of mutual, flowing social play that are salient at this time look very similar in the two groups. Observational recording in the home indicates that Kipsigis mothers and their 4-month-old infants smile and look at each other with about the same frequency as do upper-middle-class mother–infant pairs in Boston, Massachusetts.

Exactly what the behavioral changes in the baby are, and how they become encouraged by the mother's reactions, have yet to be fully documented. Smiling, however, is certainly a central feature of the changes in the baby's behavior. The frequency of smiling in normal infants rises dramatically during the third and fourth months in infants from many different cultures around the world. Figure 2.1 illustrates this for four groups of babies in Israel: those from lower- and middle-class urban families, those from a kibbutz settlement with cooperative child care arrangements, and those from a group of semi-nomadic Bedouin families in the Negev desert (Landau, 1977). The frequency of smiling by these babies, as observed in the course of a normal day, rises in a similar manner despite substantial differences in the social context of care.

The similarity in the emergence of smiling in Israeli samples, and in other even more diverse groups, suggests an underlying maturational cause – not a complete and sufficient cause, for maturation can proceed only through interaction with an environment, but still a necessary and driving force. The co-occurrence of this behavior change with a number of other developments at the same age supports the hypothesis of a broad underlying maturational factor. Important transitions at 3 to 4 months have been noted in other areas of emotion as well as cognition, motor skills, and sleep (for example,

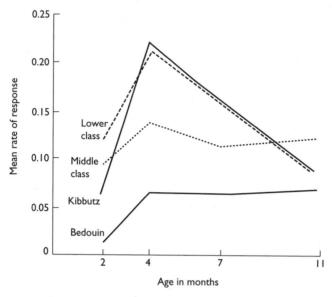

Figure 2.1 Infants from four different groups in Israel increase their rate of spontaneous
smiling in a similar way between 2 and 4 months of age

Source: Data from Landau, 1977: 389–400.

McGraw, 1946; Piaget, 1952; Spitz *et al.*, 1970). There is evidence for
changes in brain structure, most notably rapid myelinization in the cerebral
cortex and limbic (emotional) areas of the brain (Yakovlev and Lecours,
1967). Further support is available from studies of blind infants, who show an
early growth in smiling that is slightly delayed but otherwise quite similar to
development in normal infants (for example, Freedman, 1964; Parmalee,
1955).

Infant distress in response to being left by the mother also appears at a very
similar rate in a number of diverse settings. In experiments conducted in
urban America, rural Guatemala, the Kalahari desert of Botswana, and Israeli
kibbutzim, infants generally do not cry when the mother leaves until about 7
or 8 months of age, after which point distress becomes more and more frequent until a peak sometime after the first birthday (see Figure 2.2 adapted
from Kagan, 1976). The similarity here, it is argued, is not so much in the
development of a particular behavior, but rather in a cognitive ability to
detect and evaluate (and therefore sometimes to fear) unusual and unpredict-
able events (Kagan *et al.*, 1978). Regardless of whether the change is viewed
as "primarily" cognitive, emotional, or biological, or as an inseparable blend,
the data again point to a remarkably ordered emergence of emotional displays
in early life.

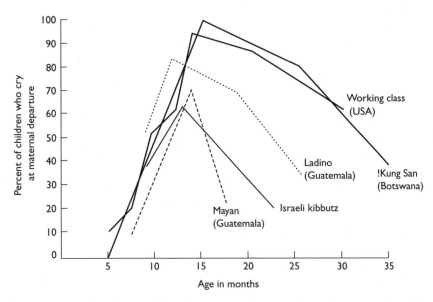

Figure 2.2 Infants from five different groups around the world show similar increases during the first year in the likelihood of crying at maternal departure in an experimental setting, but diverge during later years in the decline of this response

Source: Adapted from Kagan, 1976: 186–96.

The socialization of emotional displays

As the ability to display particular affective behaviors emerges, and especially as the ability becomes more stable and highly organized, the cultural system engages the infant's responses in particular ways. While the psychological mechanisms that lead to smiling are fundamentally universal, the opportunities and contexts for smiling in different cultures diverge. There appear to be two major pathways of cultural divergence in the emotional training of infants and young children: (1) the direct expression of parental values or beliefs, and (2) the less intentional structuring of the child's developmental niche by the physical and social resources for caretaking.

Parental values and beliefs

The most interesting aspect of parental values as they influence early socialization is that their expression is not usually a direct effort to achieve some later effect. Their expression is, rather, a more immediate reflection of adult psychological functioning. That is, values influence behavior more in the sense of "This is the way I feel like acting with my baby" or "This is the way I would like to see my baby act," rather than "I want to train my baby in this skill in order to facilitate social and economic advancement in later life."

Socialization values at this age are expressive goals in their own right, not only means to some later goal. Nevertheless, the effect of such socialization is usually to provide the infant or young child with practice in culturally appropriate social and emotional behavior.

Examples of concordance between parents' expressive interaction with infants and larger cultural values can be found from all parts of the world. In Uganda, adults and siblings talk and smile to infants more than is true in many other cultures, trying to coax a happy smile in return. It seems the natural way to play with babies. The social skills both expressed and trained in such interaction, however, are talents needed for personal advancement in the relatively mobile Baganda social order. Today, as has traditionally been the case in this group, personal skills are powerful means to gaining status and material resources. Unlike the situation in many traditional African groups, social standing can be individually earned, rather than being ascribed primarily on the basis of sex, age, or lineage (Kilbride and Kilbride, 1974; Kilbride and Kilbride, 1975).

Japanese mothers, compared to American mothers, spend large amounts of time soothing and lulling their infants, rather than stimulating them with active "chatting." The kinds of social intercourse that result are consonant with the patterns of interaction at later ages and with the larger patterns of social organization in the two societies. American mothers, partly to fulfill their own expectations of appropriate affective behavior, encourage open, expressive, assertive, self-directed behavior, while the Japanese mothers seek quiet, contented babies (Caudill and Frost, 1973; Caudill and Weinstein, 1969).

In some cases, adult beliefs about the nature of infants or about the world in general shape the emotional lives of infants. The Kwoma of New Guinea and Zinacantecans of Mexico, for example, have beliefs about supernatural threats and the vulnerability of infants that lead to keeping their babies close, quiet, and calm (Brazelton et al., 1969; Whiting, 1971). The cumulative effect on the infants' level of excitement may be substantial, even though the parents' motivations focus primarily on other matters. In contrast, many American parents in the mid-twentieth century were concerned with the possibility of lasting psychological damage that could result from excessive inhibition of "natural" feelings such as jealousy. This belief about the nature of personality development influenced their reaction to some kinds of emotional displays in their young children, for they thought it important to allow emotional conflicts to be expressed and played out where they could be discussed and managed (for example, Spock, 1968: 12).

Structural features of care

The expression and regulation of emotional behavior are also mediated by structural features of infant care that are not so obviously related to adult values or beliefs. Many aspects of a young child's environment are influenced by the way in which families are organized for other purposes. The use of child caretakers to supplement maternal care is an important example. In many societies around the world, the moment-to-moment care of a baby is given to an older sibling or other relative, typically a 7- or 8-year-old sister (Weisner and Gallimore, 1977). While attitudes within any group concerning the desirability of single versus multiple caretakers are probably consistent with the dominant pattern in that group, it would appear that aspects of social organization, such as means of economic production, family size, and mothers' work load, are more effectively related to use of child caretakers than are the values themselves. Certainly in American society over the past decades, it can be argued that maternal employment has been the driving force behind increased group care for young children, while attitudes consistently lagged behind.

In illustrating structural environmental influences on early affective development, and in the remainder of this chapter, we describe in some detail the early social life of Kipsigis children in western Kenya. It is difficult, however, to understand the integrating function of a culture's environment for children without some knowledge of the larger cultural system. Before describing structural features of the early environment in Kokwet, therefore, we will briefly present some background ethnographic information.

The Kipsigis of Kokwet

The Kipsigis of western Kenya are a Highland Nilotic people (Sutton, 1968) numbering about half a million. Traditionally they lived by herding cattle and raising simple crops; their life was semi-nomadic as they shifted pasture and field in response to the land and to sporadic fighting with neighboring groups. More permanent residence and land tenure became common in the early part of this century, encouraged by increasing contact with the British settlers and colonial administrators, especially the force of their economics and occasionally their force of arms (Manners, 1967). As in most of East Africa, the period following World War II initiated especially rapid change.

Kokwet, the Kipsigis community where we lived for 3 years in carrying out our investigation, consists of 54 homesteads spread out along 3 miles of a ridge of land formed by 2 streams that drain the Mau forest of the western highlands. To the north and east lie fine, rolling farmland and, a few hours away by dirt road, the tea estates of Kericho. To the south and west, the land dries and slopes down to the savannahs of the Mara, home of zebra and lion and of the Masai people.

The people of Kokwet have adapted successfully as farmers to the national economy. All the families are self-supporting in basic foodstuffs, with maize (corn) and milk being major components of the daily diet. Milk, maize, and pyrethrum (a daisy-like flower with insecticidal properties) are grown for cash marketing as well. Each family has about 18 acres of useful land, an unusual situation created by the initial terms of the settlement scheme set up by the Kenyan government at the time of national independence (1963). The land was purchased from a departing white settler and distributed to indigenous citizens. Neighboring lands had never been alienated for European use, and the people of Kokwet moved in from the surrounding areas. The relative abundance of fertile land in Kokwet has permitted, for the present, a continuation of the agricultural adaptation to modern life without disruptive pressures to leave the farm and seek wages in towns or plantations.

While there is no "village center" to Kokwet, households often cluster near the borders of their land to form small groups within the community. The typical round houses, with mud walls and straw roofs, overlook the families' pastures and fields most of the year, sometimes hidden by the tall maize as harvest approaches.

Despite fundamental changes in Kipsigis life, many traditional features persist in Kokwet. Social organization of the community continues to operate at the face-to-face level, with conflicts and disputes confronted and resolved in this context (Harkness *et al.*, 1981). Communal efforts among households are important for ceremonies, large projects, and some major activities, such as harvesting and weeding groups. Most adults have little or no formal education, and many families consist of one man, his two wives, and their children. While there are major divisions of role by age and sex, all members of a family participate in its maintenance through household chores, agricultural labor, and tending cattle. Most children now attend at least a few years of school, but more traditional forms of preparation for adult life continue in the home and in the larger community, for example adolescent initiation and circumcision rites for both boys and girls. Christian missions have been active in the general area for half a century, but most men and women are, in their own words, "not yet" converted.

The infant's niche in Kokwet

The infant in Kokwet is born into a physical and social setting that is different from the one familiar to Americans. Until the baby is 3 or 4 months old, the mother is almost always with the child. Most of the time, in fact, mother and baby are actually touching; the baby might be sitting propped up in the mother's lap while she prepares food, riding on her back (secured and covered with cloth) as she goes to the river for water, cradled in her arms for nursing, or straddling her hip as she moves around the yard doing chores. By the time the baby is 4 months old, a child caretaker has taken over a large share of the daytime care, holding and carrying the baby and providing entertainment, but often within sight of the mother. A little later, the mother may go to the garden, perhaps 10 minutes away, or visit a neighbor while leaving the baby with the child caretaker.

The baby's emotional life is influenced in a number of ways by this organization of care, or niche. Of particular interest here are the embeddedness of infant life in the continuing social and economic functioning of the family, and the adaptations to and by the several caretakers. A useful example is the regulation of sleep–wake behavior. Unlike many American families, Kipsigis households do not make major modifications in their living quarters or family routines to facilitate infant sleep. There is no baby's room and no nap schedule. One reason why this is possible is that care of an awake infant is more compatible with the mother's daily chores and pleasures. The Kipsigis mother can carry, hold, or entertain the baby reasonably well while sweeping the house, relaxing after the midday meal, fetching firewood, or preparing food. This is less true for the American mother, who does not have the same customary repertoire of carrying and holding practices, and whose activities include PTA meetings, balancing the checkbook, driving to the supermarket, working in an office, and watching television.

A second circumstance that contributes to the divergence in sleep–wake scheduling is the availability of other caretakers. When the Kipsigis mother needs to be free of the baby for some kinds of garden work or for her peace of mind, there is almost always a sibling caretaker, a co-wife, or another relative to take the child. She does not need to rely on the baby's sleeping for a chance to disengage from continuous care.

As one consequence of these differences in the infant's niche, Kipsigis babies do not sleep quite as much as American infants, and they do not develop long periods of sustained sleep so soon. At 4 months of age, the average Kipsigis baby sleeps just over 12 hours each day, compared to about 15 in America. The longest episode of sleep is about 4.5 hours, compared to 8 in America (Super and Harkness, 1977).

The pattern of adaptation in sleep is related to adaptations in feeding, elimination, and even social interaction. In each domain, the Kipsigis infant is likely to have briefer and less regular cycles of activity and rest, while the American baby is likely to have fewer, longer periods of sleeping, feeding, and playful interaction. The circadian flow of behavior has different patterns of tension and resolution in the two niches. The Kipsigis and American babies, in sum, are learning the emotional structure of their cultural niche.

The particular adaptations and embeddedness in each group are only part of the emotional structure of the niche. Of critical importance are the ways in which the niche can and cannot adapt to the individual characteristics of the infant, for the areas of rigidity and flexibility determine the kinds of behavior that will create upset and difficulty. For the American baby, scheduling activity by the clock may be of considerable importance to the mother because of her value system or because of her own needs. For the baby in Kokwet, adaptation to the different styles of care provided by several caretakers is essential for happy functioning of the family. Within any group, babies vary in their behavioral dispositions (Thomas and Chess, 1977). Regularity and adaptability are dimensions of variation among infants in both cultures, but their significance depends on the typical niche and its points of flexibility. In both groups, a mismatch between the needs and adaptability of the baby and those of the caretaking niche results in a situation that is stressful for all concerned. The early socialization of emotional life includes learning the sensitivities of one's niche.

Long-term adaptations to the niche play another role in emotional life, namely the building of expectations concerning what constitutes normal life and what is bizarre. While infants in Kokwet, as in other communities, are often upset when their mothers leave them for short periods, this response does not last long. They become accustomed to care by several people, and so maternal absence by itself does not occasion distress. As Figure 2.2 shows, after the universal emergence of distress at separation from mother, at about 1 year of age, there is considerable diversity among cultures in its decline in the second and third years of life. For the American and !Kung San children, for example, who are cared for almost exclusively by the mother, the distress reaction remains frequent for a relatively long time. In the other groups, however, where siblings or other persons play an important role in the day-to-day care of infants and toddlers, there is a more rapid decline in the amount of distress.

Distress at maternal departure ("separation anxiety") is often linked in developmental theory to distress at the approach of a stranger ("fear of strangers"). While the common thread of cognitive competence is important in the emergence of these two responses (Kagan *et al.*, 1978), the regulation of the reactions by features of daily life can lead to different patterns in later months. Many American children have a single caretaker but are exposed to a large number of strangers when they visit the doctor's office, the supermarket, and their older sibling's school. In Kokwet, the cast of characters for daily life remains stable and relatively small, despite the fact that two or three individuals are routinely involved in care. Informal observations suggest that fear of strangers is more intense and sustained for Kipsigis children than it is for Americans, even though distress at maternal departure is less so. In each case, the children are making equally successful adaptations to their social niche, minimizing distress in the long run and sensitizing the toddler to unusual situations. The important point for emotional development, however, is that the universal reactions are becoming differentially patterned into the structure of daily life, and that adaptation in the two settings leads to contrasting responses to the identical situation.

Summary

In summary, parental beliefs and values and the structure of infant care together provide a niche in which the baby develops an emotional life. Various features of the physical and social niche are integrated, in most cases, in a way that both reflects and reinforces larger aspects of the surrounding culture.

In the infants' adaptations to the niche can be seen the early, culturally directed organization of emotional behavior and the socialization of emotional displays.

Developmental sequences and consequences

There is a long history of speculation and inquiry in psychology concerning long-term consequences of early emotional development. Much of this work has focused on possible pathological sequelae of traumatic events or instances of extreme deprivation (Clarke and Clarke, 1976); it does not address several important issues in the continuities of normal development. In the normal case, there is not only a continuity of the mind but also some continuity of the environment. It becomes difficult, therefore, to disentangle psychological consequences of early experience from later environmental sequences.

The learning of emotional behaviors does not stop at 3 or 13 or 30, nor does the role of culture in patterning that learning. As the child grows older, he or she encounters a larger variety of social settings. Each setting has a typical cast of characters and scenario, each has a particular meaning and prescription for proper behavior; one way in which a culture socializes is in the settings it provides (Whiting, 1980). The emotional differentiation of settings in early childhood is part of the culturally regulated sequence of development. Intimately related to the differentiation of settings is the way superficially similar developmental transitions can yield divergent psychological meanings depending on the preceding and surrounding experience. Very few childhood experiences are absolute in their emotional message. The emergent patterning of emotional expression across settings, and the sequence of settings across time, are probably more important for the normal socialization of affect than learning in any one situation. In this patterning and sequencing are intertwined the values, beliefs, customary practices, and ecological forces that are integrated by the culture and that are the cultural context of development (Harkness, 1980).

Cultural divergence in the verbal expression of inner thoughts and feelings illustrates the importance of developmental sequences in socialization. Social interaction during infancy, as indicated earlier, is similar in Kokwet and American settings in the frequency of smiling and mutual regard (face-to-face interaction). The rate of vocalization in Kokwet, however, is only half the American rate; both the mothers and babies in Kokwet "speak" to each other less often than those in an American sample. While the interaction appears equally warm and affectionate in the two settings, it is quieter in Kokwet.

As the children grow through the familiar sequence of crawling, walking, talking, and other milestones of development, there is a variety of skills parents can choose to encourage. Mothers in Kokwet encourage some activities that are relatively neglected by American parents (Super, 1976), but they do not see themselves as having a major role in "teaching" a child to talk. That function, it is believed, is filled by the child's siblings. Mothers' verbal inter-action with 2- and 3-year-olds is not as frequent as that found in American homes, and has a relatively high frequency of commands. Increasingly as the child moves into early childhood, the mother's verbal communication becomes directing, comforting, and scolding rather than eliciting of verbal reply (Harkness and Super, 1977).

A particular focus of this maternal interaction is the child's initial steps toward becoming a responsible and productive member of the large house-hold. Small tasks start early through a blend of assignment and imitation – watching that the goats or calves do not approach drying produce, carrying small cans of water, helping to shell maize cobs. The father, who has had relatively little interaction with his child up to this point, joins in the affectionate responsibility for leading the child toward a maturing role in the family. It is as though the parents' traditional attitude is that children will learn to talk soon enough on their own, but they must be taught to under-stand requests and instructions and to obey them. The parents' goal for young children is verbal comprehension, not production.

Near the beginning of the transition from toddlerhood to early childhood, generally in the second year of life, the Kipsigis child has been weaned from the mother's breast for feeding, from her back for carrying and comforting, and from her bed for sleeping. Usually a younger sibling has appeared on the scene to take up those places. Interaction with adults actually decreases in the following few years, while siblings, half-siblings, and neighbor children become the main partners in social interaction. Children in the new social group range over several years in age, and while relations are ordered to some extent by the hierarchy of age and sex, a strong camaraderie develops. In this context the children appear as active and vocal as children anywhere, playing games, tussling on the ground, chasing a stray chicken, and swinging from the beams of a maize storehouse. While verbal aggression and precocity may not play the role in such children's groups that they do in some other cul-tures, there is certainly not the stricture of silence and respect found in the presence of adults.

There are two points to be made from the brief description of the social life of young children in Kokwet. First, the patterning of emotional expression in various settings is as important to affective development as is the character of expression in any one setting. Children are socialized not only into *how* they should behave, but also into how they should behave *where.*

Second, the meaning of how children should behave in different settings depends to some degree on the larger developmental sequences. The transi-tion to early childhood in America shares some characteristics with the Kip-sigis case – the pattern of interaction becomes more demanding of obedience, for example. The Kipsigis toddler, however, is already accustomed to having several important social partners to whom can be transferred some kinds of verbally expressive interaction. The meaning of the transition is affected as well by events to follow. Fewer than half of the American children witness a similar process in a younger sibling, while in Kokwet more than 80 percent see in their own family that this process is part of everyone's life.

There is a continuing sequence of niches in childhood and maturity, and each culture has its own pattern of continuities and discontinuities. In some cases, the thematic parallels are striking. The American baby who is scheduled to bottle and bed is later scheduled to school bell, and still later to time card or deadline. The Kipsigis baby whose state was more personally mediated by several people must, as an adult, accept community mediation of disputes rather than impersonal and externally imposed judgments (Harkness et al., 1981). Nevertheless, each life stage has a variety of affective settings, and an individual draws upon the variety of past experiences to know how to feel and how to express the feeling.

Conclusion

The mosaic of emotional behavior expressed by people of different cultures reflects in part their past experience. It is too simple, however, to see that residue of experience only in the shape of personality as traditionally drawn by Western psychology. Any particular expression builds on the motives and the understanding of the world acquired in a long history of culturally constituted experience. The elements of expression are universally human, but they are organized, practiced, and regulated by culture. The values and settings that started the socialization process are at least thematically related to aspects of later functioning, but the patterning and shading of feeling and expression reflect the continuing process of adaptation and growth.

[. . .]

References

Brazelton. T. B., Robey, J. S. and Collier, G. A. (1969) "Infant development in the Zinacanteco Indians of southern Mexico," *Pediatrics* 44: 274–90.

Caudill, W. and Frost, L. A. (1973) "A comparison of maternal care and infant behavior in Japanese–American, American, and Japanese families," in W. Lebra (ed.) *Mental Health Research in Asia and the Pacific*, vol. 3: *Youth, Socialization, and Mental Health*. Honolulu: University Press of Hawaii.

Caudill. W. and Weinstein, H. (1969) "Maternal care and infant behavior in Japan and America," *Psychiatry* 32: 12–43.

Clarke, A. M. and Clarke, A. D. B. (1976) *Early Experience: Myth and Evidence*. New York: Free Press.

Freedman, D. G. (1964) "Smiling in blind infants and the issue of innate vs. acquired," *Journal of Psychology and Psychiatry* 5: 17–184.

Harkness. S. (1980) "The cultural context of child development," in C. M. Super and S. Harkness (eds) "Anthropological perspectives on child development," *New Directions for Child Development* 8: 7–13.

Harkness, S. and Super, C. M. (1977) "Why African children are so hard to test," in L. Adler (ed.) "Issues in cross-cultural research," *Annals of the New York Academy of Sciences* 285: 326–31; reprinted in L. L. Adler (ed.) *Issues in Cross-Cultural Research*. New York: Academic Press.

Harkness. S., Edwards, C. P. and Super, C. M. (1981) "Social roles and moral reasoning: a case study in rural Africa," *Developmental Psychology* 17(5): 595–603.

Kagan, J. (1976) "Emergent themes in human development," *American Scientist* 64: 186–96.

Kagan, J., Kearsley, R. B. and Zelazo, P. R. (1978) *Infancy: Its Place in Human Development*. Cambridge, Mass.: Harvard University Press.

Kilbride, J. E. and Kilbride, P. L. (1975) "Sitting and smiling behavior of Baganda infants: the influence of culturally constituted experience," *Journal of Cross-Cultural Psychology* 6: 88–107.

Kilbride, P. L. and Kilbride, J. E. (1974) "Sociocultural factors and the early manifestation of sociability behavior among Baganda infants," *Ethos* 2: 296–314.

Landau, R. (1977) "Spontaneous and elicited smiles and vocalizations of infants in four Israeli environments," *Developmental Psychology* 13: 389–400.

McGraw, M. B. (1946) "Maturation of behavior," in L. Carmichael (ed.) *Manual of Child Psychology*. New York: Wiley.

Manners, R. A. (1967) "The Kipsigis of Kenya: culture change in a 'model' East African tribe," in J. H. Steward (ed.) *Three African Tribes in Transition*. Urbana, Ill.: University of Illinois Press.

Parmalee, A. H., Jr (1955) "The developmental evaluation of the blind premature infant," *Journal of Diseases of Children* 90: 135–40.

Piaget, J. (1952) *The Origins of Intelligence in Children*. New York: International University Press.

Spitz, R. A., Emde, R. N. and Metcalf, D. R. (1970) "Further prototypes of ego formation: a working paper from a research project on early development," *Psychoanalytic Study of the Child* 25: 417–41.

Spock, B. (1968) *Baby and Child Care*. New York: Pocket Books.

Super, C. M. (1976) "Environmental influences on motor development: the case of 'African infant precocity,'" *Developmental Medicine and Child Neurology* 18: 561–7.

Super, C. M. and Harkness, S. (1977) "The infant's niche in rural Kenya and metropolitan America," in L. L. Adler (ed.) *Issues in Cross-Cultural Research*. New York: Academic Press.

Sutton, J. E. G. (1968) "The settlement of East Africa," in B. A. Ogot (ed.) *Zamarii: A Survey of East African History*. Nairobi, Kenya: East African Publishing House & Longman Group.

Thomas, A. and Chess, S. (1977) *Temperament and Development*. New York: Brunner Mazel.

Weisner, T. S. and Gallimore, R. (1977) "My brother's keeper: child and sibling caretaking," *Current Anthropology* 18: 169–80.

Whiting, B. B. (1980) "Culture and social behavior: a model for the development of social behavior," *Ethos* 8: 95–116.

Whiting, B. B. and Whiting, J. W. M. (1975) *Children of Six Cultures: A Psycho-Cultural Analysis*. Cambridge, Mass.: Harvard University Press.

Whiting, J. W. M. (1971) "Causes and consequences of the amount of body contact between mother and infant," paper presented at meeting of the American Anthropological Association, New York, 18 November.

Yakovlev, P. I. and Lecours, A. (1967) "The myelogenetic cycles of regional maturation of the brain," in A. Minkowski (ed.) *Regional Development of the Brain in Early Life*. Oxford: Blackwell.

Chapter 3

A cultural perspective on the transition from prelinguistic to linguistic communication*

Bambi B. Schieffelin and Elinor Ochs

Ethnographic orientation

To most middle-class Western readers, the descriptions of verbal and non-verbal behaviors of middle-class caregivers with their children seem very familiar, desirable, and even natural. These descriptions capture in rich detail what does go on in many middle-class households, to a greater or lesser extent. The characteristics of caregiver speech (baby-talk register) and comportment that have been specified are highly valued by members of white middle-class society, including researchers, readers, and subjects of study. They are associated with good mothering and can be spontaneously produced with little effort or reflection. As demonstrated by Shatz and Gelman (1973), Sachs and Devin (1976), and Andersen and Johnson (1973), children as young as 4 years of age can speak and act in these ways when addressing small children.

From our research experience in other societies as well as our acquaintance with some of the cross-cultural studies of language socialization (Blount, 1972; Clancy, 1986; Harkness, 1975; Harkness and Super, 1977; Heath, 1983; Kulick, 1992; Miller, 1982; Philips, 1982; Schieffelin and Ochs, 1986a,b; Scollon and Scollon, 1981; Stross, 1972; Ward, 1971), the general patterns of caregiving that have been described in the psychological literature on white middle-class society are characteristic of neither all societies nor all social groups (e.g., all social classes within one society). We would like the reader, therefore, to reconsider the descriptions of caregiving in the psychological literature as *ethnographic descriptions*.

By ethnographic, we mean *descriptions that take into account the perspective of members of a social group, including beliefs and values that underlie and organise their activities and utterances*. Ethnographers rely heavily on observations and on formal and informal elicitation of members' reflections and interpretations as

* This is an edited version of a chapter that first appeared in Golinkoff, R. M. (ed.) *The Transition from Prelinguistic to Linguistic Communication*, Hillsdale, NJ: Lawrence Erlbaum, 1983.

a basis for analysis (Geertz, 1973). Typically, the ethnographer is not a member of the group under study. Further, in presenting an ethnographic account, the researcher faces the problem of communicating world views or sets of values that may be unfamiliar and strange to the reader. Ideally, such statements provide a set of organizing principles that give coherence and an analytic focus to the behaviors described.

Psychologists who have carried out research on verbal and non-verbal behavior of caregivers and their children draw on both of the methods articulated above. However, unlike most ethnographers, typically the psychological researcher *is* a member of the social group under observation. (In some cases, the researcher's own children are the subjects of study.) Further, unlike the ethnographer, the psychologist addresses a readership familiar with the social scenes portrayed.

That researcher, reader, and subjects of study tend to have in common a white middle-class literate background has had several consequences. For example, by and large, the psychologist has not been faced with the problem of cultural translation, as has the anthropologist – there has been a tacit assumption that readers can provide the larger cultural framework for making sense out of the behaviors documented. A consequence of this, in turn, is that the cultural nature of the behaviors and principles presented is not explicit. From our perspective, *language and culture as bodies of knowledge, structures of understanding, conceptions of the world, collective representations, are both extrinsic to and far more extensive than any individual could know or learn. Culture encompasses variation in knowledge between individuals, but such variation, while crucial to what an individual may know and to the social dynamic between individuals, does not have its locus within the individual.* Our position is that culture is not something that can be considered separately from the accounts of caregiver–child interactions; it is what organizes and gives meaning to that interaction. This is an important point, as it affects the definition and interpretation of the behaviors of caregivers and children. How caregivers and children speak and act towards one another is linked to cultural patterns that extend and have consequences beyond the specific interactions observed. For example, how caregivers speak to their children may be linked to other institutional adaptations to young children. These adaptations, in turn, may be linked to how members of a given society view children more generally (their "nature," their social status and expected comportment) and to how members think children develop.

We are suggesting here that sharing of assumptions between researcher, reader, and subjects of study is a mixed blessing. In fact, this sharing presents a *paradox of familiarity*. We are able to apply without effort the cultural framework for interpreting the behavior of caregivers and young children in our own social group; indeed as members of a white middle-class society, we are socialized to do this very work, that is interpreting behaviors, attributing motives, and so on. The paradox is that in spite of this ease of effort, we cannot easily isolate and make explicit these cultural principles. As Goffman's work on American society has illustrated, articulation of norms, beliefs, and values is often possible only when faced with violations, that is with gaffes, breaches, misfirings, and the like (Goffman, 1963, 1967; Much and Shweder, 1979).

Another way to see the cultural principles at work in our own society is to examine the ways in which *other* societies are organized in terms of social interaction and in terms of the society at large. In carrying out such research, the ethnographer offers a point of contrast and comparison with our own everyday activities. Such comparative material can lead us to reinterpret behaviors as cultural that we have assumed to be natural. From the anthropological perspective, every society will have its own cultural constructs of what is natural and what is not. For example, every society has its own theory of procreation. Certain Australian Aboriginal societies believe that a number of different factors contribute to conception. Von Sturmer (1980) writes that among the Kugu-Nganychara (West Cape York Peninsula, Australia), the spirit of the child may first enter the man through an animal that he has killed and consumed. The spirit passes from the man to the woman through sexual intercourse, but several sexual acts are necessary to build the child. (See also Montagu, 1937; Hamilton, 1981.) Even within a single society, there may be different beliefs concerning when life begins and ends, as the recent debates in the United States and Europe concerning abortion and mercy killing indicate. The issue of what is nature and what is nurture (cultural) extends to patterns of caregiving and child development. Every society will have (implicitly or explicitly) given notions concerning the capacities and temperament of children at different points in their development (see, for example, Ninio, 1979; Snow, de Blauw and van Roosmalen, 1979). The expectations and responses of caregivers will be directly related to these notions.

Two developmental stories

At this point, using an ethnographic perspective, we will recast selected behaviors of white middle-class caregivers and young children as pieces of one "developmental story." The white middle-class "developmental story" that we are constructing is based on various descriptions available, and focuses on those patterns of interaction (both verbal and non-verbal) that have been emphasized in the literature. This story will be compared with another developmental story: the Kaluli (Papua New Guinea), a society that is strikingly different.

One of the major goals in presenting and comparing these developmental stories is to demonstrate that communicative interactions between caregivers and young children are culturally constructed. In our comparisons we will focus on three facts of communicative interaction: (1) the social organization of the verbal environment of very young children; (2) the extent to which children are expected to adapt to situations or that situations are adapted to the child; and (3) the negotiation of meaning by caregiver and child. We first present a general sketch for each social group and then discuss in more detail the consequences of the differences and similarities in communicative patterns in these two groups.

These developmental stories are not timeless, but rather are linked in complex ways to particular historical contexts. Both the ways in which caregivers behave towards young children and the popular and scientific accounts of these ways may differ at different moments in time. The stories that we present represent ideas held in the two social groups during the 1980s.

The two stories show that there is more than one way of becoming social and using language in early childhood. All normal children will become members of their own social group, but the process of becoming social, including becoming a language user, is culturally constructed. In relation to this process of construction, every society has its own developmental stories that are rooted in social organization, beliefs, and values. These stories may be explicitly codified and/or tacitly assumed by members.

Anglo-American white middle-class developmental story

Middle class in Britain and the United States covers a broad range of white-collar and professional workers and their families, including lower-middle-, middle-middle-, and upper-middle-class strata. The literature on communicative development has been largely based on middle-middle- and upper-middle-class households. These households tend to consist of a single nuclear family with one, two, or three children. The primary caregiver almost without exception is a child's natural or adopted mother. Researchers have focused on communicative situations in which one child interacts with his or her mother. The generalizations proposed by these researchers concerning mother–child communication could be an artifact of this methodological focus. However, it could be argued that the attention to two-party encounters between a mother and her child reflects the most frequent type of communicative interaction to which most young middle-class children are exposed. Participation in two-party as opposed to multi-party interactions is a product of many considerations, including the physical setting of households, where interior and exterior walls bound and limit access to social interaction.

Soon after an infant is born, many mothers will hold their infants in such a way that they are face-to-face and will gaze at them. Mothers have been observed to address their infants, vocalize to them, ask questions, and greet them. In other words, from birth on, the infant is treated as a *social being* and as an *addressee* in social interaction. The infant's vocalizations, physical movements, and states are often interpreted as meaningful and will be responded to verbally by the mother or other caregiver. In this way, proto-conversations are established and sustained, along a *dyadic, turn-taking* model.

Throughout this period and the subsequent language-acquiring years, caregivers treat very young children as communicative partners. One very important procedure in facilitating these social exchanges is the mother's (or other caregiver's) act of *taking the perspective of the child.* This perspective is evidenced in her own speech through the many simplifying and affective features of baby-talk register that have been described and through the various strategies employed to identify what the young child may be expressing.

Such perspective-taking is part of a much wider set of accommodations by adults to young children. These accommodations are manifested in several domains. For example, there are widespread material accommodations to infancy and childhood in the form of cultural artifacts designed for this stage of life, that is baby clothes, baby food, miniaturization of furniture, and toys. Special behavioral accommodations are coordinated with the infant's perceived needs and capacities, for example, putting the baby in a quiet place to facilitate and insure proper sleep; "babyproofing" a house as a child becomes increasingly mobile, yet not aware of or able to control the consequences of his own behavior. In general, *situations and the language used in them are adapted or modified to the child* rather than the reverse. Further, the child is a *focus of attention*, in that the child's actions and verbalizations are often the *starting point* of social interaction with more mature persons.

While developmental achievements such as crawling, walking, and first words are awaited by caregivers, the accommodations noted above have the effect of keeping the child dependent on and separate from the adult community for a considerable period of time. The child is protected from certain experiences that are considered harmful (e.g., playing with knives, climbing stairs), but such protection delays his knowledge and developing competence in such contexts.

The accommodations of white middle-class caregivers to young children can be examined for other values and tendencies. Particularly among the American middle class, these accommodations reflect a *discomfort with the competence differential* between adult and child. The competence gap is reduced by two strategies. One is for the adult to simplify her or his speech to match more closely what the adult considers to be the verbal competence of the young child. Let us call this strategy the *self-lowering* strategy, following Irvine's (1974) analysis of intercaste demeanor. A second strategy is for the caregiver to interpret (Brown, 1973) richly what the young child is expressing. Here the adult acts as if the child were more competent than his behavior more strictly would indicate. Let us call this strategy the *child-raising* strategy. Other behaviors conform to this strategy, such as when an adult cooperates in a task with a child but treats that task as an accomplishment of the child.

For example, in eliciting a story from a child, a caregiver will often cooperate with the child in the telling of the story. This cooperation typically takes the form of posing questions to the child, such as "Where did you go?," "What did you see?," and so on, to which the adult knows the answer. The child is seen as telling the story even though she or he is simply supplying the information the adult has preselected and organized (Greenfield and Smith, 1976; Ochs, Schieffelin and Platt, 1979; Schieffelin and Eisenberg, 1984). Bruner's (1978) descriptions of scaffolding, in which a caregiver constructs a tower or other play object, allowing the young child to place the last block, are also good examples of this tendency. Here the tower may be seen by the caregiver and others as the child's own work. Similarly, in later life, caregivers playing games with their children may let them win, acting as if the child can match or more than match the competence of the adult.

A final aspect of this white middle-class developmental story concerns the willingness of many caregivers to interpret unintelligible or partially intelligible utterances of young children (cf. Ochs, 1982, 1991). One of the recurrent ways in which interpretation is carried out is for the caregiver to offer a paraphrase, or "expansion" (Brown and Bellugi, 1964; Cazden, 1965), using a question intonation. This behavior of caregivers has continuity with their earlier attributions of intentionality directed toward ambiguous utterances (from the point of view of the infant). For both the prelinguistic and language-using child, the caregiver provides an explicitly verbal interpretation. This interpretation or paraphrase is potentially available to the young child to affirm, disconfirm, or modify.

Through exposure to and participation in these clarification exchanges, the young child is being socialized into several cultural patterns. The first of these is a way of recognizing and defining what constitutes unintelligibility, that an utterance or vocalization may in fact not be immediately understood. Second, the child is presented with the procedures for dealing with ambiguity. Through the successive offerings of possible interpretations, the child learns that more than one understanding of a given utterance or vocalization may be possible. The child is also learning who can make these interpretations, and the extent to which they may be open to modification. Finally, the child is learning how to settle upon a possible interpretation and how to show disagreement or agreement. *This entire process socializes the child into culturally specific models of organizing knowledge, thought, and language.*

A Kaluli developmental story

The Kaluli people (population approximately 1,200) are an example of a small-scale, non-literate, egalitarian society (Schieffelin, 1976). Kaluli, most of whom are monolingual, speak the Kaluli language, a non-Austronesian verb-final ergative language (Schieffelin, 1986). They live in the tropical rain forest on the Great Papuan Plateau in the Southern Highlands of Papua New Guinea. Kaluli maintain large gardens and hunt and fish in order to obtain protein. Villages are composed of 60–90 individuals who traditionally lived in one large longhouse that had no internal walls. Currently, while the longhouse is maintained, many families are living in smaller dwellings so that two or more extended families may live together. It is not unusual then for at least a dozen individuals of different ages to be living together in one house which consists essentially of one semi-partitioned room.

Men and women utilize extensive networks of obligation and reciprocity in the organization of work and sociable interaction. Everyday life is overtly focused around verbal interaction. Kaluli think of and use talk as a means of control, manipulation, expression, assertion, and appeal. It gets you what you want, need, or feel owed. Talk is a primary indicator of social competence and a primary way to be social. Learning how to talk and become independent is a major goal of socialization (Schieffelin, 1990).

For the purpose of comparison and for understanding something of the cultural basis for the ways in which Kaluli act and speak to their children, it is important first to describe selected aspects of a Kaluli developmental story which we have constructed from various kinds of ethnographic data. Kaluli describe their babies as helpless, "soft" (*taiyo*), and "having no understanding" (*asugo andoma*). They take care of them, they say, because they "feel sorry for them." Mothers, who are primary caregivers, are attentive to their infants and physically responsive to them. Whenever an infant cries, it is offered the breast. However, while nursing her infant, a mother may also be involved in other activities, such as food preparation, or she may be engaged in conversation with individuals in the household. Mothers never leave their infants alone and only rarely with other caregivers. When not holding their infants, mothers carry them in netted bags which are suspended from their heads. When the mother is gardening, gathering wood, or just sitting with others, the baby will sleep in the netted bag next to the mother's body.

Kaluli mothers, given their belief that infants "have no understanding," never treat their infants as partners (speaker/addressee) in dyadic communicative interactions. While they greet their infants by name and use expressive vocalizations, they rarely address other utterances to them. Furthermore, mothers and infants do not gaze into each other's eyes, an interactional pattern that is consistent with adult patterns of not gazing when vocalizing in interaction with one another. Rather than facing their babies and speaking to them, Kaluli mothers tend to face their babies outwards so that they can be seen by and see others that are part of the social group. Older children greet and address the infant and, in response to this, the mother, while moving the baby, speaks in a high-pitched nasalized voice "for" the baby. Triadic exchanges such as the one shown in Figure 3.1 are typical of these situations.

When a mother takes the speaking role of an infant, she uses language that is well formed and appropriate for an older child. Only the nasalization and high pitch mark it as "the infant's." When speaking as the infant to older children, mothers speak assertively, that is, they never whine or beg on behalf of the infant. Thus, in taking this role, the mother does for the infant what

Mother	Abi
(Abi to baby)	[1] Bage!/do you see my box here?/do you see it?/do you see it?/
(high nasal voice talking as if she is the baby, moving the baby who is facing Abi):	
[2] My brother, I'll take half, my brother.	
(holding stick out)	[3] Mother, give him half/give him half/mother, my brother – here, here take half/X/
(in a high nasal voice as baby):	
[4] My brother, what half do I take? What about it, my brother, put it on the shoulder!	
[5] (to Abi in her usual voice): Put it on the shoulder.	
(Abi rests stick on baby's shoulder)	
[6] There, carefully put it on. (stick accidentally pokes baby) Feel sorry, stop.	

Figure 3.1 Example of a triadic exchange

Notes: Mother is holding her infant son Bage (3 months). Abi (35 months) is holding a stick on his shoulder in a manner similar to that in which one would carry a heavy patrol box (the box would be hung on a pole placed across the shoulders of the two men).

the infant cannot do for itself: appear to act in a controlled and competent manner, using language. These kinds of interactions continue until a baby is 4–6 months of age.

Several points are important here. First, these triadic exchanges are carried out primarily for the benefit of the older child and help create a relationship between the two children. Second, the mother's utterances in these exchanges are not based on, nor do they originate with, anything that the infant has initiated – either vocally or gesturally. Recall the Kaluli claim that infants have no understanding. How could someone with "no understanding" initiate appropriate interactional sequences?

However, there is an even more important and enduring cultural construct that helps make sense out of the mother's behaviors in this situation and in many others as well. Kaluli say that "one cannot know what another thinks or feels." Now, while Kaluli obviously interpret and assess one another's available behaviors and internal states, these interpretations are not culturally acceptable as topics of talk. Individuals often talk about their own feelings (I'm afraid, I'm happy, etc.). However, there is a cultural dispreference for talking about or making claims about what another might think, what another might feel, or what another is about to do, especially if there is no external evidence. As we shall see, these culturally constructed behaviors have several important consequences for the ways in which Kaluli caregivers verbally interact with their children, and are related to other pervasive patterns of language use that will be discussed below.

As infants become older (6–12 months), they are usually held in the arms or carried on the shoulders of the mother or an older sibling. They are present in all ongoing household activities, as well as subsistence activities that take place outside the village in the bush. During this time period, babies are addressed by adults to a limited extent. They are greeted by a variety of names (proper names, kinterms, affective and relationship terms) and receive a limited set of both negative and positive imperatives. In addition, when they do something they are not to do, such as reach for something that is not theirs to take, they will often receive such rhetorical questions such as "Who are you?!" (meaning "not someone to do that") or "It is yours?!" (meaning "it is not yours") to control their actions by shaming them (*sasidiab*). What is important to stress here is that the language addressed to the preverbal child consists largely of "one-liners" that call for no verbal response. Either an action or termination of an action is appropriate. Other than these utterances, very little talk is directed to the young child by the adult caregiver.

This pattern of adults not treating infants as communicative partners continues even when babies begin babbling. Kaluli recognize babbling (*dabedan*) but say that this vocal activity is not communicative and has no relationship to speech that will eventually emerge. Adults and older children occasionally repeat vocalizations back to the young child (ages 12–16 months), reshaping them into the names of persons in the household or into kinterms, but they do not say that the baby is saying the name nor do they wait for or expect the child to repeat those vocalizations in an altered form. In addition, vocalizations are not generally treated as communicative and given verbal expression. Nor are they interpreted by adults, except in one situation, an example of which follows.

When a toddler shrieks in protest at the assaults of an older child, mothers will say "I'm unwilling" (using a quotative particle), referring to the toddler's shriek. These were the only circumstances in which mothers treated vocalizations as communicative and provided verbal expression for them. In no other circumstances in the four families in the study did adults provide a verbally expressed interpretation of a vocalization of a preverbal child. Thus, throughout the preverbal period, very little language is directed to the child, except for imperatives, rhetorical questions, and greetings. A child who, by Kaluli terms, has not yet begun to speak, is not expected to respond either verbally or vocally. What all of this means is that in the first 18 months or so very little sustained dyadic verbal exchange takes place between adult and infant. The infant is only minimally treated as an addressee, and is not treated as a communicative partner in dyadic exchanges. One immediate conclusion is: the conversational model that has been described for many white middle-class caregivers and their preverbal children has no application in this case. Furthermore, if one defines language input as language directed to the child, then it is reasonable to say that for Kaluli children who have not yet begun to speak, there is very little. However, this does not mean that Kaluli children grow up in an impoverished verbal environment and do not learn how to speak. Quite the opposite is true. The verbal environment of the infant is rich and varied, and from the very beginning the infant is surrounded by adults and older children who spend a great deal of time talking to one another. Furthermore, as the infant develops and begins to crawl, engage in play activities, and other independent actions, these actions are frequently referred to, described, and commented upon by members of the household speaking to one another, especially by older children. Thus, the ongoing activities of the preverbal child are an important topic of talk between members of the household, and this talk about the here-and-now of the infant is available to the infant, though only a limited amount of talk is addressed to the infant. For example, in referring to the infant's actions, siblings and adults use the infant's name or kinterm. They will say, "Look at Seligiwo! He's walking." Thus the child may learn from these contexts to attend to the verbal environment in which he or she lives.

Every society has its own ideology about language, including when it begins and how children acquire it, and the Kaluli are no exception. Kaluli claim that language begins at the time when the child uses two critical words, "mother" (*nɔ*) and "breast" (*bo*). The child may be using other single words, but until these two words are used, the beginning of language is not recognized. Once a child has used these words, a whole set of inter-related behaviors is set into motion. Kaluli claim that once a child has begun to use language, he or she must then be "shown how to speak" (Schieffelin, 1990). Kaluli show their children language in the form of a teaching strategy that involves providing a model for what the child is to say, followed by the word *ɛlɛma*, an imperative meaning "say like that." Mothers use this method of direct instruction to teach the social uses of assertive language (teasing, shaming, requesting, challenging, reporting). However, object labeling is never part of an *ɛlɛma* sequence, nor does the mother ever use *ɛlɛma* to instruct the child to beg or appeal for food or objects. Begging, the Kaluli say, is natural for children; they know how to do it. In contrast, a child must be taught to be assertive through the use of particular linguistic expressions and verbal sequences.

A typical sequence using *ɛlɛma* is triadic, involving the mother, child (between 20–36 months), and other participant(s). Figure 3.2 gives an example. *In this situation, as in many others, the mother does not modify her language to fit the linguistic ability of the young child. Instead her language is shaped so as to be appropriate (in terms of form and content) for the child's intended addressee.* Consistent

---

[1] Mother → Wanu → > Binalia:[a]
Whose is it? say like that.

[2] whose is it?!/

[3] Is it yours?! say like that.

[4] is it yours?!/

[5] Who are you?! say like that.

[6] who are you?!/

[7] Mama → Wanu → > Binalia:
Did you pick (it)?! say like that.

[8] did you pick (it)?!/

[9] Mother → Wanu → > Binalia:
My G'ma picked (it)! say like that.

[10] my G'ma picked (it)!/

[11] Mama → Wanu → > Binalia:
This *my G'ma* picked! say like that.

[12] this *my G'ma* picked!/

Figure 3.2 Example of a triadic exchange using ɛlɛma

Notes: Mother, daughter Binalia (5 years), cousin Mama (3½ years), and son
Wanu (27 months) are at home, dividing up some cooked vegetables.
Binalia has been begging for some but her mother thinks that she has
had her share.
a → > = speaker → addressee.
→ > = addressee → > intended addressee.

with the ways in which she interacts with her infant, what a mother instructs
her young child to say usually has its origins not in any verbal or non-verbal
behaviors of the child, but in what the mother thinks should be said. The
mother pushes the child into ongoing interactions that the child may or may
not be interested in, and will at times spend a good deal of energy in trying to
get the child verbally involved. This is part of the Kaluli pattern of fitting (or
pushing) the child into the situation rather than changing the situation to
meet the interests or abilities of the child. Thus, mothers take a directive role
with their young children, teaching them what to say so that they may
become participants in the social group.

In addition to instructing their children by telling them what to say in
often extensive interactional sequences, Kaluli mothers pay attention to the
form of their children's utterances. Kaluli will correct the phonological,
morphological, or lexical form of an utterance or its pragmatic or semantic
meaning. Since the goals of language acquisition include a child becoming
competent, independent, and mature-sounding in his language, Kaluli use no
baby-talk lexicon, for they said (when I asked about it) that to do so would
result in a child sounding babyish, which was clearly undesirable and

counter-productive. The entire process of a child's development, of which language acquisition plays a very important role, is thought of as a hardening process and culminates in the child's use of "hard words" (Feld and Schieffelin, 1982).

The cultural dispreference for saying what another might be thinking or feeling has important consequences for the organization of dyadic exchanges between caregiver and child. For one thing, it affects the ways in which meaning is negotiated during an exchange. For the Kaluli, the responsibility for clear expression is with the speaker, and child speakers are not exempt from this. Rather than offering possible interpretations or guessing what a child is saying or meaning, caregivers make extensive use of clarification requests such as "huh?" and "what?", in an attempt to elicit clearer expression from the child. Children are held to what they say, and mothers will remind them that they in fact have asked for food or an object if when given it they don't act appropriately. Since responsibility of expression does lie with the speaker, children are also instructed with *ɛlɛma* to request clarification (using similar forms) from others when they do not understand what someone is saying to them.

Another important consequence of not saying what another thinks is the absence of adult expansions of child utterances. Kaluli caregivers will put words into the mouths of their children, but these words originate from the caregiver. However, caregivers do not elaborate or expand utterances initiated by the child. Nor do they jointly build propositions across utterances and speakers, except in the context of sequences with *ɛlɛma* in which they are constructing the talk for the child.

All of these patterns of early language use, such as the lack of expansions or verbally attributing an internal state to an individual, are consistent with important cultural conventions of adult language usage. The Kaluli very carefully avoid gossip and often indicate the source of information they report. They make extensive use of direct quoted speech in a language that does not allow indirect quotation. They utilize a range of evidential markers in their speech to indicate the source of speakers' information – for example, whether something was said, seen, heard, or gathered from other kinds of evidence. These patterns are also found in early child speech and, as such, affect the organization and acquisition of conversational exchanges in this small-scale egalitarian society.

A discussion of the developmental stories

We propose that infants and caregivers do not interact with one another according to one particular "biologically designed choreography" (Stern, 1977). There are many choreographies within and across societies. Cultural systems as well as biological ones contribute to their design, frequency, and significance. The biological predispositions constraining and shaping social behavior of infants and caregivers must be broader than thus far conceived, in that the use of eye gaze, vocalization, and body alignment are orchestrated differently in the social groups we have observed. As noted earlier, for example, Kaluli mothers do not engage in sustained gazing at, or elicit and maintain direct eye contact with, their infants, as such behavior is dispreferred, associated with witchcraft.

Another argument in support of a broader notion of biological predisposition to be social concerns the variation observed in the participant structure of social interactions. The literature on white middle-class child development has been orientated, quite legitimately, towards the two-party relationship between infant and caregiver, typically infant and mother. The legitimacy of this focus rests on the fact that this relationship is primary for infants within this social group. Further, most communicative interactions are dyadic in the adult community. While the mother is an important figure in the Kaluli developmental story, the interactions in which infants are participants are typically triadic or multi-party. As noted, Kaluli mothers will organize triadic interactions in which infants and young children will be oriented away from their mothers toward a third party.

This is not to say that Kaluli caregivers and children do not engage in dyadic exchanges. Rather, the point is that *such exchanges are not accorded the same significance as in white middle-class society*. In white middle-class households that have been studied, the process of becoming social takes place predominantly through dyadic interactions, and social competence itself is measured in terms of the young child's capacity to participate in such interactions. In Kaluli [. . .] households, the process of becoming social takes place through participation in dyadic, triadic, and multi-party social interactions, with the latter two more common than the dyad.

From an early age, Kaluli children must learn how to participate in interactions involving a number of individuals. To do this minimally requires attending to more than one individual's works and actions, and knowing the norms for when and how to enter interactions, taking into account the social identities of at least three participants. Further, the sequencing of turns in triadic and multi-party interactions has a far wider range of possibilities *vis-à-vis* dyadic exchanges, and thus requires considerable knowledge and skill. While dyadic exchanges can only be ABABA . . . , triadic or multi-party exchanges can be sequenced in a variety of ways, subject to social constraints such as speech act content and status of speaker. For Kaluli children, triadic and multi-party interactions constitute their earliest social experiences and reflect the ways in which members of these societies routinely communicate with one another.

Conclusions

This chapter contains a number of points but only one message – that the process of acquiring language and the process of acquiring socio-cultural knowledge are intimately linked. In pursuing this generalization, we have formulated the following proposals:

The specific features of caregiver speech behavior that have been described as simplified register are neither universal nor necessary for language to be acquired. White middle-class and Kaluli children become speakers of their languages within the normal range of development, and yet their caregivers use language quite differently in their presence.

The use of simplified registers by caregivers in certain societies may be part of a more general orientation in which situations are adapted to young children's perceived needs. In other societies, the orientation may be the reverse – that is, children at a very early age are expected to adapt to requirements of situations. In such societies, caregivers direct children to notice and respond to others' actions. They tend not to simplify their speech and frequently model appropriate utterances for the child to repeat to a third party in a situation.

The cross-cultural research raises many questions. The extent to which we are developing culturally specific theories of development needs to be considered. To add to what we know, we must examine the prelinguistic and linguistic behaviors of the child and the ways in which they are continually and selectively affected by the values and beliefs held by those members of society who interact with the child.

It is tempting to speculate about what differences these differences make. Cross-cultural research invites that. However, at this point in our research it seems premature to focus on answers. Instead we prefer to use these data to generate questions – questions that will suggest new ways to think about language acquisition and socialization. And when we identify a new phenomenon or find old favorites missing – such as the absence of expansions and lack of extensive modified speech to the child in diverse societies – we must identify the socio-cultural factors that organize and make sense of communicative behaviors. Because these behaviors are grounded in culturally specific norms, we can expect that the reasons for the "same" phenomenon will be different.

While biological factors play a role in language acquisition, socio-cultural factors have a hand in this process as well. It is not a trivial fact that small children develop in the context of organized societies. Cultural conditions for communication organize even the earliest interactions between infants and others. Through participation as audience, addressee, and/or "speaker," the infant develops a range of skills, intuitions, and knowledge, enabling him or her to communicate in culturally preferred ways. The development of these competences is an integral part of becoming a competent speaker.

References

Anderson, E. S. and Johnson, C. E. (1973) "Modifications in the speech of an eight-year-old to younger children," *Stanford Occasional Papers in Linguistics* 3: 149–60.

Blount, B. (1972) "Aspects of socialization among the Luo of Kenya," *Language in Society* 235–48.

Brown, R. (1973) *A First Language: The Early Stages*. Cambridge, Mass.: Harvard University Press.

Brown, R. and Bellugi, U. (1964) "Three processes in the child's acquisition of syntax," *Harvard Educational Review* 34: 133–51.

Bruner, J. S. (1978) "The role of dialogue in language acquisition," in A. Sinclair, R. J. Jarvella, and W. J. M. Levelt (eds) *The Child's Conception of Language*. New York: Springer-Verlag.

Cazden, C. (1965) "Environmental assistance to the child's acquisition of grammar," unpublished Ph.D. dissertation, Harvard University.

Clancy, P. (1986) "The acquisition of communicative style in Japanese," in B. B. Schieffelin and E. Ochs (eds) *Language Socialization Across Cultures*. New York: Cambridge University Press.

Feld, S. and Schieffelin, B. B. (1982) "Hard talk: a functional basis for Kaluli discourse," in D. Tannen (ed.) *Analyzing Discourse: Talk and Text*. Washington, DC: Georgetown University Press.

Geertz, C. (1973) *The Interpretation of Cultures*. New York: Basic Books.

Goffman, E. (1963) *Behavior in Public Places*. New York: Free Press.

Goffman, E. (1967) *Interaction Ritual: Essays on Face-to-Face Behavior*. Garden City, New York: Anchor Books.

Greenfield, P. M. and Smith, J. H. (1976) *The Structure of Communication in Early Language Development*. New York: Academic Press.

Harkness, S. (1975) "Cultural variation in mother's language," in W. von Raffler-Engel (ed.) *Child Language, Word 27*: 495–8.

Harkness. S. and Super, C. (1977) "Why African children are so hard to test," in L. L. Adler (ed.) *Issues in Cross-Cultural Research. Annals of the New York Academy of Sciences* 285: 326–31.

Heath. S. B. (1983) *Ways with Words: Language, Life and Work*. London: Cambridge University Press.

Irvine, J. (1974) "Strategies of status manipulation in the Wolof greeting,", in R. Bauman and J. Sherzer (eds) *Explorations in the Ethnography of Speaking*. New York: Cambridge University Press.

Kulick, D. (1992) *Language Shift and Cultural Reproduction: Socialization, Self and Syncretism in a Papua New Guinea Village*. New York: Cambridge University Press.

Miller, P. (1982) *Amy, Wendy and Beth: Learning Language in South Baltimore*. Austin, Tex.: University of Texas Press.

Montagu, A. (1937) *Coming into Being among the Australian Aborigines: A Study of the Procreative Beliefs of the Native Tribes of Australia*. London: Routledge.

Much, N. and Shweder R. (1979) "Speaking of rules: the analysis of culture in breach," in W. Damon (ed.) *New Directions for Child Development: Moral Development 2*. San Francisco, California: Jossey-Bass.

Ninio, A. (1979) "The naive theory of the infant and other maternal attitudes in two subgroups in Israel," *Child Development* 50: 976–80.

Ochs, E. (1982) "Talking to children in Western Samoa," *Language in Society* 11: 77–104.

Ochs, E. (1988) *Culture and Language Development: Language Acquisition and Socialization in a Samoan Village*. Cambridge: Cambridge University Press.

Ochs, E. (1991) "Misunderstanding children," in N. Coupland, H. Giles, and J. Wiemann (eds) *"Miscommunication" and Problematic Talk*. London: Sage.

Ochs, E., Schieffelin. B. B., and Platt, M. (1979) "Propositions across utterances and speakers," in E. Ochs and B. B. Schieffelin (eds) *Developmental Pragmatics*. New York: Academic Press.

Philips, S. (1982) *The Invisible Culture*. New York: Longman.

Sachs, J. and Devin, J. (1976) "Young children's use of age-appropriate speech styles," *Journal of Child Language* 3: 81–98.

Schieffelin, B. B. (1986) "The acquisition of Kaluli," in D. Slobin (ed.) *The Crosslinguistic Study of Language Acquisition*, vol. 1. Hillsdale, NJ: Lawrence Erlbaum Associates.

Schieffelin, B. B. (1990) *The Give and Take of Everyday Life: Language Socialization of Kaluli Children*. New York: Cambridge University Press.

Schieffelin, B. B. and Eisenberg, A. (1984) "Cultural variation in children's conversations," in R. L. Schiefelbusch and J. Pickar (eds) *Communicative Competence: Acquisition and Intervention*. Baltimore, MD: University Park Press.

Schieffelin, B. B. and Ochs, E. (1986a) *Language Socialization Across Cultures*. New York: Cambridge University Press.

Schieffelin, B. B. and Ochs, E. (1986b) "Language Socialization," *Annual Review of Anthropology* 15: 163–191.

Schieffelin, E. L. (1976) *The Sorrow of the Lonely and the Burning of the Dancers*. New York: St Martin's Press.

Scollon, R. and Scollon, S. (1981) "The literate two-year old: the fictionalization of self. Abstracting themes: a Chipewyan two-year-old," in R. O. Freedle (ed.) *Narrative, Literacy and Face in Interethnic Communication*, vol. VII: *Advances in Discourse Processes*. Norwood, N.J.: Ablex.

Shatz, M. and Gelman, R. (1973) "The development of communication skills: modifications in the speech of young children as a function of listener," *Monographs of the Society for Research in Child Development* 152, 38 (5).

Snow. C., de Blauw, A., and van Roosmalen, G. (1979) "Talking and playing with babies: the role of ideologies of childrearing," in M. Bullowa (ed.) *Before Speech: The Beginnings of Interpersonal Communication*. Cambridge: Cambridge University Press.

Stern, D. (1977) *The First Relationship: Infant and Mother*. Cambridge, Mass.: Harvard University Press.

Stross, B. (1972) "Verbal processes in Tzeltal speech socialization," *Anthropological Linguistics* 14(1).

von Sturmer, D. E. (1980) "Rights in nurturing," unpublished M.A. thesis, Australian National University, Canberra.

Ward, M. (1971) *Them Children: A Study in Language Learning*. New York: Holt, Rhinehart & Winston.

Chapter 4

Shared care for children*

Elly Singer

How can we provide good day care for our children? What demands should be made about the quality of day care? Millions of parents face questions like these when seeking day care for their child. Child care professionals and the authorities responsible for day care also have to find answers, but there are few well-founded answers available.

Over the last two decades, the number of mothers working outside the home has grown rapidly throughout the West, though proportions of pre-school children in day care vary markedly from nation to nation. Thus in the United States the proportion was 58 per cent in 1990 and was predicted to be 67 per cent by 1995, whereas in The Netherlands only 24.8 per cent were in day care in 1985, rising to 30 per cent in 1995 (Singer, 1992). While the proportion of children in day care has been exploding, scientific interest has been mainly on effects: is day care good or bad for children? Thus, in the 1970s, much research was done on the possible positive effects of child care centres for the language use and cognitive development of children in disadvantaged situations (Consortium for Longitudinal Studies [CLS], 1983; Zigler and Anderson, 1979). The 1970s also saw research where negative expectations were expressed about day care that was necessitated by mothers working outside the home. Researchers asked whether child care children were more often 'insecurely' attached than those raised at home. Only since the 1980s has research focused on the quality of child care. What factors within the family situation or within the day care situation determine whether the care experience is good or bad for a child? At last research was being carried out on the questions asked by parents who want good day care for their children. Why had it taken so long for developmental psychologists to pick up the questions asked by working parents?

The most obvious explanations are in terms of the personal values and standards of the researchers, and the lack of interest shown by the people

* This is an edited version of an article that appeared in *Theory and Psychology*, 3(4): 129–149, 1993. Reprinted by permission of Sage Publications Ltd.

responsible for research funds. I will show that there is also 'theoretical resistance': shared care is at loggerheads with a number of central assumptions in present theories about early child development because it breaks radically with the pattern of the traditional family. Therefore, we have to construct theories that take into account the fact that children grow up within two or more contexts. For example, a number of current concepts, such as maternal 'sensitivity', are concerned only with a dyadic relationship. Is such a concept adequate for describing the quality of the caretaker's behaviour when this takes place within the context of a network of relationships between a group of children and other caretakers?

This chapter is written from a social constructionist perspective. My theoretical starting-point is to recognize that 'the child' whom the psychologists study is a social invention: 'the child' is a nexus of power relations, policy concerns and value investments. Very often we are scarcely aware of just how deeply our theories, concepts and research questions are anchored in moral and social–political choices and problems. For this reason, I start with a brief sketch of historical roots of developmental theories in the pedagogical philosophy of the eighteenth and nineteenth centuries – traditional answers to the question how, and on the basis of which values and standards, shall I raise my child (see Singer, 1992, for an extended history)? I show how theories about the importance of early childhood and of strong emotional bonds developed as part of much broader moral and social theories about the reform of children from different social classes.

In the second part of the chapter, I place present research trends in the field of child care into their social–political context. In spite of the claim to universality in dominant theories, these are, at most, only applicable within a traditional, Western, middle-class upbringing. They are context-specific pedagogies, theories of how children *should* be brought up in a traditional middle-class family. Moreover, because they claim universality, 'untruths' are produced about parents and children who 'differ' from middle-class norms.

In the last part of the chapter, I show how work from a social constructionist perspective is forming new theory and research in the field of child care. Psychologists can make an increasingly important contribution to the 'invention of a new child', to use Kessen's (1979) language. However, they must realize that they will not have either the first or the last word in this project.

The historical roots of theories about day care

Ambivalence towards mothers

Since at least the eighteenth century, pedagogues, psychologists and social reformers have dreamed of improving society by freeing the child from the bad influences of parents, servants and others with no understanding of upbringing. Rousseau, Pestalozzi, Owen, Froebel and Montessori saw the child as inherently good, but it would remain so only if properly brought up.

Proper upbringing meant upbringing based on knowledge of the needs and natural development of children. To this end, Pestalozzi (1746–1827) and Froebel (1782–1852) designed developmental theories consisting mainly of religiously inspired contemplations on the 'essence' of the child and the 'godly laws of development'. According to Pestalozzi, the child needed maternal love in which the finest of all feelings was reflected: the love of and belief in the Creator. Without maternal love, the child's instinctive impulses would develop into 'a thousand imaginary and artificial needs; that would send us from one pleasure to another and eventually end in complete selfishness' (Pestalozzi, 1818/1956, p. 140). Both these pedagogues backed up their contemplations by so-called exemplary observations. Froebel (1826/1928, p. 147), for instance, described in detail how the 'good mother' helps her child to exercise his abilities: 'for instance, pointing to the light: "There is the light," – taking it away: – "Now it's gone".' At the same time, the mother should help her child to experience the divinity of things.

From the end of the nineteenth century, the religious themes slowly disappeared and observation became more important; writers tried to discover the truth about children through empirical research. However, they still had a common belief in the purity of the child, carrying the potential for a better society if only it were well brought up. For nineteenth-century pedagogues, the first years of childhood determined the entire life. 'The power of first impressions' was supposedly so great that wrong impressions during early childhood had to be avoided at all cost (Van Calcar, 1861). This, of course, immediately raised the question of the competence of the parents, particularly the mother. If first impressions were so influential, could we leave upbringing to mothers? From answers to this question, a deep-rooted ambivalence towards mothers becomes apparent, even to this day.

On the one hand, mothers are idealized: good mothers make a better society through their children. On the other hand, mothers are rigorously scrutinized and held responsible for the 'bad behaviour' of their (adult) children: truancy, immorality, criminality, behavioural problems and psychological disorders. Hence, for the past two centuries, experts on upbringing and policy-makers have sought ways in which to teach mothers through mother groups and parent courses how 'healthy' children can develop 'normally' – preferably without altering the framework of family upbringing with mother at home. Child care facilities were, and still are, seen as a way of improving and complementing family upbringing. Hence nineteenth-century infant schools were often aimed at preventing criminality and immorality. Froebel, for instance, saw his 'kindergarten' as an institution for the 'cultivation of family life' and elevation of humanity. In the kindergarten, expert guidance could be given to mother and child. Froebel worked out graduated exercises based on children's games, and designed simple educational apparatus, 'gifts', to enable children to learn the elementary laws of physics and the eternal law of God. This method supposedly followed the child's 'natural' development, and, therefore, had to be strictly followed.

A hundred years after Froebel, American child psychologists rediscovered child care centres as a way of raising family upbringing to a higher level. First, in the 'human relationship laboratories' of the 1920s (Davies, 1933), children could be studied in nursery schools while parents/mothers learnt how to bring up their children in a scientifically responsible fashion; and again, in the 1960s, psychologists within 'Project Head Start' proposed child care centres as a way of benefiting children from 'disadvantaged' environments, by compensating for 'bad' home upbringing. Hence, from Froebel's pre-industrial Europe to modern America, the scientific approach to day care has relayed the same ambivalent message to mothers: mothers, you must take care of your children, but we doubt your capability to do so. You need scientific advice and scrutiny.

Maternal love and mental health

After the Second World War, there was an upsurge of psychological interest in maternal love. Psychologists made no direct link between maternal love and moral issues, but rather an indirect link through the concept 'health', which was seen as universal and value-free. Nevertheless, 'unhealthy' development supposedly led to disturbed and anti-social behaviour.

During the 1950s, writers like Winnicott and Bowlby based their theories on 'object relations' theory. Following the psychoanalyst Klein (1975), they started from the premise that the small child is torn between feelings of love and hate for its primary carer, the mother; but, contrary to Klein, Winnicott and Bowlby held the mother responsible for the way in which children learn to live with these conflicting emotions. They designed a management model for controlling these strong emotions. The mother was the 'psychic organizer' of the child. Thus Winnicott (1964/1981, p. 62) explained to mothers that babies could feel 'wild tigers and lions' inside them. The mother could not hope to take away all the sources of anger, but she could be 'good enough'. In other words, she had to be calm, empathic, tolerant and permanently available, so that the child could make good all the hateful things he had done to her in his aggressive fantasies.

In the 1960s, Bowlby gave up his earlier theory in favour of what he called 'attachment theory' (Singer, 1992). In the new theory, the conflict between the emotions of love and hate was replaced by a field of tension between two opposing behavioural tendencies: the search for the proximity of the attachment figure and the exploration of the outside world (Bowlby, 1988, pp. 120–123). The child had to conquer this conflict with the help of a permanently available, sensitive and responsible mother or carer. The child needed the feeling of being in control of the mother or parent figure. If the child left the carer, he or she knew that they would remain available. If mothers, fathers or carers were not sensitive or responsive, children would develop an 'insecure' attachment: they would become anxious/resistant 'clingers' or anxious/avoidant children who were 'indifferent' or 'disobedient'. Hence a connection was once again made between a bad attachment to the mother and ineducability of the children (Bowlby, 1988, pp. 119–136; Winnicott, 1984). As Mulder (1827) put it 150 years earlier, children who are not worried about separation from their mother or about losing her love miss the psychological basis for love and the fear of God: they know no 'God or command'.

Attachment theory as a pedagogy

Attachment theory offers a culturally specific model for regulating emotions and behaviour and for internalizing moral concepts (Singer, 1992: Walkerdine and Lucey, 1989). Such a model can justly be called a pedagogy. The theory answers such questions as, How can I help my children to handle their emotions? and, How can I bring them up to be obedient, yet at the same time to behave independently?

As presented within attachment theory, the regulation of emotions fits neatly with Western culture, where a clear distinction is made between 'inside' and 'outside' the home, between 'dependence' and 'independence'. Dependence is experienced within the family environment and satisfied by an ever-available mother, whilst independence and self-confidence are expected in the outside world. Or, more precisely, a secure dependence on or attachment to the mother paves the basis from which the outside world can be explored, independently and autonomously. Note that other cultures have very different ways of dealing with the need for dependence and independence. For example, in some African cultures, 2-year-olds are separated quite abruptly from their mothers (LeVine, 1983). The actual care and training of children after infancy is then delegated to others in the family, particularly older children.

According to attachment theory, the mother plays a central role in the development of (self-)discipline and (self-)confidence, but in order to give the child the feeling of controlling the behaviour of the mother (figure), the mother's power should remain as far as possible invisible. For instance, Stayton, Hogan and Ainsworth (1971) wrote that a cooperative mother will never enforce her will upon a child: if she has to intervene, she is very good at 'mood setting', which means that the child will accept her wishes as something he wants himself. In this way, a mother's own will, her (career) wishes, activities and thoughts, are cast in a negative light, as characteristics of a non-sensitive mother – they should be hidden. Conceptualized in this way, self-confidence is something for which the child has no model in the mother. In fact, it is based on an illusion. The mother must act as though she has no power. If her power becomes visible, it is thought to be 'unnatural' and dangerous for the child's self-confidence.

In present day theories about socio-emotional development, the moral question, as a rule, remains implicit. The laws of attachment behaviour have supposedly developed during the evolution of humankind. The 'healthy basis' is supposedly both natural and universal. It is this claim of universality that makes it theoretically impossible to speak both of differences in subcultures and of moral choices. Anything that does not conform is quickly dubbed 'pathological'. Hence, moral questions are not placed outside attachment theory. The 'healthy basis' the theory defines inscribes values and standards that mothers must live by if their children are not to grow up 'anti-social and a menace' (Ainsworth, Bell and Stayton, 1974). Like its European forebears, attachment theory is at heart a pedagogy.

Values in research on effects

Nowhere is the role of values and social–political choices as visible as in child care research. The rise and fall of 'waves of research' into day care have very little to do with 'scientific progress', but everything to do with changes in the social–political context. I will clarify this by examining 'three waves' of research into day care in the United States and the shifting values defining them. It is the narrowness of these values that has led research into the quality of child care to fall into a rut: they are at odds with the diversity of values alive in practical shared care.

First wave: the claim of expertise is not fulfilled

During the 1960s, as a consequence of the racial unrest in various American cities, 'Project Head Start' was set up. It was a political initiative, liberally backed by federal funds. The aim was to give children from disadvantaged backgrounds better chances at school and in society.

Head Start was based on theories emphasizing the influence of the environment on human development. Research showed that the programmes had immediate positive effects on the children, but that very often these disappeared within a few years, or were much less spectacular than expected (e.g. Clarke-Stewart and Fein, 1983; CLS, 1983). These disappointing results led to a heated debate about the relative influence of nature and nurture on development. Are poor (black) people inferior due to hereditary disposition, or is their position the result of racism and discrimination? In general, the scientists involved in Head Start did not drop their environmentalist claim that they could bring up children better than parents, but the interventions should preferably start at the infant stage, continuing until primary school, and should also include the home situation by influencing the mothers:

We can safely assume that it is never too early in the child's life to educate families on his needs as he develops . . . the earlier the intervention and the longer it lasts, the better.

(Palmer and Anderson, 1979, p. 460)

The mother also had to be influenced: after all, she would remain the most important upbringer for years, whilst teachers had contact with the child for only a limited period of time.

At a theoretical level, this was translated into the so-called 'ecological intervention model' by Bronfenbrenner (1979), in which he suggested that interventions should give parents some immediate support in situations where a multitude of problems and poverty made progress seem hopeless. Bronfenbrenner proposed many means of family support, varying from child day care to better housing, health care and working conditions and welfare payments for mothers.

Partly as a consequence of Bronfenbrenner's work, the importance of environmental factors in thinking about development has become generally accepted amongst psychologists. The causal model is now often visualized in the form of complex interwoven diagrams, with manifold arrows symbolizing the mutual influencing processes between, for instance, 'attachment biography of the parents', 'work', 'marriage satisfaction', '(in)secure attachment of child' and 'school success' (e.g. Belsky, 1984).

Bronfenbrenner also stressed that researchers need to account for the way in which those involved in interventions viewed their own situation and the programme that was meant to change it. This has scarcely been worked out at a theoretical level, however, although it is not that psychologists do not see that relating to the values, standards and possibilities of parents is absolutely crucial and that without this, mothers will give up (Gray and Wandersman, 1980); children will not feel at home with the programme (Ogilvy, Boath, Jahoda and Schaffer, 1992; Tizard and Hughes, 1984); and mothers will not retain their self-esteem (Moore, 1982). But it has never become generally acceptable to take parents' own values of upbringing and reality as a starting-point for theory or research. Most psychologists do not accept that children from poor families need different (psychological) abilities to survive than middle-class children. They do not see that other values apply in worlds where there is no certainty of the basic requirements of life, such as a doctor in the case of illness, sufficient food or adequate housing. If psychologists are to intervene effectively, these values would have to be recognized in their programmes. They would have to distance themselves from their claim of being more expert than parents, and to acknowledge that their theories can yield no neutral advice. But this is rare.

Second wave: the value of a 'secure attachment' under attack

Research into the negative effects of child care on the bond between mother and child is usually based on Bowlby's attachment theory. Does it seem from this research that daily recurring separations from the mother are really damaging? 'No', concluded various researchers in reviews published around 1980 (e.g. Clarke-Stewart and Fein, 1983). It seemed that child care children were just as securely attached as children growing up at home.

In the late 1980s, however, debate about the damaging effects of day care sparked up again. On the basis of new research, Belsky (1988) came to the conclusion that full-time baby care harmed emotional development. Of the children who had spent more than 20 hours a week in day care before the age of 1, 41 per cent were scored as insecurely, and often resistantly, attached to their mother in the Strange Situation, compared with 26 per cent of the children who spent less than 20 hours a week in care. Besides this, Belsky argued that other research showed that schoolchildren with day care experience were more aggressive and disobedient than home-bred children. Attachment theory tells us that this sort of behaviour is the result of insecure attachment. All this, says Belsky, points to an emotional disturbance in children who experienced full-time day care as babies.

Belsky's reasoning provoked a strong reaction (Clarke-Stewart, 1988; Lamb and Sternberg, 1990). Methodological shortcomings were pointed out in the research he quoted, along with the existence of much research data that opposed his reasoning. For example, Swedish research showed that schoolchildren with full-time day care experiences as babies are much better in the social–emotional field than children brought up at home (Andersson, 1992).

A debate also developed about how the 'insecure attachment' of children with day care experience should be interpreted. In this discussion, pedagogic values and standards were of critical importance. Clarke-Stewart (1988) questioned what was actually meant if day care children were more often scored as 'insecurely/resistantly' attached in the Strange Situation. Does 'resistant behaviour' when mother re-enters, having left her child alone in an unfamiliar room, point to an 'anxious attachment to mother'? Or is it possible that day care children are blasé about their mothers going away and returning? This would mean that these children do not 'avoid' their mothers out of anger or revenge, but because in their world nothing 'strange' has occurred in the Strange Situation. After all, this test was originally intended for American middle-class children growing up at home. It is most likely that day care children develop a 'working model' in order to feel secure that differs from that of home-reared children. Perhaps they are orientated less towards their mother as a source of safety and more towards other children. Or perhaps they are more independent slightly earlier than children growing up at home. For instance, day care children are apparently more skilful in initiating social relationships with their peers (Howes, 1987a). It is possible that the care-takers in a day care centre discourage 'clinging behaviour' and demands for attention more than do mothers at home (Ainsley, 1990, p. 45). Therefore, 'resistant' behaviour in children with day care experience need not necessarily point to a 'disturbance'. Many Dutch parents and day care professionals see 'independence' as an important aim of day care centres (Miltenburg and Singer, ongoing research).

A similar discussion is taking place about research into the social behaviour of schoolchildren with day care experience (Clarke-Stewart, 1988). On what grounds do researchers judge a child to be aggressive, maladjusted or disobed-ient? Could these children not just as well be described as being independent, assertive and having their own point of view? According to Clarke-Stewart, middle-class children of working mothers are brought up with different values and standards than those of the traditional family. She says:

> day care children as a group are developmentally advanced in the social realm, just as they are in the intellectual realm, which is why they are also more determined to get their own way and they do not always have the social skills to achieve this smoothly, which is why they are also more aggressive, irritable, and non-compliant.
>
> (Clarke-Stewart, 1991, p. 50)

If so, there may be no question of pathology as stated by Belsky, but rather of a greater independence and assertiveness as a result of a different style of upbringing and different values. These children learn a different way of regu-lating their needs for dependence and independence than those who, accord-ing to the attachment theory, are considered 'healthy', because the parents do not share the values on which the attachment theory is based. The two sets of children belong to different pedagogic subcultures.

Third wave: the impossibility of a universal answer to the question of quality

For too long researchers have been asking the wrong questions. They should not be asking whether child care is bad for children. 'The challenge is to make quality day care a reality' (Lamb and Sternberg, 1990).

From the start of the 1980s, research has been carried out into key indica-tors of child care quality. This line of research directly corresponds to the practical questions raised by parents and policy-makers, who already concede the necessity of child care. The central questions are:

> Can we identify reliable components of good quality care? What are they? What is their relation to children's family environments?
>
> (Phillips, 1987, p. ix)

Research has been carried out into the effects of wide differences in child care quality on children's development. Sometimes it has concerned a comparison of the effects of various forms of care, such as in-home care versus family day care; sometimes it has concerned quality characteristics such as group size or teacher:child ratio. Besides this, attention has been paid to issues concerning children's child care history (e.g. age of entry, length of time in child care) and family background, as these interact with aspects of quality. Very often such research is very complex, with many variables being correlated in order to unravel the relations between aspects of quality, family backgrounds, children's child care experience and children's development.

Researchers mainly identify 'quality' with characteristics of care facilities that correlate with favourable scores on developmental tests, for example: *structural characteristics*, such as group size and adult:child ratio (with babies a maximum of 1:4); *process characteristics*, such as positive and stimulating behaviour from the teachers; and *characteristics of cooperation with parents*, such as basic agreement on values and standards. Probably few parents would be surprised by these results. Thus it is surprising that the proof to back them up is so weak. The connections shown are low in significance and are not found consistently. Some quality characteristics have negative as well as positive effects. The researchers agree on the importance of the variables so crucial for policy-makers, such as teacher:child ratio, but in their concrete advice they vary considerably.

Why the inconsistencies and weak relations? These can partly be explained by the different indices used for measuring in the various studies. There are, of course, no standard indices for measuring interactions between children in a group, emotional bonds between children or the educative values of toys and space in a child care centre. A second explanation is that the sort of facility used varies depending on the socio-economic and cultural back-grounds of the family. As Goelman and Pence say, a large number of children are in a ' "worst of both worlds" situation: They come from low-resource families and attend low quality family day care' (1987, p. 101). Apart from this, different facilities have different aims: sometimes the aim is purely to offer care, sometimes it is social development and sometimes encouraging cognitive development is the main aim. All this means that any link found between quality characteristics and developmental scores is a product of a specific social context. Thus it is unsurprising that different links are found in different places.

What does this context-dependence mean for the sort of knowledge about quality that can be gained through scientific research? Researchers have dif-ferent answers to this question. Some, such as Howes, Phillips and White-book (1992), simply ignore the problem. They retain their conviction that 'research must provide thresholds for quality variables as well as demonstrate linear relations between quality and outcome' (1992, p. 449). Howes makes strong statements about 'high quality centres' distinguished by, amongst other things, shorter opening hours and a higher degree of adult participation in the socialization (Howes, 1987b, pp. 84–86). However, from her research we see that 'high quality centres' are mainly used by parents under relatively little stress. Perhaps parents under relatively larger amounts of stress cannot use these centres because the opening hours are too short, or the costs too high. Howes see this, but does not find it sufficient reason to rethink her definition of 'quality'. Hence, she chooses to ignore the fact that her 'high quality', when seen from the perspective of poor parents and children, is 'low quality', because they are unable to use it. Without the 'low quality centres', quite a lot of children would probably be without adequate care.

Clarke-Stewart draws a different conclusion to Howes: psychologists ought to study the limits beyond which variations in care make a big difference for children's development.

> I would guess that detrimental effects of extremely low scores on meas-ures of regulable variables would be stronger and more meaningful than the beneficial effects of extremely high scores, for instance.
>
> (Clarke-Stewart, 1987, p. 116)

With her emphasis on the low limits, Clarke-Stewart arrives at a much more modest parcel of demands for quality. For instance, she pleads for an adequate adult:child ratio for older pre-schoolers, probably 1:12. Howes wanted 1:7!

Clarke-Stewart (like Scarr, 1992) retains the idea that there are universal causal relations between environmental influence and normal development, but she is more modest in her statements about what constitutes good and bad in upbringing. She gives parents and teachers much more room to man-oeuvre than Howes, for instance. But this point of view also has disadvan-tages. There is a danger that the sort of research favoured by Clarke-Stewart would not come up with anything new: do we really need research to prove that one caretaker to ten babies is insufficient? More seriously, nothing has been done about the fact that choices and variations in values, standards and styles of upbringing, seen from the perspective of parents and children, do matter. Bringing up children without dealing with values is a form of neglect.

Towards a fourth wave: notes on context-bound theories of shared care

In the past, developmental psychologists all too often started out from the presupposition that, on the basis of their universal knowledge, they were the only ones qualified to make statements about what was good for the 'normal' development of the child. In so doing, they often ignored parents' wants and denied the upbringing situation of most children. The basis for psychological theories was formed by visions of the ever-available, loving and encouraging mother, so that the use of child care facilities could only be seen as an aberration.

In spite of the concept of 'non-judgemental' science, research in this area is strongly embedded in specific pedagogic values. In other words, theories are not universal, but bound to a limited purview. In order to produce knowledge in the future that is based on the reality of parents and children who make use of day care, I think two steps are necessary:

1   The claim to superiority must be relinquished. Psychologists must explicate their own values and standards, and place themselves at the service of formally authorized upbringers (usually the parents) and their children.
2   Work must begin on (new) context-bound theories that offer an insight into the developmental processes under the new pedagogic conditions of shared care for children.

Relinquishing the claim to superiority: who determines what?

The question of who determines the standard of what is good for children is a political question. It is a question not so much of who is in possession of the truth, but of who determines how children should be brought up. In Western countries, parents have prime authority. Therefore, the 'quality' of child care facilities must first be measured against what parents expect, and not against the scores children achieve in developmental-psychological tests. Further- more, parents delegate a measure of responsibility to others. So substitute upbringers need their own sphere of influence to be recognized – as do the authorities who regulate child care settings. Psychologists have at most a supplementary or facilitating role to play.

Assuring the effectiveness of facilities means solving problems of com- munication and organization. How can parents make their demands known? How can parents retain authority/participation in the upbringing of their child, even if part of this takes place somewhere else? Such questions need attention from researchers who wish to intervene in child care. For example, Moore (1982) found that, during the last two decades, many black families have learned that some well-intentioned programmes, if not administered correctly, can be much more destructive than supportive, largely because the original researchers and the subsequent planners have not had a positive view of the families they were trying to help. In Sweden, a country with an exten- sive subsidized child care system, the domination of standards by develop- mental psychologists has led to the exclusion of immigrant and working-class children from child care: these parents did not feel at home in the 'high quality centres' (Broberg and Hwang, 1991). Middle-class children can also suffer if the parents' authority in their upbringing is impaired. Swedish sociologist Liljestrom (1983) shows that the domination of the professional perspective in day care leads to timidity, insecurity and a bad conscience in both parents and workers.

If experts alone establish the rights and wrongs of day care, both parents and children may be hurt; but relinquishing the claim to privileged expertise will not be easy. It is a claim deeply anchored in two centuries of scientific thought on children, in which so-called universal 'truths' were confused with the right to establish standards, as I have already shown. So how can psychologists play a more modest and helpful role in the development of good quality child care facilities?

Local knowledge and collaborative research

First, psychologists must research their own position in local and/or international discussions of child care. In this connection, developmental psychologists could learn much from anthropologists and sociologists. Their studies clarify how the knowledge of psychologists, professionals and parents function at a local level. Think of the already classic study by Joffe (1977) with the significant title *Friendly Intruders*, which analyses the conversations between (white) teachers and (black) mothers in a few American day care centres. Studies like this show how psychological 'truth' comes to be institutionalized in rules and regulations (Mozere and Aubert, 1977).

In the second place, clear collaborative working relations between policymakers, practitioners, parents and psychologists at local levels are of great importance. In countries where child care was always encouraged by governments, there is often a long tradition of this kind. In the former German Democratic Republic, for instance, there were close working relationships between policy-makers, practitioners and multidisciplinary teams of researchers (Weigl and Weber, 1991). Research projects originated from practical experience rather than from a clearly outlined pedagogical or theoretical position. The chief benefit of this material was to redirect the work in nurseries from nearly exclusive medical care to pedagogical aims and to provide the basis for a unified approach for nursery educators. Good examples of this are the 'fundamental principles' constituting the basis of the process of language acquisition (for instance that 'mechanisms of language acquisition are closely linked to practical activities'); and guidelines for settling the child into the nursery after admission.

In a country like The Netherlands, similar forms of collaboration are impossible at the moment: a government establishing pedagogic aims is quite unthinkable. Besides this, the political will to make child care a government responsibility is lacking. For this reason, in our research (Miltenburg, Singer and Van Unen, 1992) we have emphasized the process of democratic decision-making and the listing of definitions of quality found among the various parties concerned. In this way, fundamental conflicts become evident: for instance, between the importance attached to continuity in the caretaker–child relationship (psychologists, professional workers, parents) and the opening hours adapted to working hours (of businesses, parents). No policy for guaranteeing continuity seems to be acceptable to all parties. We also found that in Holland only lip-service is paid to the importance of continuity in relationships between children. In the Dutch situation, this knowledge of the diverse definitions of quality is important because even the most basic political decisions still have to be made about how to work towards a national system of child care and quality control. Which aspects require negotiations? How can we develop a system that meets all the different quality demands?

Once child care is in place, psychologists have the important task of locally researching its effects on carers, children and parents. Do different kinds of local facilities meet the claims they make to parents and children? Are there undesirable side-effects? A great deal of this sort of research has been carried out in Sweden (Hwang, Broberg and Lamb, 1991). Such research may involve continuing collaboration with parents and practitioners, as in the 'partnership research' of Helen Penn in Scotland, which was carried out within the framework of a major reorganization of services to young children (Bradley and Sanson, 1992).

Context-bound developmental theories

As research on day care becomes more collaborative and local, theoretical discourse must also grow more context-bound. This is because it must take into account the particular histories and moral values of parents, children and others involved in the child care enterprise under investigation. Nevertheless, three central questions must be addressed in any study of socio-emotional development, however local.

First: *How do children organize their security? How do children build up their internal household?* Children in day care grow up in a less restricted and self-evident world than children at home. At a very young age they come into contact with changing caretakers and groups of children, and upbringing situations that can be quite different from those at home. How these children organize their security is less obvious because of the many changes, and, perhaps, because it is more difficult than for children at home. This is also apparent from the very little available research in this field. For children from the age of 6 months, for instance, getting used to a day care centre appears to be a stressful event (Hwang, Broberg and Lamb, 1991; Singer, 1991). Many children adapt themselves in a few days and are happy to explore the new environment; but for some children this process of adaptation can last several weeks and, in exceptional cases, more than five months. Nevertheless, they all manage to feel comfortable after a while. In so doing, they may give us insight into what has been called the 'social construction of emotions' (Harré, 1986). For if, as Harré says, emotions are 'assessments', actions that incorporate the meaning given to a person or thing in a specific situation, we might hazard that a child's emotional life may be quite differently organized at day care than at home.

Such an idea opens space for defining the differences between children in terms other than 'abnormal' or 'normal': searching for the proximity of mother may not be the only 'normal' way of searching for security. Besides this, it allows us to ask how adults support or hinder their children in achieving security. For example, some children new to child care are unable to organize the strange space cognitively and become anxious. Teachers often anticipate this by taking children around the space and giving them their own corner. Children may be frightened by the strong emotional reactions of other children. Teachers sometimes offer certain rituals in order to regulate these outbursts. Children can often tell what they do in these difficult circumstances. A 3-year-old boy told me exactly how he coped with the changeover to a new group. Was he going to miss his teachers? 'Oh no', he answered. 'Now the teachers in my new group are the nicest.'

The second question is linked to the first: *How do children organize being together?* That children should feel secure is, of course, a minimal requirement of upbringing. Up to now, for young children 'belonging' was primarily defined within the family, and in particular by the mother–child relationship. Day care raised the question of how young children (babies and toddlers) can form bonds outside the family, and also the question of how children themselves define their relationships. Is every child they play with more than once a 'friend'? Or do they distinguish, just like adults, between friends and acquaintances? And what do separations and interruptions in these sorts of relationships mean for children?

In order to address this question, we need a theoretical language that is suited to understanding children's functioning in their time and situation. Current dyadic models used to describe parent–child interactions are insufficient. Within the family, Dunn and Kendrick (1982) have carried out pioneering work by researching complex interactions between sisters, brothers and parents; but hardly any research of this kind has been done in child care settings. An exception are the studies of peer relations among babies and toddlers in day care centres in France and Italy (Corsaro and Emiliani, 1992). These studies show that a basic aspect of peer culture is children's creation and sharing of a stable set of activities or routines. Routines seem to be very important because they involve activities that the children consistently produce together; thus, peer routines are communal, recurrent and predictable. Even 1-year-olds seem to enjoy making rules together, for instance by playing peek-a-boo. Rules at that age are spontaneous and bound to concrete situations, but even then they give the children the joy of sharing and controlling their environment. Creating and sharing rules are crucial for children's feeling of being together.

The third question is implied by the first two. It is concerned with adults:

How do parents and substitute upbringers organize their relationship with the children at emotional and moral levels? Within the traditional family it seemed clear: the mother had to be physically and emotionally available as a basis from which the child could explore the environment independently. Normally this was thought to be taken care of by nature, by 'maternal instinct'; but mothers' working outside the home has necessitated a redefinition of the division of caring tasks between mothers and fathers, something taking place only very slowly and involving great conflicts (Hochschild, 1989). A close bond with one's own child is apparently not self-evident, but something that takes time, effort and attention. Parents can also suffer from the fear of 'separation', and have to learn 'the art of saying goodbye' (Hock, McBride and Gnezda, 1989; Singer, 1991). The division of tasks between the upbringers or substitute upbringers is also at issue. Dutch research has shown that parents take it for granted that their children form their emotional attachments at home, and that the teachers at the day care centres play a socializing and disciplinary role (teaching social rules and good manners) (Singer, 1991).

Finally, there is the emergent problem of authority over the child: what influence do parents lose if they use child care facilities? This question becomes more urgent as the gap between home upbringing and substitute upbringing widens, or as the parents feel themselves more and more powerless.

Conclusion: developmental theories and standards of upbringing

Developmental theories always have a normative, pedagogic basis. This often remains implicit because theories are phrased in causal terms that render specific social motivations invisible: the theories are presented as objective and universal. Because of their hidden assumptions about the 'home-bound' mother, current theories do not apply to children in shared care. Hence, I have suggested, theoretical work in developmental psychology must become self-consciously situation-specific. Does my approach solve the problem of the link between developmental theories and standards of upbringing? It does, insofar as it makes space for differences in development to be considered without these being judged as 'normal' or 'pathological' from a superior scientific point of view.

At an extreme, my view would lead to total relativism, where every development is a valuable development; but the fact remains that people always judge. Statements about development are not simply 'bound' to situations – they depend on the inevitably value-laden perspective from which a situation is seen. Anna Freud's (1951/1969) famous study of young children who survived concentration camps without adults to take care of them might be used to show, for instance, how children can develop under extreme circumstances. However, she describes the children from the perspective of the psychoanalyst, the expert upbringer: she sees severely disturbed children suffering from, amongst other things, an extreme fear of being separated from one another; but these children were not psychotic, and Anna Freud cannot understand why. If she had had the perspective of the children, she might have seen something quite different: adequate survival strategies. She might have had to concede that fear of separation from one another in the old situation (the concentration camp) was a realistic danger for the children, and that separation in the new situation was a realistic threat. For, in the end, it was Anna Freud's aim to separate the children from each other in order for them to be able to form 'normal' bonds with foster parents.

In the long run, child psychology always involves a question of which 'truth' and whose 'judgement' counts the most – at once an ethical question and a question of power. Yet the truth of the psychologist should never be put, as a matter of course, above that of the parent – just as the truth of the parent should not be set above that of the child, or the truth of the man above that of the woman. The value of a scientific statement about children never depends on psychologists alone. As far as shared care is concerned, even greater modesty is required: as of now, developmental psychologists have no adequate way of understanding shared care. If the illusion of universal know-ledge is broken, the social arrears of developmental psychological concepts come plainly into view. We really must have a major rethink!

References

Ainsley, R. C. (1990). Family and center contributions to the adjustment of infants in full-time day care. In K. McCartney (Ed.), *Child care and maternal employment: A social ecology approach* (pp. 39–53). San Francisco, CA: Jossey-Bass Inc.

Ainsworth, M. D. S., Bell, S. M. and Stayton, D. J. (1974). Infant–mother attachment and social development: socialization as a product of reciprocal responsiveness to signals. In M. P. M. Richards (Ed.), *The integration of a child into a social world* (pp. 99–135). Cambridge: Cambridge University Press.

Andersson, B. E. (1992). Effects of day care on cognitive and socio-emotional competence of thirteen-year-old school-children. *Child Development*, 63, 20–36.

Belsky, J. (1984). The determinants of parenting: a process model. *Child Development*, 55, 83–96.

Belsky, J. (1988). The 'effects' of infant day care reconsidered. *Early Childhood Research Quarterly*, 3, 235–272.

Bowlby, J. (1988). *A secure base: Clinical applications of attachment theory*. London: Tavistock.

Bradley, B. and Sanson, A. (1992). Promoting quality in infant day care via research: conflicting lessons from 'The day care controversy'. *Australian Journal of Early Childhood*.

Broberg, A. and Hwang, C. P. (1991). Day care for young children in Sweden. In E. C. Melhuish and P. Moss (Eds), *Day care for young children: International perspectives* (pp. 75–101). London and New York: Tavistock/Routledge.

Bronfenbrenner, U. (1979). *The ecology of human development*. Cambridge, MA: Harvard University Press.

Clarke-Stewart, K. A. (1987). In search of consistencies in child care research. In D. A. Phillips (Ed.), *Quality in child care: What does research tell us?* (pp. 105–120). Washington, DC: NAEYC.

Clarke-Stewart, K. A. (1988). The 'effects' of infant day care reconsidered: Risks for parents, children, and researchers. *Early Childhood Research Quarterly, 3*, 292–318.

Clarke-Stewart, K. A. (1991). Day care in the USA. In P. Moss and E. Melhuish (Eds), *Current issues: Day care for young children* (pp. 35–60). London: HMSO.

Clarke-Stewart, K. A. and Fein, G. G. (1983). Early childhood programs. In H. Mussen (Ed.), *Handbook of child psychology. Formerly Carmichael's manual of child psychology. Vol. II: Infancy and developmental psychology* (pp. 917–999). New York: Wiley.

Consortium for Longitudinal Studies. (1983). *As the twig is bent . . . Lasting effects of preschool programs*. Hillsdale, NJ: Erlbaum.

Corsaro, W. A. and Emiliani, S. (1992). Child care, early education, and children's peer culture in Italy. In M. E. Lamb, K. J. Sternberg, C. P. Hwang and A. G. Broberg (Eds), *Child care in context: Cross-cultural perspectives* (pp. 81–115). Hillsdale, NJ: Erlbaum.

Davis, M. D. (1933). *Nursery schools: Their development and current practices in the United States*. Washington, DC: Washington University Press.

Dunn, J. and Kendrick, C. (1982). *Siblings: Love, envy and understanding*. London: Grant McIntyre.

Freud, A. with Dann, S. (1969). An experiment in group upbringing. In A. Freud, *Indications for child analysis and other papers* (pp. 163–229). New York: Hogarth. (Original work published 1951.)

Froebel, F. W. A. (1928). *Froebel's opvoeding van den Mensch, vertaald door J. M. Telders*. Groningen: Paedagogische bibliothek. (Original work published 1826.)

Goelman, H. and Pence, A. (1987). Effects of child care, family, and individual characteristics on children's language development: the Victoria day care research project. In D. A. Phillips (Ed.). *Quality in child care: What does research tell us?* (pp. 89–104). Washington, DC: NAEYC.

Gray, S. W. and Wandersman, L. P. (1980). The methodology of home-based intervention studies: problems and promising strategies. *Child Development, 51*, 993–1009.

Harré, R. (Ed.) (1986). *The social construction of emotions*. New York: Blackwell.

Hochschild, A. (1989). *The second shift: Working parents and the revolution at home*. New York: Viking Press.

Hock, E., McBride, S. and Gnezda, M. T. (1989). Maternal separation anxiety: Mother–infant separation from the maternal perspective. *Child Development, 60*, 793–802.

Howes, C. (1987a). Peer interaction of young children. *Monographs of the Society for Research in Child Development*, 53 (1, Serial No. 217).

Howes, C. (1987b). Quality indicators in infant and toddler child care: the Los Angeles study. In D. A. Phillips (Ed.), *Quality in child care: What does research tell us?* (pp. 81–88). Washington, DC: NAEYC.

Howes, C. (1991). Caregiving environments and their consequences for children: the experience in the United States. In E. C. Melhuish and P. Moss (Eds), *Day care for young children: International perspectives* (pp. 185–198). London and New York: Tavistock/Routledge.

Howes, C., Phillips, D. A. and Whitebook, M. (1992). Thresholds of quality: implications for the social development of children in center-based child care. *Child Development, 63*, 449–160.

Hwang, C. P., Broberg, A. and Lamb, M. E. (1991). Swedish childcare research. In E. C. Melhuish and P. Moss (Eds), *Day care for young children: International perspectives*. London: Tavistock/Routledge.

Joffe, C. E. (1977). *Friendly intruders: Childcare professionals and family life*. Los Angeles: University of California Press.

Kessen, W. (1979). The American child and other cultural inventions. *American Psychologist, 34*, 815–820.

Klein, M. (1975). *Love, guilt and reparation and other works 1921–1945*. London: Hogarth.

Lamb, M. E. and Sternberg, K. J. (1990). Do we really know how day care affects children? *Journal of Applied Developmental Psychology, 1*, 351–379.

Lamb, M. E., Sternberg, C. H., Hwang, C. H. and Broberg, A. G. (Eds) (1992). *Child care in context*. Hillsdale, NJ: Erlbaum.

LeVine, R. A. (1983). A cross-cultural perspective on parenting. In M. D. Fantini and R. Cardenas (Eds), *Parenting in a multi-cultural society*. New York: Longman.

Liljestrom, R. (1983). The public child, the commercial child and our child. In F. S. Kessel and A. W. Siegel (Eds), *The child and other cultural inventions* (pp. 124–152) Houston Symposium No. 4). New York: Praeger.

Miltenburg, R., Singer. E. and Van Unen, L. (1992). *Kwaliteitseisen aan kinderopvang: Meningen van sleutelfiguren in woord en geschrift*. Amsterdam: SCO.

Moore, E. (1982). Day care: a black perspective. In E. F. Zigler and E. W. Gordon (Eds), *Day care, scientific and social policy issues* (pp. 413–443). Boston, MA: Auburn House.

Mozere, L. and Aubert, G. (1977). *Babillage . . . Des crèches aux multiplicités d'enfants* (Recherches No. 27). Paris: Fontenay-sous-Blois.

Mulder, H. (1827). *Opmerkingen de wenken voor opvoeders en onderwijzers*. The Hague.

Ogilvy, C. M., Boath, E., Jahoda, G. and Schaffer, H. R. (1992). Staff–child interaction styles in multi-ethnic nursery schools. *British Journal of Developmental Psychology, 10*, 85–97.

Palmer, F. H. and Anderson, L. W. (1979). Long-term gains from early intervention: findings from longitudinal studies. In E. Zigler and J. Valentine (Eds), *Project Head Start* (pp. 433–466). New York: Free Press.

Pestalozzi, J. H. (1956). *Brieven over de opvoeding van het jonge kind, gericht aan J. P. Greaves*. Amsterdam. (Original work published 1818.)

Phillips, D. A. (Ed.) (1987). *Quality in child care: What does research tell us?* Washington, DC: NAEYC.

Scarr, S. (1992). Developmental theories for the 1990s: development and individual differences. *Child Development, 63*, 1–19.

Singer, E. (1991). *Kijk op kinderopvang, ervaring van ouders*. Utrecht: Jan van Arkel.

Singer, E. (1992). *Child care and the psychology of development*. London and New York: Routledge.

Stayton, D. J., Hogan, R. and Ainsworth, M. D. (1971). Infant obedience and maternal behavior: the origins of socialization reconsidered. *Child Development, 42*, 1057–1069.

Tizard, B. and Hughes, M. (1984). *Young children learning, talking and thinking at home and at school*. London: Fontana.

Van Calcar, E. (1861). *Onze ontwikkeling of de magt der eerste indrukken*. Amsterdam.

Walkerdine, V. and Lucey, H. (1989). *Democracy in the kitchen*. London: Virago.

Weigl, I. and Weber, C. (1991). Research in nurseries in the German Democratic Republic. In E. C. Melhuish and P. Moss (Eds), *Day care for young children: International perspectives* (pp. 56–74). London and New York: Tavistock/Routledge.

Winnicott, D. W. (1981). *The child, the family, and the outside world*. Harmondsworth: Penguin. (Original work published 1964.)

Winnicott, D. W. (1984). *Deprivation and delinquency*. London and New York: Tavistock.

Zigler, E. and Anderson, K. (1979). An idea whose time had come: the intellectual and political climate. In E. Zigler and J. Valentine (Eds), *Project Head Start: A legacy of the war on poverty* (pp. 3–19). New York: Free Press.

Part II

Making sense of relationships

Chapter 5

The child's need to learn a culture*

Colwyn Trevarthen

A natural curiosity for meaning

My title refers to the innate need that children have to live and learn *in* culture, as fish swim in the sea and birds fly in the air, not to the acquired or cultivated need of the scholar to describe and explain *about* culture. Scholars customarily think of cultural activity as the accumulated language, arts, sciences, customs, institutions and other creations of a cooperation stretching back over historical time, physical and mental objects refining the discoveries and creations of untold generations. How could a young child have more than a passive place in such a sophisticated cosmos of artificial tools, ideas and symbols?

This seems to be a misleading way to approach the process of human development and human life. Watching and listening to infants and toddlers, I have come to the view that being part of culture is a need human beings are born with – culture, whatever its contents, is a natural function. The essential motivation is one that strives to comprehend the world by sharing experiences and purposes with other minds, and that makes evaluations of reality, not as a scientist is trained to do by experimenting to eliminate differences of understanding so that reality can be exposed free of human attitudes and emotions, but in active negotiation of creative imaginings that are valued for their human-made unreality. Culture, with language and music as media expressing the need, is an invention of human thoughts, an ordered fantasy that communities of people have agreed to endow with meaning. Even science cannot escape distortion of its 'truth' by theory. It observes through a lattice of ideas imposed on it from historical, social, political and other varieties of cultural meaning. It seems that the child's preferred prescientific interest in the values and purposes that other people invent will persist as an inescapable drive in the most rational of adult activities disciplined by conventions of objectivity. In the end, physics is a kind of poetry.

Of course, infants and preschool children, acting as intelligent individuals,

* This is an edited version of an article that appeared in *Children and Society*, 9(1), 1995. Reproduced by permission of John Wiley & Sons Limited.

show investigative curiosity and a desire to solve problems and learn with experiment, comparison and thought. Jean Piaget (1962) emphasized this aspect of mental growth, and he made a significant advance in psychological theory by demonstrating how a child's acts, accommodating to events and assimilating sensory effects, are deployed with increasing strategic wisdom to build up predictive and representational schemata in the mind. He did not, however, understand the power of interpersonal or intersubjective processes by which cooperative awareness is achieved. In consequence, he could make only an awkward explanation of symbols and cultural knowledge in general. Both Henri Wallon in France (Nadel, 1993) and Lev Simonovitch Vygotsky (1962, 1967) in Russia gave awareness of persons and their communication a primary place in the development of thinking. For Wallon, imitation was a means of negotiating purposes and points of view. Vygotsky perceived the child as seeking support through communication for accomplishing tasks just beyond reach, and he demonstrated that talk, including the imaginative talking to him- or herself, makes it possible for a child to improve control of actions or create adventurous thoughts, and above all to take in the different knowledge and points of view of companions.

Meanings, it must be said, are discovered in our community by people comparing, negotiating, persuading, showing their interests to others. We can construct together only by allowing turns in initiative. These cooperative skills have a strong innate foundation, as is made clear by the way in which very young infants become involved in 'protoconversational' exchanges of expression with other persons, and by the rapid development of enjoyment in games in which events and actions on objects are made to be part of rhythmic expressions and their use is negotiated in interactions.

Infants can learn, at least from about four months of age, to join in musical or periodic games and dance-like body play, if partners are willing to watch the infant's own forms of expressions of fun and imitation. The adult has to enjoy acting like an enhancing mirror, and be prepared to have the game played back by the baby. From the interactive rituals of these games with their teasing and jokes comes, by a remarkable internally generated change in the infant's thinking at about nine months after birth, an eagerness to perceive and act *vis à vis* the shared world as others do. This causes objects and actions on them to be endowed with common interest, and the baby, still far from using language, starts to notice trappings of culture, like clothes, books, toys, ways of posing and gesturing, and to use them for 'showing off' the knowledge gained.

We see nothing like this behaviour in any animal, even the socially very clever apes. One-year-old children are profiting from development of the amazing appetite for common knowing, the rudiments of which showed from birth, and from the desire that develops in them during the first year to have fun in games that involve friendly teasing. They transform their communicative interest to take an active, responsible place in the community of arbitrary meanings that the older members of the family and familiar work-a-day community take for granted.

The point of these introductory remarks is to make clear that when we try to understand how young children, who are not realistic or logical in their thinking, come to learn about the culture they have been born into, we have to ask what makes them want to see things our way. Why do they eagerly learn the language and all the other peculiar habits and beliefs of our community, when no other species can do it? Similarly, why was this remarkable human intelligence, and its emotional underpinnings, not understood?

Limitations of a utilitarian and individualist psychology

It has been the tradition in our highly organized societies, with a culture based upon transmitted literacy, to regard rational understanding as higher than intuition; and, with the rise in scientific realism, intelligence has been equated with a capacity for rational problem-solving. The effect of this cultural trend is particularly clear in our psychology. Most of academic psychology is concerned with attempts to explain the individual thinker's cognition and learning. It is preoccupied with one subject's processing and storing of information. Social psychology has found, however, that simple individualistic learning theories do not explain human behaviour. It has had to ask more and more questions about motivations, and about what happens to motives in groups. Unfortunately, this has led to a fascination with role-playing and issues of conformity or rebellion. It seems to me that the positive curiosity about what can be achieved cooperatively in companionship, through conversational negotiation, has still to be elucidated.

The psychology textbooks that our students read, most from the USA, are lively and full of facts, but they give a strange account of the forces that lead a child to become a citizen. Apparently, the two main tasks are to construct an emotionally secure self-image and then to acquire independent literate and rational thinking that can be put to effect in economically useful work. Observing the progress of a happy child in an affectionate and busy family, surrounded by a responsive community of other similar families, can lead one to a different prospectus for human intelligence.

By following the development of cognition and communication together through infancy, it becomes clear how the 'scientific' motives that Piaget was concerned with are modulated and transformed by the interpersonal skill by which the infant develops negotiation of ideas with others.

Although it may not always seem so, human life is essentially cooperative. People expect to be able to share ideas about the world and to coordinate their interests and actions so that they can accomplish things that one person could never do alone. Understanding of language and every kind of symbol needs this kind of participatory consciousness. It is not enough to be intelligent, in the sense of being able to solve problems; we have to be able to see intelligence in others, and in the effects and artefacts that they produce. We could not even have symbols for language or for thinking if we did not have insight into one another's motives, experiences, intentions and feelings (Vygotsky, 1962; Werner and Kaplan, 1963). These are not trivial achievements. Children have to come ready to learn through sharing of other persons' states of consciousness and the contents of their memories.

Jerome Bruner (1983) once said that all education is conversational. I think conversational intelligence is the hallmark of a human mind, and the necessary motivator of cultural learning. It is an intelligence that tries to negotiate with other minds to share the process of conscious awareness and purposeful thinking itself.

Lessons from infant development

I base my account on 25 years of research into the development of communication, play and cooperation in the first year of life, supplemented by less systematic explorations of how the conversational and playful infant we have come to know develops into a toddler and preschool child (Trevarthen, 1979, 1980, 1982, 1987, 1988, 1993; Trevarthen and Hubley, 1978; Trevarthen and Logotheti, 1987). At the end of this development, on the eve of entry into the 'big' school where instruction is more formal, most children have accumulated an immense fund of culturally relevant knowledge, and learned to talk with a large vocabulary and a proper grammar. I believe that the essential motivation for this remarkable early learning can be seen in the first months after birth when the baby seeks to engage in protoconversation with his or her mother.[1]

Young infants have a number of extraordinary abilities, most of which were unrecognized by psychological or educational theory until recently. In the right communicative situation, a newborn may be a proficient imitator of the expressions of other persons. They read emotions in the face or voice with surprising precision, and can even hear and learn to prefer subtle differences

---

1   Note that throughout this chapter I refer mainly to the importance of mothers. I do so because, almost always, the principal caregiver of a young baby is his or her mother, and almost all the research has been done with mothers. There is also evidence that infants' initial preferences are to communicate with their mother, whose voice has become familiar to them *in utero*. These infant preferences are in turn usually strongly reinforced by nurturant maternal attention during the early days and weeks of life. Fathers, grandparents, siblings and other caregivers can play a highly significant part in the young child's social world, and their role often increases in importance, depending on local circumstances and cultural traditions and services for infant and preschool care, but my starting point is the experience of very young infants, most of whom soon come to recognize their mother as their principal companion in communication and learning.

in speech that identify their mothers and even the language that she speaks. Two-month-old children express their willingness to enter protoconversations with many coordinated expressions and gestures that a sympathetic parent readily takes as real efforts to 'talk'.

Growing curiosity about the world, and a new companionship

A three-month-old may show great absorption in a mother's handling of a toy while still too young to control his or her reaching to grasp the object of interest. Interest in objects seen or heard, and attempts to touch them with the hand, become stronger and better controlled, as do associated emotions of Piaget's 'concern at failure' in 'accommodation' to an object or event, or 'joy in mastery' of a known object, the properties of which the mind has 'assimilated' and can predict. Although the baby usually does not yet seek eye contact with the mother to confirm or elaborate communication around the object, 'moods' of interest in the play are signalled to her by squeals, growls, yells, raspberries, intake and expulsion of breath, laughter, or various sounds of impatience or annoyance. At the same time as the baby watches the mother's hands, he or she listens to the vocal 'gloss' that the mother is likely to give her movements when she is presenting a toy in play.

In the second six months, infants coordinate their self-centred orientation to events with a partner's other-centred orientation. For example, to follow a mother's pointing towards an object in a shared space/time frame, the baby must conceive the mother's line of attention and orientation and find a place and thing to which it leads from the mother's body. 'Checking' behaviour, by which the baby directs attention to the eyes, face, voice or hands of the partner (or to various combinations of these), shows how the infant's growing awareness of how to coordinate with the other person's mind is coupled to a need for specific information on expressed details of their feelings, interests and intentions. After six months, infants are increasingly aware of the possibility that what they are about to do can be qualified by how their mothers will feel about it. All these games of mutual interest set a groundwork for joint appreciation of reality and for communication by symbols and language.

Developmental psychologists have devised experiments that prove that infants can categorize experiences, strive to solve problems concerning the appearances and disappearances of objects, and remember events over considerable periods of time. By six months a baby is both eager to explore surroundings and ready to play lively games with a familiar playmate. Communication also must change to assimilate the competing interests of this increasing adaptation of the infant's consciousness and intentions to objects that can be explored, manipulated and assimilated, but not communicated with. The new vigour and variety of the infant's body activity, with effects in body experience or feelings of movement, gain increasing part in control of the repertoire of expressions that the infant likes to play with. These new manifestations of infant enthusiasm in play are incorporated into new and more elaborate games that mothers create to gain the infants' willing and joyful participation. We have traced how the mother and her baby develop a companionship out of lively routines of playful teasing. Other companionships may be developing, too, with fathers, grandparents, siblings and friends.

Universals in the infancy of music

Compared to early protoconversations, games with three- to six-month-old children are livelier, on a faster beat, more forceful, much more varied in emotional colour and organized to fill longer stretches of time. These laws of play are shown beautifully in the songs that mothers discover themselves singing to babies over three months of age. Recently we have found that mothers do not restrict their entertainments to traditional ditties. Many perform dance and song for their babies using their own favourite rock or folk music, in forms that exhibit the same universal features as those made for babies, especially in the ways in which they are made by a happy mother. Babies are introduced very early into the popular music of the day. Micro-analysis of videos reveals that the mother's performances not only excite the interest and emotions of the infant, who watches eagerly, anticipates with 'dread' and laughs with joy at appropriate places, they also give the infant a rhythmic 'story' to learn, with introduction, build-up, climax and resolution. The mother has to capture the interest of an individual with much in mind. She may be considered to succeed by engaging with universal poetic and aesthetic parameters in the infant's motivation, parameters that remain as universals in adult poetry and music. The innate musicality of infants, and its importance in communication before words, has become the focus of researchers' attention in the last few years. This should enhance the status of shared musical experience for preschool children (Bjørkvold, 1992).

Obviously, for whatever reason, we have underestimated the poetic and musical awareness of young infants, and this points to the non-verbal abilities all humans must possess, and the kind of rhythmic and emotional machinery they must have in their heads, if they are to interact mentally and make sense of one another's feelings, actions, ideas and opinions. The unconscious level of communication, regulating the tone of interpersonal contact, obviously has importance in all cooperative work, including teaching and being taught.

Jokes, teasing and self-awareness: negotiating to signal emotions and initiatives, and to test companionship

Close observation of tricks, jokes, naughtiness and 'mucking about' shows that, before nine months, infants gain pleasure from a kind of 'play fighting' with their preferred playmates (Reddy, 1991). This is an important manifestation of intersubjective assertiveness that clearly paves the way to negotiation of initiative in protolanguage. The very wide range of mannerisms, expressions, actions and ritual performances that are 'shown off' by infants as 'jokes' or 'tricks' when they are between six and twelve months of age gives us a broad scope for interpretation of 'infant semiotics'. These are socio-dramatic posturings, clown expressions, musical performances (with rudimentary 'singing' and 'dancing'), conventional acts of etiquette, declamatory posturings, destructive and uncooperative actions, and many others. All these displays increase in subtlety and complexity in the second year, but they start in the first. It should be emphasized that such acts of communication are not simply framed or 'scaffolded' by the partner, although they are learned at first by imitation in interaction; rather they are recreated by the child out of this favourable intersubjective learning situation.

This kind of pretentious communication seems to be linked in development with a suspicious fear of an unfamiliar and potentially unsympathetic or uncomprehending stranger. The baby, while capable of infectious joy in play with a trusted partner, may show extreme mistrust leading to expressions of fear and crying with an unfamiliar person who approaches and invites communication. Thus the developing social consciousness of a seven- to eight-month-old is manifested simultaneously in pretending or joking with 'friends', and in sensitivity to incomprehension or ridicule by a stranger.

Sharing experience of the world and learning to cooperate meaningfully

A one-year-old distributes attention strategically between multiple goals, and willingly follows gestural and vocal signs of how to manipulate objects in new combinations. At this age, babies express themselves in 'protolanguage', combining vocalizations, facial expressions and gestures to declare interests to partners. These developments in cooperating through communication accompany advances in memory of objects and events, and in the ability to hold back the impulse to move in response to every attractive stimulus. The baby is becoming more intelligent, more 'world wise' and more cautious and deliberate, as well as more communicative. His or her attempts to act 'properly' with them are greeted with approval by parents, who praise both the interest and the 'cleverness' of the actions. These uses and meanings become frames for the perception of any new thing, and the child starts fantasy play in which all sorts of materials and objects are imagined to be useful as food, tools, dress, etc. The child also gains favourite possessions that become part of daily rituals. In the next few years, play becomes richer in imagery and memory. It becomes the driving force of the child's mental work.

One-year-old infants are starting to walk, and the increased mobility in the second year assists a much wider exploration and manipulation of the environment. The most remarkable, most human, developments in this time, however, are those that build a shared cultural awareness, one that is profoundly influenced by what other people do, and by what they express in emotion, gesture and speech.

Into the coded world of language

If an 18-month-old is presented with a collection of new, but commonplace, play objects – dolls; clothes; model vehicles or miniature pieces of furniture, such as tables and chairs, a bath or a bed; implements like dishes, cups and saucers, knives, spoons and forks, combs, brushes and so on; books, pictures, pencils – these objects will be recognized for what they 'properly' are. The toddler's play may seem egocentric, because the child characteristically turns his or her back to the mother most of the time and may shrug off any recommendation she may offer as to what should be done with the toys, and may say 'No!' to her. However, what the mother shows or says is picked up and it does influence what the toddler attends to and plays with. The mother can help set up a shared pretend situation – giving the dolly a cup of tea, or a bath, for example – and the child will cooperate to the extent of accepting a simple 'play frame' supplied by the mother. The actions are not elaborated with much cooperation, however, and it is highly characteristic of 18-month-old children to assert independence or separateness and to limit their own contribution to the ideas of play. Cooperation is better developed in fantasy play with the mother a few months later.

At this age, for most children, knowledge of what things mean, or what they communicate, greatly exceeds what can be said. Comprehension of what the mother says is much more evident than it was a few months before, but it is dependent on 'the pragmatic and interpersonal context', which is to say that the child's grasp of the meaning of some names that others give to things, or some actions they describe verbally, depends on a richer mental grasp of what can be done with such things, and especially on how they, or things or actions like them, have been shared with others previously.

An audio recording of the talk that accompanies a mother's play with her toddler reveals the importance of prosody and intonation in this communication (Ferrier, 1985). It also reveals that the mother is identifying strongly with the child's imagination and apparent purposes. A mother's talk is given lively inflection, and the animation of her voice highlights shared moments of enjoyment, triumph, curiosity, surprise, difficulty, disappointment, annoyance, sadness, and so on, in clearly distinct ways. For his or her part, the child, while making only poorly articulated attempts at speech, controls a range of protolanguage vocalizations with subtle and appropriate intonation. Different messages (questions, declarations, imperatives, exclamations of varying emotion) are clearly conveyed by appropriate modulations of pitch, quality and loudness. The child's prosody is rich and appropriate.

Gestural communication is also well developed, with both mother and child making and responding to a wide variety of expressive diectic (place indicating) and praxic (object using) movements of the hands that are coupled to body movements, posturings and facial and vocal expressions. The intersubjectivity of two-year-old children is certainly rich and subtle, and they communicate in ways that bring their consciousness and understandings together.

Infants obviously develop awareness, emotions and intentions in companionship with familiar and sympathetic persons months before they understand words, and they come to understand words in the context of shared awareness and purposes before they produce any. A one-year-old can copy arbitrary expressions, manners, actions and roles and can match objects with their uses. They eagerly share what they know before they talk. Approximations to words come within this 'acting to mean'. At one year, an infant may comprehend 40–100 words and produce 0–20, all acquired in shared purposeful action, and the early vocabulary reflects both differences in motives of children and the style and speech of older companions, especially, in most cases, the mother. Some children acquire names for objects and actions on objects first; others use interpersonal, social and self-referred phrases more.

A rapid 'explosion' of vocabulary starts about 20 to 30 months after birth, but there are large individual differences in this learning, as there are in temperament at this 'difficult' age. The first 'telegraphic' two- or three-word sentences do not appear to be linked to awareness of language rules before about 30 months (Locke, 1993). They are part of rituals of shared interest in familiar targets. The 'vocabulary explosion' occurs when the child has a new compulsion to share items and narratives of experience, as well as a desire to identify categories that 'need' to be named. This is an age when toddlers like to imitate in games with their peers, and, when words are not so readily found or understood, when imitative play is used as a way to negotiate ideas and actions. Nadel (1993) has shown that three-year-olds in a playgroup can share ideas by imitating actions and selecting the same toys. They may have little language, but they can show interest in one another by exchanging imitations. This immediate imitation falls off with four-year-olds, who have more speech and can negotiate play themes by talking, arguing and story-telling together.

The rise in vocabulary, grammatical facility and awareness of language rules and phonology continues with maximum rapidity between three and five years. As children begin to master conventions of regular grammatical forms, they start to think of explanations free of their own feelings and desires, or the feelings and desires they sympathetically attribute to others. At the same time, at three to four years, they can begin to talk about events from other persons' points of view. The child learns how to think in and about language, and this is facilitated by school instruction in the use of text and narrative form, and how to avoid ambiguity in explanations and stories. These language skills make increasing demands on strategic or analytical use of memory, and on subtle expression of others' knowledge and states of mind. They are consolidated by the regular grammatical and phonological rules that have become customary in the language community over generations, and these become increasingly attractive to the child after three years.

There is no doubt that, for a child who knows what words are and who can share speech with others easily, talking about acts can make them stronger and their goals clearer. In an article entitled 'Why children talk to themselves', Laura Berk (1994) reviews studies that demonstrate how talking out loud can help a young child organize behaviour and master new skills. The theory of Vygotsky (1967), that development of 'inner speech' from talking to oneself about tasks to be performed is crucial to learning how to think about acting, and to profiting from the advice of companions and teachers, is strongly supported by this work. The way in which toddlers get into language, however, should alert us to the fact that speech can be imitated or 'parroted' without much comprehension (Locke, 1993). Getting beyond this mimicry of speech sounds to using the language to think and plan needs the backing of other people who are willing to join in games of give and take with words. Objects and actions, and feelings about them, come to life as genuine topics of joint interest (Tomasello, 1988). The adult speaker who wants to teach has to be a willing listener too.

I believe that language is a powerful motivator if it is carried on with others in mutual awareness and mutual respect, in tried and tested relationships of 'confident confiding'. The same is true for music, which is just as powerful, and more immediately accessible. It would appear that we have yet much to learn about the power of musical performance in improvised interactions for motivating and consolidating skills.

A most interesting set of temperamental developments occurs near the end of the second year, and these have been shown to be independent of large cultural differences in the upbringing of young children. Although they have been attributed to a maturation in memory and cognition, their description strongly suggests a fundamental change in self-awareness related to the new understanding of cooperation and shared responsibility for meaningful interaction.

Jerome Kagan (1982) showed that 20-month-olds show a heightened anxiety about broken or defective things, about naughty (punishable) acts, and about potential criticism, especially from a stranger about inability to understand something or do a prescribed task. I suggest that this manifestation of a more aware and vulnerable 'me', in George Herbert Mead's sense (1934), a new self-consciousness, is connected to the great advance in vocabulary and self-assurance that the child will show after two years.

What preschool can offer for moral and cultural development

My research leads me to be curious about what children *want* to do – about their motivation. We cannot understand learning unless we have a clear idea of motivation. Human learning is different from that of animals because its motivation is different. The classical assumption has been that children learn because they are taught, as if the purpose of their learning was outside them. A young child has been compared with any other intelligent animal that learns. Undoubtedly, what a child has to learn is from the world and from other people, but the nature of human learning is unique. It is driven by a different kind of curiosity than that which other animals possess. It is both imitative and creative and it makes greater use of communication. The child's motives can be traced by observing how communication and exploratory behaviour develop hand in hand from infancy.

The developments in the first year, and then into language in the second year, show that learned codes for meaning are natural developments of a powerful motivation to give experiences emotional values that match the feelings of other people, and this can include teachers and peers in nursery school. A three-year-old is a socially aware person who is capable of making and keeping friends and of negotiating interesting cooperations and tests of understanding with a wide range of acquaintances. The world is full of interesting things and offers endless experiments to be carried out. Categories of experience may be defined in the course of individual discoveries and rational analysis, but every aspect of this seemingly private cognitive activity is open to qualification by what other people feel and do. Infants and toddlers are active, inquisitive learners from other people – they are adapted in their psychological make-up to what Barbara Rogoff (1990) calls 'apprenticeship in thinking'. Given that others are willing to negotiate the terms of sharing, and even speechless toddlers can be expert at this, then mutual learning can advance joyfully.

Young children obviously make sense by sharing. They use their emotions and other people's emotions to fix categories of experience that are important in cooperating. They are adept at expressing communicable ideas by means of signs – gestures, postures, vocalizations that are situated in a negotiated context of intersubjectivity – well before they can say the words of the mother tongue. Their awareness of reality and learning is aesthetic, dramatic and moral because it is built through communication with the motives and emotions of other persons. Provided that they can maintain relationships of trust and understanding, there is no reason why this learning cannot be carried out with many persons outside the family, and groups of other children offer a particularly rich context for testing feelings and ideas. Indeed, the evidence is overwhelming that well-organized preschools, where interest in the community and its culture is alive, can bring great and lasting benefits (Sylva, 1994). This is what we would predict from the abilities that infants show to learn through cooperation.

Rational cognitivists, and I would include both Freud and Piaget, as well as Descartes, find it easiest to imagine the young infant as a biological and mental isolate, mentally shapeless and boundaryless at birth. Even when, as in Freud's case, emotions become the primary focus of concern, a rationalist has to treat them as products of a state of equilibrium in cognition – in what can be perceived, remembered, thought about. As soon as one looks at how people actually, vitally communicate, form relationships, make contracts and work and learn together, not as thinking units, but as beings that need to complement and adjust to one another as partners in consciousness and activity, emotions take on a more central, positive role.

I believe that we must use our new knowledge of infancy to formulate a different concept of the socio-cultural super-ego. Both Piaget and Freud describe the process of socialization as a training, suppression or 'dressage', of the originally egocentric motives of individuals who are forced to change because they have to live together and take in other people's ideas, and obey the society's established rules. Infants, who are innate companions and cooperators, show us the need for a more positive theory. They show that emotions and their communication have a central regulatory role in cognitive growth, that they are not only in the service and 'defence' of the individual self.

References and further reading

Berk, L. E. (1994) 'Why children talk to themselves', *Scientific American*, November 1994, 60–65.

Bjørkvold, J.-R. (1992) *The Muse Within: Creativity and Communication, Song and Play from Childhood through Maturity*. New York: HarperCollins.

Bruner, J. S. (1972) 'The nature and uses of immaturity', *American Psychologist*, 27, 687–708.

Bruner, J. S. (1983) *Child's Talk: Learning to Use Language*. New York: Norton.

Donaldson, M. (1978) *Children's Minds*. London: Fontana/Collins.

Dunn, J. (1988) *The Beginnings of Social Understanding*. Cambridge, Mass.: Harvard University Press.

Dunn, J. (1993) *Young Children's Close Relationships: Beyond Attachment*. London: Sage.

Ferrier, L. J. (1985) 'Intonation in discourse: Talk between 12-month-olds and their mothers' *in* Nelson, K. ed. *Children's Language*, Vol 5. Hillsdale, New Jersey: Erlbaum.

Garvey, C. (1982) 'Communication and the development of social role play' *in* Forbes, D. and Greenberg, M. T. eds *Children's Planning Strategies*. New Directions for Child Development, Vol. 18. San Francisco: Jossey-Bass.

Gottman, J. M. (1983) 'How children become friends', *Monographs of the Society for Research in Child Development*, Vol. 48 (3, serial No. 201).

Halliday, M. A. K. (1975) *Learning How to Mean*. London: Edward Arnold.

Hartup, W. W. (1983) 'Peer relations' *in* Mussen, Paul H. ed. *Handbook of Child Psychology, Vol. IV: Socialization, Personality and Social Development*. New York: Wiley.

Howes, C. (1983) 'Patterns of friendship', *Child Development*, 54, 1041–53.

Hubley, P. and Trevarthen, C. (1979) 'Sharing a task in infancy' *in* Uzgiris, I. ed. *Social Interaction During Infancy*. New Directions for Child Development, Vol. 4, 57–80. San Francisco: Jossey-Bass.

Kagan, J. (1982) 'The emergence of self', *Journal of Child Psychology and Psychiatry*, 23, 363–381.

Locke J. L. (1993) *The Child's Path to Spoken Language*. Cambridge, Mass. and London: Harvard University Press.

Mead, G. H. (1934) *Mind, Self and Society*. Chicago: University of Chicago Press.

Mueller, E. and Vandell, D. (1979) 'Infant–infant interaction' *in* Osofsky, J. D. ed. *Handbook of Infant Development*. New York: Wiley.

Nadel, J. (1993) 'The development of communication: Wallon's framework and influence' *in* Vyt, A., Block, H. and Bornstein, M. eds *Francophone Perspectives on Structure and Process in Early Mental Development*. Hillsdale, New Jersey: Erlbaum.

Nadel, J. and Camaioni, L. eds (1993) *New Perspectives in Early Communicative Development*. London: Routledge.

Nadel-Brulfert, J. and Baudonniere, P.-M. (1982) 'The social function of reciprocal imitation in 2-year-old peers', *International Journal of Behavioural Development*, 5, 95–109.

Papousek, M. and Papousek, H. (1981) 'Musical elements in the infant's vocalization: Their significance for communication, cognition and creativity' *in* Lipsitt, L. P. and Rovee-Collier, C. K. eds *Advances in Infancy Research*, Vol. 1. Norwood, New Jersey: Ablex.

Piaget, J. (1962) *Play, Dreams and Imitation in Childhood*. London: Routledge & Kegan Paul.

Pope, C. (1994) *Baby Monthly*. London: BBC Books.

Reddy, V. (1991) 'Playing with others' expectations: Teasing and mucking about in the first year' *in* Whiten, A. ed. *Natural Theories of Mind*, 143–158. Oxford: Blackwell.

Rogoff, B. (1990) *Apprenticeship in Thinking: Cognitive Development in Social Context*. New York: Oxford University Press.

Shugar, G. W. and Bokus, B. (1986) 'Children's discourse and children's activity in the peer situation' *in* Mueller, E. C. and Cooper, C. R. eds *Process and Outcome in Peer Relationships*, Orlando, Florida: Academic Press.

Stambak, M., Ballion, M., Breaute, M., and Rayna, S. (1985) 'Pretend play and interaction in young children' *in* Hinde, R. A., Perret-Clermont, A.-N. and Stevenson-Hinde, J. eds *Social Relationships and Cognitive Development*. Oxford: Clarendon Press.

Stern, D. N. (1985) *The Interpersonal World of the Infant: A View from Psychoanalysis and Development Psychology*. New York: Basic Books.

Sylva, K. (1994) 'School influences on children's development', *Journal of Child Psychology and Psychiatry*, 35, 135–170.

Tomasello, M. (1988) 'The role of joint attentional processes in early language development', *Language Sciences*, 10, 69–88.

Trevarthen, C. (1979) 'Communication and cooperation in early infancy. A description of primary intersubjectivity' *in* Bullowa, M. ed. *Before Speech: The Beginning of Human Communication*, 321–347. London: Cambridge University Press.

Trevarthen, C. (1980) 'The foundations of intersubjectivity: Development of interpersonal and cooperative understanding in infants' *in* Olsen, D. ed. *The Social Foundations of Language and Thought: Essays in Honor of J.S. Bruner*, 316–342. New York: W.W. Norton.

Trevarthen, C. (1982) 'The primary motives for cooperative understanding' *in* Butterworth, G. and Light, P. eds *Social Cognition: Studies of the Development of Understanding*, 77–109. Brighton: Harvester Press.

Trevarthen, C. (1987) 'Sharing makes sense: Intersubjectivity and the making of an infant's meaning' *in* Steele, R. and Threadgold, T. eds *Language Topics: Essays in Honour of Michael Halliday*, Vol. 1, 177–199. Amsterdam and Philadelphia: John Benjamins.

Trevarthen, C. (1988) 'Universal cooperative motives: How infants begin to know language and skills of culture' *in* Jahoda, G. and Lewis, I. M. eds *Acquiring Culture: Cross-Cultural Studies in Child Development*, 37–90. Croom Helm.

Trevarthen, C. (1993) 'Playing into reality: Conversations with the infant communicator', *Winnicott Studies*, Number 7, Spring, 1993: 67–84. Karnak Books Ltd.

Trevarthen, C. and Hubley, P. (1978) 'Secondary intersubjectivity: Confidence, confiding and acts of meaning in the first year', *in* Lock, A. ed. *Action, Gesture and Symbol*, 183–229. Academic Press.

Trevarthen, C. and Logotheti, K. (1987) 'First symbols and the nature of human knowledge', *in* Montangero, J., Tryphon, A. and Dionnet, S. eds *Symbolisme et Connaissance (Symbolism and Knowledge)*, Cahier No. 8, Jean Piaget Archives Fondation. Geneva: Jean Piaget Archives Fondation.

Uzgiris, I. C. (1984) 'Imitation in infancy: Its interpersonal aspects', *in* Perlmutter, M. ed. *Parent–Child Interaction and Parent–Child Relations in Child Development*. The Minnesota Symposia on Child Psychology, Vol. 17. Hillsdale, New Jersey: Erlbaum.

Vygotsky, L. S. (1962) *Thought and Language*. Cambridge, Mass: The MIT Press.

Vygotsky, L. S. (1967) 'Play and its role in the mental development of the child', *Soviet Psychology*, 5(3), 6–18.

Werner, H. and Kaplan, B. (1963) *Symbol Formation*. New York: Wiley.

Winnicott, D. W. (1965) *The Maturational Process and the Facilitating Environment*. Hogarth.

Chapter 6

Young children's understanding of other people

Evidence from observations within the family*

Judy Dunn

In infancy, babies are apparently both interested in and responsive to the emotions and behavior of other people. They are born predisposed to attend to stimuli with the characteristics of the human face and voice, and they develop quickly "remarkable abilities to perceive the actions and expressions of other people" (Spelke and Cortelyou, 1981). They learn rapidly about stimuli that change in a manner that is contingent upon their own behavior – as does the behavior of other people interacting with them. By 2 months of age, they respond differently to a person who intends to speak to them than to one who speaks to someone else (Trevarthen, 1977). By the second half of their first year, they have begun to share a common communicative framework with other family members, and, as we have learned from the elegant experimental studies of *social referencing* (Klinnert, Campos, Sorce, Emde, and Svejda, 1983), in situations of uncertainty, they monitor the emotional expressions of their mothers and change their behavior appropriately in response to those expressions. As the work of those studying early language has shown particularly clearly, their comprehension of social procedures is surprisingly subtle. Bruner, for example, has persuasively argued that children have mastered the culturally appropriate use of requests, invitations, and reference well before they are correctly using the conventional linguistic forms (Bruner, 1983).

It seems, in common-sense terms, highly adaptive for babies to develop early in life some grasp of the intentions, feelings, and actions of the all-important members of their family world. However, this growing sophistication about the social world, documented in babies who have hardly begun to talk, stands in notable contrast to the limitations in much older children's understanding of other minds, which have been revealed by experimental research focused on the "metarepresentational" level of reflection on others. This experimental work underlines the deficiencies in 3- and 4-year-olds'

* This is an edited version of a chapter that appeared in D. Frye and C. Moore (eds) *Children's Theories of Mind: Mental States and Social Understanding*, Hillsdale, NJ: Lawrence Erlbaum Associates, 1991.

ability to conceptualize how others think and perceive the world. The discrepancy between the emphasis on infants' social sensitivities and these limitations in older children's understanding of other minds – at least when faced with questions about hypothetical others – raises several serious questions. If preschool children are so limited in their ability to understand others, how do they manage to function effectively in the complex world of the family? Is it possible that there are differences between children's understanding of others (at least their practical, "ready-to-hand" understanding [Packer, 1986]) in their intimate emotional family world, on the one hand, and their ability to reflect on and talk about the minds and actions of the hypothetical others that are the focus of most experimental studies, on the other hand? Does the ability to recognize the emotional states of others develop well in advance of the ability to conceptualize their thoughts? In this chapter, I consider the nature of children's understanding of familiar others during the transition from infancy to childhood, with a discussion of evidence from naturalistic observations of children within their families.

With these naturalistic data, we cannot, obviously, make such clear-cut inferences about details of children's problems in understanding others as is possible with the experimental research reported in Frye and Moore (1991). However, such naturalistic observations do have three important *a priori* advantages. First, we are able to study children in social settings that have real emotional significance for them. It is now well documented that very young children's abilities can be gravely underestimated if the children are studied in task settings that do not make "human sense" to them (Donaldson, 1978). Second, with unstructured observation, we are able to monitor and study the comments and inquiries about other people that are generated by the children themselves – rather than those that are imposed by the adult psychologist. Thus, we gain a window on what the child finds interesting or puzzling about others. Finally, by studying the context in which children perform at their most mature, we may be able to generate hypotheses about the key processes that contribute to developmental change in the domain of interest.

The findings that I discuss (described fully in Dunn, 1988) are drawn from three longitudinal studies of secondborn children in their second and third years: six children followed at 2-month intervals through the second year, six followed similarly through their third year, and 43 families studied when the secondborn children were aged 18, 24, and 36 months. The families were middle- and working-class families living in and around Cambridge in England, and all the observations, which were unstructured, were made while the children were at home, playing, fighting, and talking with their mothers and siblings. Examples are also cited from an ongoing study of children in Pennsylvania. Our strategy was to examine a number of different features of the children's behavior within their families. It would clearly be foolish to attempt to draw general inferences about children's social understanding from a focus on just one feature of their behavior; rather, we studied the children within a range of social situations, with different social partners, and in very different emotional contexts. The following domains were systematically studied: disputes, prosocial behavior, response to distress in others, cooperation and play, jokes, and conversations about others.

Two issues stand out from these studies. The first is the evidence for the children's growing ability, over the second and third years, to understand the feeling states, intentions, and behavior of others. The second is that the results give some useful indications of which processes may be important in these developments. Two, in particular, are discussed in the second section of the chapter: the role of discourse about others' feelings and intentions and the significance of affective experience in such developments. More generally, the implications of the way in which children's growing understanding is used in their family relationships are considered.

Children's understanding of others in the second and third years

Disputes

Within each domain that we studied – disputes, jokes, empathetic and proso-cial behavior, cooperation, pretend play, and conversations about other people – we found evidence for children's growing grasp of the feelings of others, of their intended actions, and of how social rules applied to other people and to themselves. In disputes, for example, the children showed a growing sophistication in teasing – actions that demonstrated a practical grasp of what would upset or annoy a particular person. Early in the second year, acts that we categorized as teasing were pretty simple; for example, children in disputes with their older siblings often seized or removed their siblings' transitional object or most special toys, or attempted to destroy something that had special significance for the siblings. In the course of the second year, such teasing acts became more frequent and more elaborate. One 24-month-old, for instance, whose older sister had three imaginary friends called Lily, Allelujah, and Peepee, would, in the course of disputes with this sister, announce that *she* was Allelujah. It was an act that was reliably followed by anger or distress on her sister's part, and it was also an act of notable sophistication for a 24-month-old, because it involved both some grasp of what would upset her sister and a transformation of her own identity.

Our analysis of disputes between the siblings showed, too, that early in the second year the children's attempts to enlist the aid of their mothers on their own behalf differed sharply according to whether the siblings had acted in an aggressive or hostile fashion first or whether they themselves had done so. The probability that the children would appeal to their mothers was high (66%) if the sibling had been the first to act in an aggressive or teasing manner. In contrast, they rarely appealed to their mothers for help in incidents when they *themselves* had acted in such way: in only 4% of such incidents did they do so. Such a distinction in the children's behavior, and indeed the evasive actions that second-year children take to avoid future punishment (see Dunn, 1988), indicate some anticipation of the mothers' actions, although, of course, they imply no elaborate understanding of the mothers' *minds*. This grasp of how other people can be expected to behave in relation to social rules becomes strikingly evident during the third year, when children's language abilities increase. Our analysis of disputes showed, for example, that *blaming* the sibling for incidents in which the child might be in trouble, and drawing the attention of the mother to the sibling rather than the self, are both common by 36 months – demonstrating a ready anticipation of how the mother will respond to another's transgression. The children's justifications showed, then, that notions of responsibility and of blame are well in place by 36 months, and that these were used frequently by the children, revealing an effective grasp of how their mothers would react to cultural breach.

Particularly illuminating were the *excuses* that the children used in their attempts to avoid disapprobation. The nature of the excuses that the children used in disputes showed an increasingly elaborate grasp of how social rules applied to different people in different contexts and of how these rules could be questioned. For our present purposes, it is excuses of intent that are of special interest. In our culture, we see as crucial the distinction between acts that are intended to harm others or transgress rules of conduct and acts that have similar consequences but are accidental (Darley and Zanna, 1982). The question of when children begin to make this distinction is, however, a matter of some dispute. Piaget (1965) considered that there was "some reason to doubt whether a child of 6–7 could really distinguish an involuntary error from an intentional lie . . . the distinction is, at the best, in the process of formation" (p. 145). In contrast to this view, Shultz (1980) reported observations that children as young as 3 may make such a distinction. The children in our studies made the excuse that they "didn't mean to" rather infrequently during the observations. However, among the incidents when they did refer to intentions were some that involved children as young as 26 months:

Example 1: Child aged 26 months (Study 3)

Child climbs on Mother to investigate light switch:
M: You're hurting me!
C: Sorry. Sorry. I don't mean to.

This example could be interpreted as a "rote-learned" strategy for getting out of trouble, rather than evidence that the child really understood the significance of his intentions for his mother. For several of the earliest examples of the references to intentions, such explanations in terms of the child having learned to repeat phrases without understanding their meaning can be offered (cf. Astington, 1991). However, the wide variety of situations and the appropriateness with which these phrases are used should be borne in mind: it should be noted that there is not one example of such a phrase being used inappropriately. The children in both the Cambridge and Pennsylvania studies very clearly understood the significance of the phrase that an act (either against them or by them) had been done *on purpose*, and they used this in their attempts to obtain comfort or help, to good effect. The following example comes from an observation of a 33-month-old girl in the Pennsylvania study, who came crying to her mother after her brother had deliberately bitten her on the forehead:

Example 2: Child aged 33 months (Pennsylvania study)

C:	Look what Philip did!
	He bited me!
	(crying)
M:	He bit you on the head?
C:	Yes.
M to Sib:	Philip is that true?
S:	No.
C to M:	Yes!
	On purpose!
M to C:	He did it on purpose?
C:	Yes!
M to Sib:	Come on over, Philip.
Sib to M:	I didn't do it on purpose Mom.
C to M:	Yes he did.

In the course of the third year, the children's references to intentions – usually but not always their own – were more clearly expressed and are not easily explained simply in terms of the children having learned a "formula" that works without any grasp of the significance of the reference to intention. In the example that follows, the 33-month-old is resisting his mother's attempts to get him down off the settee by referring to his own honorable intentions (cleaning the TV set):

Example 3: Child aged 33 months (Study 3)

M:	Get off!
C:	(sits down on the settee still): Look. I'm not – (stands up). Mummy. I'm not – I'm not standing on there. I'm trying to get a paint off (rubs TV).
M:	——
C:	I going try and get a paint off. All I'm trying to do is – there.

This child's repeated attempts to get out of trouble by mentioning his good intentions surely reflects some notion that his mother's view of the action will differ according to the nature of those intentions. His "creative" use of his own worthy goal (getting the paint off) as a justification for employing particular means (staying on the settee) is very unlikely to have been learned as a rote formula, and with this reference to a goal as justification for means we have the necessary elements of an understanding of intention as set out by Frye (1991).

The same general point is supported by the finding that children sometimes made excuses that a transgression was made in *pretend*. They also commonly made excuses on grounds of *lack of control*, or *incapacity*. In their claims to be too tired to pick up their toys or their refusal to help their mothers on the grounds that they have a headache or – quite simply – are still "a baby," we see that they have begun to understand that their mothers will apply rules differently according to the intention, incapacity, or lack of control of the transgressor.

Two further points concerning these excuses and attempts to blame others should be noted. The first is that the children made reference to the needs and intentions of others as well as themselves in their attempts to get their way. In the next example, for instance, the boy refers to his mother's needs in an attempt to blame his sister and exclude her from the football game he was enjoying with his mother:

Example 4: Child aged 36 months (Study 2)

Child and Mother are playing with soccer ball. Sibling attempts to join game by kicking ball when it comes near her.

C to Sib: No! It's Mummy's go again. No! It was Mummy's go again.
M: Chrissie (sib) did it for me.
C: I'll put this ball away. I'm going to put it away if Chrissie's going to spoil it for Mummy.

Martin, the 36-month-old boy in this example, refers to a principle of justice and to his mother's enjoyment – all in the service of his own interest.

This matter of the importance of the child's interests brings us to the second point raised by these early discussions of rights, intentions, and the behavior of others. This is that the children's grasp of these issues of how people respond to rule violations, blame, and responsibility appears to be a very practical one. This is not a trivial point. Their understanding is of how excuses and justifications can be used to reach their own ends in the complex world of the family. They apply this understanding differently in different relationships, according to the nature of that relationship and their needs within that relationship. This differentiation of their behavior according to whether it is their father, mother, or sibling with whom they are interacting was apparent in each of the domains we examined – whether disputes, cooperative play, prosocial behavior, or propositional discussion; and it underlines the point that children's understanding of those other family members – what will annoy or please them, what will enlist their aid or attention, how they will react to excuses and justifications, under what circumstances they can be expected to cooperate or punish – is an increasingly differentiated understanding. This matter of the practical use to which the children put their understanding of others – and the adaptive importance of that understanding within the family – is one we return to later, when we consider the developmental processes that may contribute to these developments.

Cooperative pretend play

The analysis of children's behavior in cooperative play, in response to others' distress, as humorists, and in conversation about others, provides further evidence on the nature of their understanding of the other people in their world. During the third year, children's participation in joint pretend play, for example, changed dramatically. Between 18 and 24 months, they joined their older siblings' pretend play as compliant participants who obeyed (usually) the managerial – and often dictatorial – instructions of their siblings (Dunn and Dale, 1984). In the course of the third year, their cooperation became a far more active affair, in which they were innovative actors who not only anticipated the goals and intentions of their partner in play, but who, in their own original contributions, demonstrated some understanding of the intentions and feelings of the pretend "other" whose role they were enacting. In the example that follows, the 30-month-old girl was playing a game of mothers and babies with her older sister. The game began with a command from the older sister to "pretend you're a baby or my mummy." The sequence was not unusual in its length or complexity. It lasted for 140 conversational turns, and Annie, the younger sister, made a number of contributions to the play narrative, relevant to her role as baby. She also acted both compliantly and noncompliantly:

Example 5: Child aged 30 months (Study 3)

Child's innovations in the joint pretend play, for her role as Baby:
  Makes babbling noises.
  Crawls.
  Says she can't put slippers on: "I'm baby."
  Designates "baby bed."
  Asks for porridge.
  Plays guitar in a way she designates as "a babby way . . . Me babby."
  Addresses sibling as "Mummy."
  Acts naughty with the guitar.

Pretends to get lost.

Snores.

In answer to sibling enquiring why she is crying ("What's wrong babbu?") replies "Me can't get to sleep."

Instructs sibling on what she should say, as Mummy.

Child's disputes and noncompliance with sibling over course of pretend play:

When told to babble and not to cry, cries.

Criticizes sibling's action in terms of role: "No you not a baby."

Denies that they are both tired in the game.

Refuses to go on "Mummy's" knee.

Child's compliance with sibling's actions or suggestions in the game:

Sibling says go to sleep: Child pretends to sleep.

Sibling gives "drink": Child pretends to drink.

Sibling gives "food": Child pretends to eat it.

Such innovations in joint pretend became increasingly evident from the middle of the third year. The ability to imagine being another person with intentions and feelings that are different from one's own is surely important evidence for children's growing understanding of others – evidence that parallels the signs of children's ability to deceive. Now, it has been plausibly argued that there is a major change in children's ability to reflect on others' minds and behavior during the third year (Wellman, 1988). It has been shown, for instance, that children first begin to talk about mental states in themselves and others – about knowing, remembering, forgetting – during the second half of the third year (Shatz, Wellman, and Silber, 1983; Wellman, 1988). It has been argued by Wellman, on the basis of experimental and naturalistic studies, that after two-and-a-half years, children begin to have an understanding of mind that is a coherent and interconnected set of concepts that make a distinction between mental and physical entities (Wellman, 1988). The evidence from these pretend episodes supports the argument that such capacities indeed develop markedly during the third year. (It should be noted, however, that close study of the six individual children in our study does not support the idea that there is a sudden shift in understanding at 28–30 months; rather, the changes appear gradually, and there are marked individual differences in the timing of their development.) Further support for the idea that there is a major change in children's understanding of other minds around the middle of the third year comes from two other sources: first, our analyses of the children's conversations about other people and, second, the analysis of children's interventions in conversations between other family members.

Conversations about others

From the transcripts of the observations of the six children observed at 2-month intervals during their third year, we examined all the children's questions about other people, categorizing such inquiries according to whether they were about the whereabouts, actions, or inner states of the people concerned or about the application of social rules to those others. Figure 6.1 shows that inquiries about inner states and social rules were absent during the first months of the third year but showed a sharp increase in the second half of that year.

A similar analysis of the 43 children in the larger study as 36-month-olds provided an encouraging replication of these findings, with very similar proportions of questions about the inner states and feelings of others. What is particularly notable about such conversations, for our present concern, is that a relatively high proportion of the conversations included discussion of the cause or consequence of the feelings or inner state of the person discussed (Dunn, Brown, and Beardsall, 1990). The rise of questions about others at this time and our analysis of the pragmatic context of such questions indicate that, as their ability to reflect on other minds develops there is a growth of "disinterested" curiosity about others. It seems that as children's ideas about others become more elaborate, there are more issues for them to clarify with questions.

A strikingly parallel set of findings, again highlighting children's interest

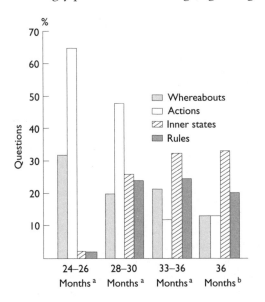

Figure 6.1 Percentage of questions about other people

Notes: a Study of 6 children
         b Study of 43 children

in the inner states of others during the second half of the third year, came from an analysis of the children's narratives about other people during the third year. As with the questions about others, narratives about other people became increasingly focused on inner states and social rules during the second half of that year (Figure 6.2).

The results from our study of children's interventions in conversations also provide relevant evidence – in this case evidence for children's growing ability to understand the focus of others' interests. Much of the talk in families with small children is not directed to the children; the ability to participate effectively in such conversations is a developmental achievement of major importance. Analyses of the children's interventions in talk between their mothers and siblings in the third year show that the children attempted to join the conversations between others from early in the third year; however, such interventions were frequently not relevant to the topic of the others' talk, and although the children often *interrupted* the others' talk, they did not make a contribution of new or relevant information to that previous conversation. In the course of the third year, however, their interventions became increasingly relevant and contributed new information to the topic of the previous interlocutors' talk (Dunn and Shatz, 1989). The results highlighted the salience of the conversation between other family members for young children, their increasing skill at joining such conversations in a relevant fashion, and their adeptness at turning the focus of such talk to their favorite subject – themselves.

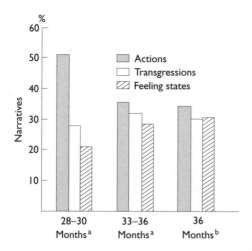

Figure 6.2 Percentage of narratives about actions, transgressions, and feelings

Notes: a Study of 6 children
       b Study of 43 children

Jokes

A further instance of the children's sensitivity to the interests and feelings of the different people in their social world was provided by an analysis of the children's humor. Even before they are using many words, children find the behavior of others in their world a source of amusement, as they do jokes that can be pointed out and shared with others. Sharing a joke implies, at some level, an expectation that another person will also find this distortion of the expected absurd or comic. What our examination of the children's jokes showed was that children made different jokes to their siblings than to their mothers or the observer. With parents, play with naming jokes, true–false assertions, transgressions of social rules, and with the emotional dynamics of their relationships stood out:

Example 6: Child aged 24 months (Study 1)

M: Do you like your Mummy, John?
C: No yes! (smiles)
M: No yes? No yes?
C: No yes!

With their siblings, the children enjoyed and developed ritual insults, scatalogical jokes, and word play on forbidden topics. The results strongly suggest that, by 36 months, children already have a considerable and differentiated understanding of what familiar others will find funny or offensive.

The developmental course of children's understanding of others in the second and third year

In summary, the results of these observations within the family suggest the following course of development: children's understanding of others' feelings grows early in the second year from an "affective tuning" to the distress or amusement of others (see Stern, 1985) to a grasp of how certain actions lead to disapproval or anger in others, how certain actions can comfort other family members (see Yarrow, Zahn-Waxler, and Chapman, 1983), and what actions can be a shared source of amusement with others. They respond empathetically to others' distress early in the second year, and they show in both their nonverbal and verbal behavior much interest in the feeling states of others. With increasing explicitness, they show curiosity about and understanding of the causes of pain, anger, distress, pleasure, dislike, fear, comfort in others. They play with and joke about these feelings in others and tell stories about them.

They also, during the second year, show increasing sensitivity to the goals and intentions of others – understanding that is evident in their disputes, pretend, narratives, and questions. Understanding of mental states, as opposed to emotional states and intended actions, appears to develop somewhat later, during the second half of the third year.

Of course, the limitations of this early understanding of others' emotions, intentions, and mental activity are notable. We have little evidence for the ability to recognize the nuances of the "social" emotions (embarrassment, shame or guilt), and experimental studies show that children of this age do not grasp the idea that people can experience combinations of emotions (Harris, 1989). It is obvious that children in their third year could have only a rudimentary understanding of the causes of adult emotions, and that their grasp of the intentions of others will be limited to the intentions of others in familiar contexts. Similarly, as Wellman has cogently argued, although they understand that human action is governed by wishes, beliefs, and attitudes, they do not have a concept of mind as an interpreting processor of information. (Johnson and Wellman, 1982; Wellman, 1988). What remains particularly unclear is the extent to which their early understanding of mental states is dependent on the familiarity of the person and context. This matter of the family context, in which the earliest signs of understanding others are observed, brings us to the issue of what processes may be involved in the development of such abilities. I have discussed elsewhere (Dunn, 1988) several themes that stand out as important contributors; here, I discuss just two: the emotional context of family interactions and the significance of family discourse.

The possible importance of the emotional context

In considering the ways in which family interactions might play a special role in fostering the development of social understanding, it is surely important to examine the possible role of affective experience. One provocative set of findings here came from our analysis of the disputes between children and their mothers and siblings (Dunn and Munn, 1987). We were interested in the relations between the emotions that the children expressed during the disputes, the topic of these disputes, and the likelihood that they would *reason*, rather than behave in a less mature way (such as resorting to hit or howl). The results showed that as 18-month-olds they were most likely to be angry or distressed in disputes over the topic of rights and interests (usually their own!). The emotional significance of these disputes might lead one to predict that as 3-year-olds they would be most likely to regress to hitting and howling, rather than to reason in mature fashion when frustrated in conflict over these issues.

The results told a very different story. Eighteen months later, when the children were 36 months old, it was in these disputes over rights and interests that they showed their most "mature" behavior, by marshalling justifications and excuses for their actions. The children, that is, showed their most mature behavior over the issues that their earlier emotional behavior had suggested they cared most about. One inference from these findings might be that children use their intelligence on what matters most to them emotionally. Another, which is not incompatible with the first, is that the experience of mild distress and anger during these family conflicts may actually contribute to the children's learning – that the arousal they experience may heighten their vigilance and attentive powers. (See Arsenio and Ford, 1985, and Masters, Barden, and Ford, 1979, for parallel arguments based on experimental studies.)

Yet another possibility is that the mothers' behavior during these conflicts was an important influence. Our analyses showed that mothers were indeed more likely to reason with children in conflicts in which the younger child was distressed or angry than in incidents in which the child was not upset. They were, too, more likely to use reasoning in conflicts over rights than in disputes over other topics. It could be, therefore, that what the children are learning is that it is more appropriate and practically successful to use reasoning and justification in certain kinds of dispute than in others. We cannot, on the basis of our observations, assess separately the plausibility of these different possibilities; yet, the observations make clear that, in real life, the emotional state of the child, the salience of the topic, and the mothers' articulation of reasons and excuses are closely linked in the children's experience (see also Miller and Sperry, 1987). It could well be that it is this combination of a powerful cognitive and affective experience that contributes to the children's developing grasp of the way in which social rules and others' behavior are linked.

The general point is that the distress, anger, and amusement that the children show highlight the importance of the frustration of goals and the pleasure in shared positive experience for children, and our findings suggest that these emotions may contribute to the learning that takes place. This is not to argue that the development of understanding takes place only in such contexts. It is evident that in older children passages of intellectual search often occur in calm, reflective exchanges between children and adults (Tizard and Hughes, 1984). Nevertheless, there may well be special significance in the emotion-laden exchanges in the family – exchanges in which it is clearly of great importance for the child to learn how others will behave and think. Because these are settings that are rarely studied by psychologists, they are unlikely to be given prominence in accounts of cognitive development. A further general point is that the new understanding of others' mental states and intentions has great significance for their strategies in conflict and in situations where their own goals are frustrated (Dunn, 1988). The adaptive importance of their new capability to understand other people is highlighted in these findings on the links between emotion, conflict, and justification.

The possible significance of family discourse

The second theme that should be highlighted in any consideration of the processes that are important in the developments in understanding of others is the contribution of family discourse about others. The evidence from studies in both the United States and Britain shows that young children in our cultures grow up in a world in which there is much conversation within families about the feelings and behavior of others and about their motives, intentions, and the permissibility of their actions. Messages – implicit and increasingly explicit – about such matters are conveyed to them each day in a wide variety of ways (see also Shweder, Mahapatra, and Miller, 1987). Children are participants in conversations about such matters from a very early age; they monitor, comment on, and join in such discussions between others, and they question, joke about, and argue as to the causes and consequences of the feelings and behavior of others. It appears very likely that children's differentiated understanding of other minds is influenced by such discourse. Here, the analysis of individual differences supports such a contention. Differences between families in the frequency and extent of discussion of others' feelings, motives, and behavior are striking; in our studies in Cambridge, correlations were found between such differences in the first three years of children's lives and in a variety of "outcome" measures, such as the child's own participation in conversation about inner states (Dunn, Bretherton, and Munn, 1987), their friendly behavior towards their younger siblings (Dunn and Kendrick, 1982), and, most strikingly, their performance three to four years later on affective perspective-taking tasks (Dunn, Brown, and Beardsall, 1990).

Conclusion

In conclusion, let us return to the questions raised at the outset. The first question concerned how, if their ability to understand others is as limited as was formerly supposed, preschool children relate to others and manage their lives within the complex social world of the family. Here, the results of our observations are unequivocal. By 36 months of age, the children "managed" their family lives very effectively: they anticipated and manipulated the reactions of others, "read" their emotions, used others to reach their own ends, and influenced the feeling states of others intentionally and practically by teasing, comforting, and joking. They questioned and disputed the application of social rules to themselves and others and they successfully redirected blame onto others.

The second question concerned the possible differences in children's abilities within the family, as well as their capacities in more formal and less familiar settings. The direct comparisons that would allow us to answer the question have not yet been made. However, the very early ages at which children can recognize and respond to the feeling states and intentions of other family members lead one to predict that such comparison would show the children more capable within the familiar and emotionally significant context of the family. It appears, indeed, that the more carefully the experimental setting is designed to be relevant to the children's emotional interest, the better their understanding and performance are in such settings (Donaldson, 1978). It should be noted, however, that the abilities that we have documented and discussed here concern primarily the children's abilities to understand and inquire about others' feelings, behavior, and intentions, rather than their cognitive processes. Our third question concerned the issue of whether the ability to recognize and reflect on *emotional states* develops well before the ability to understand and reflect on *other minds*. It appears, from the evidence of children within their families, that this is probably so. This conclusion is, perhaps, unsurprising, given the accessibility of people's emotional expression and behavior and – even more significantly – given the adaptive importance of understanding the emotional state of others with whom one shares a family world and upon whom, as a small child, one is emotionally dependent.

References

Arsenio, W. F., and Ford, M. E. (1985). The role of affective information in social–cognitive development: Children's differentiation of moral and conventional events. *Merrill-Palmer Quarterly, 31*, 1–17.

Astington, J. W. (1991). Intention in the child's theory of mind. In D. Frye and C. Moore (Eds), *Children's theories of mind: Mental states and social understanding*. Hillsdale, NJ: Lawrence Erlbaum Associates.

Bruner, J. (1983). *Child's talk*. New York: Norton.

Darley, J. M. and Zanna, M. P. (1982). Making moral judgements. *American Scientist, 70*, 515–521.

Donaldson, M. (1978). *Children's minds*. London: Fontana.

Dunn, J. (1988). *The beginnings of social understanding*. Cambridge, MA: Harvard University Press.

Dunn, J. and Dale, N. (1984). I a Daddy: Two-year-olds' collaboration in joint pretend with mothers and siblings. In I. Bretherton (Ed.), *Symbolic play: The development of social understanding* (pp. 131–158). New York: Academic Press.

Dunn, J. and Kendrick, C. (1982). *Siblings: Love, envy and understanding*. Cambridge, MA: Harvard University Press.

Dunn, J. and Munn, P. (1987). The development of justification in disputes with mother and with sibling. *Developmental Psychology, 23*, 791–798.

Dunn, J. and Shatz, M. (1989). Becoming a conversationalist despite (or because of) having a sibling. *Child Development, 60*, 399–410.

Dunn, J., Bretherton, I., and Munn, P. (1987). Conversations about feeling states between mothers and their young children. *Developmental Psychology, 23*, 132–139.

Dunn, J., Brown, J., and Beardsall, L. (1990). Family talk about feeling states, and children's later understanding of others' emotions. *Developmental Psychology, 26*.

Frye, D. (1991). The origins of intention in infancy. In D. Frye and C. Moore (Eds) *Children's theories of mind: Mental states and social understanding*. Hillsdale, NJ: Lawrence Erlbaum Associates.

Harris, P. L. (1989). *Children and emotion*. Oxford: Blackwell.

Johnson, C. N. and Wellman, H. M. (1982). Children's developing conceptions of the mind and brain. *Child Development, 53*, 222–234.

Klinnert, M. D., Campos, J. J., Sorce, J. F., Emde, R. N., and Svejda, M. (1983). Emotions as behavior regulators: Social referencing in infancy. In R. Plutchik and H. Kellerman (Eds), *Emotion: Theory, research and experience* (Vol. 2, pp. 57–86). New York: Academic Press.

Miller, P. and Sperry, L. L. (1987). The socialization of anger and aggression. *Merrill-Palmer Quarterly, 33*, 1–32.

Masters, J. C., Barden, R. C., and Ford, M. E. (1979). Affective states, expressive behavior, and learning in children. *Journal of Personality and Social Psychology, 37*, 380–390.

Packer, M. J. (1986, January). Social interaction as practical activity: Implications for social and moral development. *Proceedings of the conference on social process and moral development*, Miami, FL.

Piaget, J. (1965). *The moral judgement of the child*. New York: Free Press.

Shatz, M., Wellman, H. M., and Silber, S. (1983). The acquisition of mental verbs: A systematic investigation of the first reference to mental state. *Cognition, 14*, 301–322.

Shultz, T. R. (1980). The development of the concept of intention. In A. Collins (Ed.), *Minnesota symposium on child psychology* (Vol. 13, pp. 131–164). Hillsdale, NJ: Lawrence Erlbaum Associates.

Shweder, R. A., Mahapatra, M., and Miller, J. G. (1987). Culture and moral development. In J. Kagan and S. Lamb (Eds), *The emergence of moral concepts in young children* (pp. 1–83). Chicago: University of Chicago Press.

Spelke, E. S. and Cortelyou, A. (1981). Perceptual aspects of social knowing: Looking and listening in infancy. In M. E. Lamb and L. R. Sherrod (Eds), *Infant social cognition* (pp. 61–84). Hillsdale, NJ: Lawrence Erlbaum Associates.

Stern, D. (1985). *The interpersonal world of the infant*. New York: Basic Books.

Tizard, B. and Hughes, M. (1984). *Young children learning*. London: Fontana.

Trevarthen, C. (1977). Descriptive analyses of infant communicative behaviour. In H. R. Schaffer (Ed.), *Studies in mother–infant interaction* (pp. 227–270). London: Academic Press.

Wellman, H. M. (1988). First steps in the child's theorizing about the mind. In J. W. Astington, P. L. Harris, and D. R. Olson (Eds), *Developing theories of mind* (pp. 64–92). Cambridge, England: Cambridge University Press.

Yarrow, M. R., Zahn-Waxler, C., and Chapman, M. (1983). Prosocial behavior. In P. H. Mussen (Ed.), *Handbook of child psychology: Volume 4. Socialization, personality and social development* (pp. 469–545). New York: Wiley.

Chapter 7

Development of intersubjectivity in social pretend play*

Artin Göncü

The attainment of intersubjectivity, or shared understanding, is a central issue in psychosocial development. One activity in which young children may exhibit intersubjectivity is pretend play, in which they construct shared representations without the assistance of adults. My goal in this chapter is to examine the development of intersubjectivity in this activity.

Investigations of the development of intersubjectivity focus on adult–child interaction (Bretherton, 1991; Hay *et al.*, 1991; Rogoff *et al.*, 1984), particularly between mother and infant (Kaye and Charney, 1980; Trevarthen, 1979). The little work that does address intersubjectivity among peers largely deals either with non-pretend play interaction of toddlers (Brenner and Mueller, 1982) or problem-solving interaction of school-age children (Rogoff, 1990). Despite the observation that 'play is inherently intersubjective' (Trevarthen, 1989, p. 3), there is no systematic analysis of intersubjectivity in pretend play. Although theories of social pretend play exist (Piaget, 1946/1962; Vygotsky, 1978), they do not address how children develop shared understandings.

In exploring the development of intersubjectivity in social pretend play, I examine the claim emerging from theory (Piaget, 1946/1962; Vygotsky, 1978) and empirical observation (Parten, 1932) that pretend play becomes social – that is, shared – only after 3 years of age. First, I examine the concept of intersubjectivity, including its developmental origins and mechanism. Second, a conceptual analysis of social pretend play as an intersubjective activity is proffered. Third, existing empirical evidence is examined in light of this analysis. Finally, an agenda for future research is proposed.

* This is an edited version of an article that appeared in *Human Development*, 36, 1993.

The concept of intersubjectivity

Defining intersubjectivity

[. . .]

There is some consensus among scholars that intersubjectivity refers to shared understanding among the participants of an activity (Bretherton, 1984, 1991; Göncü, 1993; Kaye, 1982; Newson, 1977, 1978; Rogoff, 1990; Rogoff *et al.*, 1984; Rommetveit, 1979, 1985; Trevarthen, 1979, 1988; Wertsch, 1984). According to Trevarthen (1988), intersubjectivity is achieved through recognition and coordination of intentions in mother–infant communication. Such coordination is accomplished by two activities that occur simultaneously – adoption of a shared focus of attention and agreement on the nature of communication.

The framework offered by Trevarthen for considering intersubjectivity may be applied fairly directly to older children. A shared focus of attention serves as a starting point for joint activity and enables the participants to expand their existing knowledge and understanding to new situations (Rogoff, 1990; Vygotsky, 1978; Wertsch, 1985). For example, mothers and children initiate a problem-solving activity first by focusing on a part of the problem, before relating it to the general purpose of the activity (Rogoff and Gauvain, 1986; Wertsch, 1984). Similarly, children negotiate with one another about how to expand their pretend play after adopting a topic of joint interest and familiarity (Sutton-Smith, 1980).

Agreement on the nature of communication goes hand in hand with agreement on the activity to be shared. When people agree to engage in a specific activity, they also agree to engage in communication that is unique to that activity. Such agreements are evident in both the interactive roles adopted by the participants and the dialogic devices they use. For example, when mothers help their children in problem-solving situations, they guide children by means of instruction (Rogoff and Gauvain, 1986; Wertsch *et al.*, 1980). However, they become spectators to their children, or follow their children's leads, when they engage in pretend activity with them (Dunn, 1988; Miller and Garvey, 1984).

Furthermore, participants use different verbal and non-verbal devices in communicating their intentions, depending on the activity. Mothers use directives in an instructional situation, but they use declaratives in the enactment of pretend roles with their children. Similarly, the linguistic devices preschool children use in pretending with their peers are different from those they use in non-pretend dialogues (Garvey and Kramer, 1989). Thus, by engaging in a given category of activity, participants implicitly share an understanding that there are different categories of activities and each category has its own system of communication (Bateson, 1955). However, to further our understanding of intersubjectivity, particularly in pretend play, we need to distinguish between choosing the category of activity and the system of communication used within that activity. We later return to this issue.

Developmental origins of intersubjectivity

Intersubjectivity is thought to originate in mother–child interaction (Kaye, 1982; Trevarthen, 1988). Trevarthen (1988) claims that during the prelinguistic stage of life, sharing takes place only within the context of affective expression in mother–child interaction (primary intersubjectivity). In other words, intersubjectivity is experienced in terms of affect actually present in the current interaction. For example, smiles in mother–infant play indicate the joy jointly experienced in the interaction, with each person aware of the other's joy (Trevarthen, 1988).

After about 9 months of age, however, a transformational shift occurs. Due to the development of language that symbolizes the shared reference, the mother–child pair is now able to share experiences about other people, objects, and events. Trevarthen and Hubley (1978) call this secondary intersubjectivity. After having learned to share an experience in terms of affect they currently feel, children use language to construct a shared reference to objects and other people not present in the current interaction. Evidence for secondary intersubjectivity can be found in 2-year-old children's play dialogue with their mothers (Budwig *et al.*, 1986; Dunn, 1988; Göncü, 1987a; Kaye and Charney, 1980; Miller and Garvey, 1984; Sutton-Smith, 1980).

Existing studies of intersubjectivity do not address its development in peer interaction. However, it has been suggested that the accomplishment of sharing meaning with adults on the basis of symbols enables children to use symbolic means to share experiences with other children (Budwig *et al.*, 1986; Trevarthen, 1989). That is, secondary intersubjectivity attained in mother–child interaction prepares a child to share meanings with peers. Using their new symbolic competence, children construct and develop intersubjectivity in peer interaction by negotiating their ideas and experiences. This linguistic development of intersubjectivity in peer interaction may be a gradual and a continuous process that does not involve further transformational shifts. A similar conceptualization of peer interaction can be found in non-pretend play research involving toddlers (Brenner and Mueller, 1982; Eckerman *et al.*, 1989).

Mechanisms in the construction of intersubjectivity

There is a compelling argument that construction of a shared world is accomplished through a process called *prolepsis* (Rommetveit, 1979; Stone, 1993; Stone and Wertsch, 1984). Prolepsis entails two related presuppositions by participants in a dialogue. The first is the presupposition that the dialogue in which they are engaged is sincere. This presupposition of trust, perhaps the most important prerequisite for the construction of intersubjectivity, implicitly expresses the participants' willingness to make an effort to understand one another.

The second is the speaker's presupposition that the listener has some knowledge that is not yet introduced in the interaction but is essential to the topic being introduced. In the terms of Rommetveit (1979), 'Intersubjectivity has in some sense to be taken for granted in order for it to be achieved. It is based on faith in a mutually shared world' (p. 96). Since the speaker is presupposing, or taking for granted, certain things, the listener needs to fill in these gaps. Therefore in the ensuing interaction, the listener begins to test the accuracy of his or her assumptions about the gaps left by the speaker. If the communication is successful, the listener constructs the knowledge that the speaker presupposes. In the case of an ideal intersubjectivity, the listener comes to adopt the perspective of the speaker as his or her own.

Understanding and changing of perspectives is not limited to one of the participants (Stone, 1993). All participants adopt the roles of speaker and listener. Therefore, each participant brings his or her own presuppositions to the interaction, and each participant must construct the knowledge that the others presuppose.

Construction of intersubjectivity is thus a dynamic process. In other words, intersubjectivity changes from one point to another as a result of continuous knowledge exchange and negotiation between partners (Forman, 1987; Rogoff, 1982; Rommetveit, 1985).

[. . .]

The development of social pretend play as an intersubjective activity

The most distinctive feature of pretend play is that it is a representational activity (Erikson, 1972; Piaget, 1946/1962; Vygotsky, 1978). When children pretend, they use physical or psychological means to represent the meaning of another entity. For instance, when a child announces herself to be a mother, she uses words and actions to represent the mother role.

In order to pretend with other players, children must agree on the reference of pretense and the appropriate ways of executing such pretend reference (Wolf, 1984). For example, when two children in their joint play pretend to be mothers, they try to reach a consensus about what constitutes motherness and how mothers act (Göncü, 1987b). In this process, children discover the commonalities in their understanding of motherness and possibly also change their initial understanding of motherness to produce closer agreement.

In order to understand how children achieve intersubjectivity in social pretend play, we can make use of Trevarthen's (1988) discussion of early mother–child intersubjectivity. First, we can use the construct of a joint focus of attention. Achieving intersubjectivity in pretend play involves children's adoption of a joint focus of attention that is representational in nature and affective in origin. However, we need to extend Trevarthen's approach by distinguishing between metacommunication and communication, since development of the focus of attention in social pretend play requires co-ordination of intentions at these two levels. Following Bateson (1955), metacommunication refers to children's reaching agreement on the nature of the activity – that is, that they are engaged in pretend play. The other level – communication – involves coordination of particular intentions through discourse.

Current play theory offers a developmental hypothesis only about the joint adoption of a pretend focus. The hypothesis is that pretend play representations become social only after 3 years of age and that social pretend play increases between 3 and 6 years of age (Fein, 1981; Rubin et al., 1983). Underlying this hypothesis is Piaget's (1946/1962) claim that children attain collective symbolism as a stage after solitary play, beginning in the third year of life. Collective symbolism is achieved as a result of negotiations of personal and idiosyncratic symbols with peers. Through these negotiations, play symbols begin to carry similar meanings for all the players.

Others offer observations that are consistent with Piaget's. For example, Vygotsky (1978) states that children negotiate the rules of pretend play around 3 years of age, implying that social pretend play with peers does not occur before this age.

Finally, in her seminal study, Parten (1932) provides observations indicating that cooperative play including joint construction of symbols, rules, planning, and division of labor increases in frequency after age 3. Parten's observations have been confirmed by various researchers (Fein et al., 1982; Rubin et al., 1976; Rubin and Krasnor, 1980; Rubin et al., 1978).

These efforts to examine the development of social pretend play are limited by lack of discussion of the mechanism by which children construct intersubjectivity in pretend play. Here I seek to propose such a mechanism, using the concept of prolepsis. The first presupposition entailed in prolepsis – that dialogue is sincere – is a prerequisite for social pretend play to take place. However, I devote my attention to the second presupposition – that in their pretend play children take for granted that their partners share their knowledge, leaving implicit some of their meaning. Doing so obliges children to make and test assumptions about what their partners mean, thus creating intersubjectivity.

In using the mechanism of prolepsis to explain children's construction of intersubjectivity, we can borrow from anthropological (Bateson, 1955) and sociological (Goffman, 1974) theories. To address how children communicate understandings with one another in the pretend mode of interaction, we can borrow from developmental psycholinguistics and discourse analysis (Bruner, 1975; Olson, 1980). I propose to extend the developmental hypothesis regarding the adoption of shared pretend focus to include metacommunication and communication. Children's negotiation of idiosyncratic symbols necessitates not only a joint pretend focus but also engagement in metacommunication about the activity and communication within the pretense. Therefore, it is plausible to seek support for a threefold hypothesis: children's social pretend play becomes shared with respect to its *focus*, its *metacommunication*, and its *communication* only after 3 years of age.

Development of a shared pretend focus

Although play theory does not address the social origins of pretend play, insights regarding the origins of pretense in general help in conceptualizing how children construct a shared pretend focus. According to many theorists, a child pretends in order to understand and regulate his or her own affective life (Fein, 1989; Gaskins and Göncü, 1988); The reasons for playing can vary from an illusory fulfillment of a tendency that cannot be fulfilled in real life (Vygotsky, 1978) to reconstructing an emotionally significant experience to gain mastery over it (Erikson, 1972; Piaget, 1946/1962). Based on this thesis, I propose that children's recognition of the similarity in their affective needs creates a joint focus in their pretend activity.

[. . .]

Although limited in number, there are studies of preschool children showing that representations in pretend play derive from children's unique experiences of affective significance. For example, Heath (1983) cites a 22-month-old girl who recreated her conversation with Heath about having ice cream the previous day. Field and Reite (1984) reported that, following the arrival of a sibling, 2- to 5-year old first-born children expressed envy, aggression, and anxiety in their play. Children reveal such feelings, for example, in pretending that their mothers and siblings are in traffic accidents. Similarly, Rosenberg (1983; cited in Bretherton, 1989) found that the content of pretend play of securely and insecurely attached children varies in theme elaboration and nurturance, with identifiable themes of separation and abandonment more prevalent in the pretense of insecurely attached children.

Existing evidence thus supports the theory that the origin of pretense is affective. In light of this evidence, it is plausible to argue that children come to social pretend play because of their need and desire to share experiences of affective significance with their peers. Social pretense is an arena in which private affective concerns become public in a playful manner.

Children thus make the proleptic presupposition that their partners will have experiences of their own, leading them to understand the specific subject matter proposed for pretend interaction. For example, when a girl says in a stern tone, 'You're the mother, I am the mother, and we don't have no children,' she is assuming that her friend will understand this overture based on the friend having a related experience (Göncü, 1987b).

[. . .]

If there is no similarity in the experiences or needs of players, or when the similarity is not perceived, the communication comes to an end. A powerful illustration is provided by the unsuccessful efforts of a 3-year-old girl in her play with friends (Corsaro, 1983). The girl tried to reconstruct her experience of viewing her baby brother on a television screen. The child's friends ignored her overtures, due to their unfamiliarity with such an experience. In the ensuing play, the children enacted a different play script, one familiar to all of them.

Agreeing on a pretend play proposal makes intersubjectivity possible on at least two grounds. First, it sets the stage for negotiation of differences deriving from individual children's understanding. This negotiation leads to the development of shared event representations. These representations, often referred to as scripts, are cognitive structures containing the elements essential for representation of a given event (Bretherton, 1989; Göncü, 1987b; Nelson and Seidman, 1984). Joint construction of a script reveals children's developing ability to identify commonalities in their individual experiences. Existing research indicates that at about 3 years of age, children begin to develop such scripts (Göncü, 1987b, 1989), and that between 3 and 5 years of age, pretend scripts become increasingly elaborate (Garvey and Berndt, 1975; Sachs *et al.*, 1984; Miller and Garvey, 1984; Nelson and Seidman, 1984).

A second way in which agreeing on a pretend proposal makes intersubjectivity possible is that it enables children to negotiate the joint pretend representation of affect. There is evidence that children negotiate the affect associated with the pretend script, as well as the script itself (Göncü, 1987b). Representation of festive events requires agreement on happiness, while pretense of frightening ones requires the appropriate enactment of fright (Garvey and Berndt, 1975).

Perceiving some minimum level of affective similarity among the experiences of all players is necessary for constructing a shared focus of attention. Research with 3- to 5-year-olds indicates that by age 3, children are able to negotiate a joint pretend focus. However, to confirm that 3 years of age is a milestone in beginning to negotiate a joint pretend focus with peers, its absence in younger children must be demonstrated. Recent work on sibling interaction, for example by Dunn (1988), indicates that children as young as 18 months engage in rudimentary forms of scripted pretend play with their older siblings. This finding raises the possibility that children younger than 3 years of age may construct a shared pretend focus with peers as well as siblings.

Metacommunication about pretense

A mutual pretend focus is necessary but not sufficient for social pretend play. It also must be communicated that a pretend play message is to be interpreted as such, rather than as a literal message. Bateson (1955) refers to such communication as metacommunication. For example, when a 4-year-old girl claims to be having a baby in the middle of a preschool classroom, she is only inviting her friends to join her play, not expressing a belief that she is in real labor.

The metacommunication indicates the changing form of interaction from non-play to play, and provides a ludic interpretive frame for the activity (Bateson, 1955; Goffman, 1974). The proleptic presupposition involved in metacommunication is this: children expect that their peers speak a play language that is distinct from non-play language (Bretherton, 1984; Garvey, 1977; Giffin, 1984; Kessel and Göncü, 1984). Used effectively, this metacommunication conveys a desire to have fun by playing with representations. Therefore, only when there is a mutual understanding about the meaning of metacommunicative messages will children's interaction be pretend play. [. . .]

To explore the hypothesis that social pretend play becomes intersubjective after 3 years of age, Göncü and Kessel (1984, 1988) examined verbal metacommunication in the pretend play of 3- and 4½-year-old preschool dyads. Seven types of verbal metacommunication were identified, following the work of Garvey and Berndt (1975) and Schwartzman (1978). These are invitations (direct requests for joint pretend play), plans (proposing a course of action for ensuing pretend activities), transformations (symbolic representations of experiences), acceptances and negations of transformations, object claims (expression of possession of play materials), and terminations (expressing disinterest in or ending joint play). The hypothesis that social pretend play becomes intersubjective after 3 years of age leads to the expectation that 4½-year-olds will express significantly more acceptances and fewer negations than 3-year-olds. However, the results showed both of these categories to be relatively infrequent, and there were no significant age differences in either of them. Nor were age differences found in the remaining five categories. At both ages, the metacommunicative category of highest frequency was transformations (65 percent), followed by object claims (13 percent), and plans (12 percent). Given the absence of developmental differences in type or quantity of verbal metacommunicative messages during the preschool years, Göncü and Kessel suggest that future research needs to focus on non-verbal forms of metacommunication to document fully how preschool children develop a shared pretend play language.

In summary, existing findings indicate that children develop a common understanding of acceptable metacommunicative behavior in pretending with peers at an early age. However there is a discernable pattern in the

development of metacommunication. Children below 3 years of age communicate their intentions regarding play in terms of pretend enactments,
such as feeding the baby (Fein *et al.*, 1982; Howes *et al.*, 1989). Between 3
and 5 years of age, children communicate their intentions in terms of verbal
communication, as well as pretend enactments (Göncü, 1987b, 1989; Nelson
and Seidman, 1984; Bretherton, 1989). Thus, what emerges after 3 years of
age is not metacommunication itself but a new type of metacommunicative
message, one that is differentiated from the actual enactment.

Communication within pretense

The study of metacommunication allows us to examine how children
determine the plane of communication as play and how they reach other
metacommunicative agreements. However, there remains the issue of how
children coordinate their intentions regarding specific pretend ideas. A
complete analysis of intersubjectivity should include an examination of
how children make and test the proleptic of presupposition that their partners
are familiar with specific pretend proposals. Only then is it possible to
determine how children relate to and expand one another's imaginative
worlds.

Analysis of how children communicate their ideas within specific pretend
play activity has begun. Such efforts stem from work on intentionality in
mother–child discourse (Bruner, 1975), as well as the study of intentionality
in children's non-pretend dialogues (Torrance and Olson, 1985). The purpose
of this line of work is to understand how partners respond to one another in
expanding their dialogue. In a notable example, Kaye and Charney (1980)
analyze the dialogic turns of mothers and their 2-year-old children to illustrate
the different ways in which partners create and expand their play dialogue.

Research focusing on the communication of intentions in the pretend play
of children reflects a similar approach, of identifying how children express
their own intentions and respond to those of their partners. For example,
Howes (1985, 1987; Howes *et al.*, 1989) examines how infants and young
children relate to one another's play intentions. She finds a predictable developmental pattern, with pretend play communication becoming reciprocal
and complementary around 3 years of age.

Howes *et al.* (1989) show that pretend actions do not get responses from
the partner when they first appear (at 12–15 months of age). Subsequently,
partners perform similar pretend actions in each other's presence (15–20
months). This phase is followed by one in which partners engage in
sequenced pretend activities as they engage in social exchanges (20–24
months). Still later, partners engage in pretend activities with similar themes,
but the actions of partners are not integrated with one another (24–30
months). Finally, partners adopt complementary pretend roles such as doctor–
patient (30–36 months), revealing their developing ability to understand and

expand a partner's intentions. Howes (1987) reports that the frequency of complementary pretend play does not vary significantly between 3 and 5 years of age. However, she notes that her coding scheme, based only on the presence or absence of complementary turn-taking, may not have captured the complexities of older children's play dialogues found by previous researchers (Garvey, 1974; Garvey and Berndt, 1975).

In fact, several studies of children's pretend play dialogues do show significant age changes during the preschool years. For instance, Garvey (1974) identifies two primary ways in which preschoolers respond to their partner's play turn – they either repeat the partner's utterance or complement it. According to Garvey, repeating implies acknowledging the partner's intentions, while complementing indicates both accurate interpretation of the partner's intention and appropriate extension in the child's own turn. Based on qualitative analyses, Garvey concludes that in the range of 3–5 years of age, older children are more likely to complement and younger children are more likely to repeat their partners' utterances.

In the Göncü and Kessel (1984, 1988) research the 3- and 4½-year-old preschoolers' utterances were coded according to the way in which children express knowledge and respond to their partners within pretend play, using four categories from previous research (Garvey, 1974; Kaye and Charney, 1980; Torrance and Olson, 1985). In decreasing order of intersubjectivity, these categories are turnabouts (acknowledging and extending the partner's previously expressed intention), responses (acknowledging the partner's intention), demands (extending the partner's intention), and unlinked utterances (making an utterance not relevant to the partner's previously expressed intention). The hypothesis that older children would make significantly more turnabouts and significantly fewer unlinked utterances was supported. In a second phase of this work, we double-coded utterances for metacommunication, as well as communication, to determine the degree of intersubjectivity of the metacommunicative utterances coded as transformations, plans, and object claims. Older children expressed these metacommunicative utterances as turnabouts more often than did younger children. Thus, after 3 years of age, developmental differences in intersubjectivity occur more in the coordination of intentions within pretend play communication than in the coordination of intentions in metacommunication.

Conclusions

The emerging picture is that intersubjectivity in pretend play develops on three planes simultaneously. First, the origin of intersubjectivity in social pretend play appears to be *affective*. Children engage in play to share emotionally significant experiences with their peers. Second, children *metacommunicate* to create an agreement or joint understanding that identifies the nature of the enterprise as pretend play. Third, children use actions and language as *communicative* devices to jointly construct the playful representation of experience.

Three years of age appears to be a landmark in the development of verbal intersubjectivity in social pretend play. At this age, children adopt a shared pretend focus and begin to mark their interaction explicitly as pretend play (metacommunication), as well as to relate to one another's intentions within the pretend activity (communication) with increasing degrees of relevance. From 3 to 5 years of age, children understand and expand one another's ideas with increasing frequency, reflecting their developing tacit agreement and shared knowledge regarding the joint-event representations in question.

There is, however, some evidence that children express metacommunicative and communicative messages in social pretend play as early as 18 months of age. During this period between 18 months and 3 years, children appear to communicate in and about their pretend play by means of non-verbal exchanges such as exaggerated movements, facial gestures, and voice inflection, as well as brief verbal exchanges. This kind of engagement in metacommunication and communication presumes the adoption of a joint pretend focus. Therefore, it is plausible to argue that intersubjectivity in social pretend play occurs earlier than claimed in previous theories of play (Piaget, 1946/1962; Vygotstky, 1978). What may happen at about age 3 is not the emergence of intersubjectivity, but a change in the prominence of different communicative means by which intersubjectivity is constructed.

Based on the emerging evidence, I propose that children have the motivation to share their worlds in pretend play very early in life. The proleptic presupposition that other children will understand something about what is a significant experience and how to share it in a playful way emerges around 2 years of age. The emergence of young children's ability to construct shared understandings in pretend play coincides with the emergence of their ability to construct shared understandings in non-representational experiences, of both playful and serious sorts. With regard to the former, Hartup (1983) indicates that 2-year-olds have the ability to engage in game interactions by giving one another the non-verbal message that what they do is acceptable because it is fun. With regard to the latter, Radke-Yarrow *et al.* (1983) note that children try to help others who are distressed by offering affective non-verbal comfort. These commonalities point to an important achievement by young children. As they share experiences of affective significance in real life (in a non-representational mode), children also share affectively significant experiences in the representational mode of play.

The present conceptualization of social pretense as an intersubjective activity leads to two sets of proposals for future research. The first set addresses questions regarding the activity of social pretend play itself. The second set involves comparing social pretend play with other childhood activities, to examine how children share meanings with their peers in different kinds of activities.

With regard to the first set of questions, conceptualizing the motivation for social pretend play as the need to share emotionally significant experiences points in several directions. The immediate question is what experiences of affective significance children share in this activity. To answer this question, we need to inquire what children do in their play and why they do it. For the most part, our existing knowledge of what children do in pretend play is based on direct or indirect play proposals that researchers make to children. We do not know what children bring to social pretend play when left to their own devices. In order for us to understand what is important for children to share, we need to observe them in their own naturally occurring activity. The question of why certain children jointly represent a given experience instead of others can be answered only by determining the unique affective significance of that experience for these children. Thus, understanding the motivational origins of social pretense requires us to conduct studies that focus on the ways in which emotional experiences of children find their expression in pretend play. Such studies need to be both comprehensive of events that take place in children's lives and longitudinal. Only by means of such studies will it be possible to establish the relation between social play representations and children's experiences.

With regard to the second set of questions, comparing social pretense with other activities, current research suggests that intersubjectivity may develop at different rates in different activities. For example, Tudge and Rogoff (1989) claim that young preschoolers do not benefit from peer interaction in solving structured, closed-ended, problems presented to them in laboratory settings. However, it is still unclear what variables are responsible for differences in intersubjectivity across different domains. For example pretend play activity is free-flowing in nature, in contrast to structured, laboratory, problem-solving activity, in which children are expected to reach predefined solutions. Another critical difference might be the relative affective motivation of children in these activities. Only by investigating these and other such issues will it be possible for us to understand better how children make and share meaning with their peers.

References

Bateson, G. (1955). A theory of play and fantasy. *Psychiatric Research Reports*, 2, 39–51.
Brenner, J. and Mueller, E. (1982). Shared meaning in boy toddlers' peer relations. *Child Development*, 53, 380–391.
Bretherton, I. (Ed.) (1984). *Symbolic play: The development of social understanding*. New York: Academic Press.
Bretherton, I. (1989). Pretense: The form and function of make-believe play. *Developmental Review*, 9, 383–401.
Bretherton, I. (1991). Intentional communication and the development of an understanding of mind. In D. Frye and C. Moore (Eds), *Children's theories of mind: Mental states and social understanding* (pp. 49–75). Hillsdale NJ: Erlbaum.

Bruner, J.S. (1975). From communication to language: A psychological perspective. *Cognition*, 3, 255–287.

Budwig, N., Strage, A., and Bamberg, M. (1986). The construction of joint activities with an age-mate: The transition from caregiver-child to peer play. In J. Cook-Gumprez, W. Corsaro, and J. Streeck (Eds), *Children's worlds and children's language* (pp. 83–108). Berlin: Mouton.

Corsaro, W. (1983). Script recognition, articulation, and expansion in children's role play. *Discourse Processes*, 6, 1–19.

Dunn, J. (1988). *The beginnings of social understanding.* Cambridge MA: Harvard University Press.

Eckerman, C.O., Davis, C.C., and Didow, S.M. (1989). Toddler's emerging ways of achieving social coordinations with a peer. *Child Development*, 60, 440–453.

Erikson, E. (1972). *Play and development.* New York: Norton.

Fein, G. (1981). Pretend play: An integrative review. *Child Development*, 52, 1095–1118.

Fein, G. (1989). Mind, meaning, and affect: Proposals for a theory of pretense. *Developmental Review*, 9, 345–363.

Fein, G., Moorin, E.R., and Enslein, J. (1982). Pretense and peer behavior: An intersectoral analysis. *Human Development*, 25, 392–406.

Field, T. and Reite, M. (1984). Children's responses to separation from mother during the birth of another child. *Child Development*, 55, 1308–1316.

Forman, E. (1987). Peer relationships of learning disabled children: A contextualist perspective. *Learning Disabilities Research*, 2, 80–90.

Garvey, C. (1974). Some properties of social play. *Merrill-Palmer Quarterly*, 20, 160–180.

Garvey, C. (1977). *Play.* Cambridge MA: Harvard University Press.

Garvey, C. and Berndt, R. (1975). Organization of pretend play. Paper presented at the annual meeting of the American Psychological Association, Chicago IL.

Garvey, C. and Kramer, T. (1989). The language of social pretend play. *Developmental Review*, 9, 364–382.

Gaskins, S. and Göncü, A. (1988). Children's play as representation and imagination: The case of Piaget and Vygotsky. *The Quarterly Newsletter of the Laboratory of Comparative Human Cognition*, 10, 104–107.

Giffin, H. (1984). The coordination of meaning in the creation of a shared make-believe reality. In I. Bretherton (Ed.), *Symbolic play: The development of social understanding* (pp. 73–100). New York: Academic Press.

Goffman, E. (1974). *Frame analysis: An essay on the organization of experience.* Cambridge MA: Harvard University Press.

Göncü, A. (1987a). The role of adults and peers in the socialization of play during preschool years. In G. Casto, F. Ascione and M. Salehi (Eds), *Current perspectives in early childhood research* (pp. 33–41). Logan UT: Early Intervention Research Institute Press.

Göncü, A. (1987b). Toward an interactional model of developmental changes in social pretend play. In L. Katz (Ed.), *Current topics in early childhood education* (Vol. 7, pp. 108–125), Norwood NJ: Ablex.

Göncü, A. (1989). Models and features of pretense. *Developmental Review*, 9, 341–344.

Göncü, A. (1993). Development of intersubjectivity in the dyadic play of preschoolers. *Early Childhood Research Quarterly*, 8(1), 99–116.

Göncü, A. and Kessel, F.S. (1984). Children's play: A contextual-functional perspective. In F.S. Kessel and A. Göncü (Eds), *Analyzing children's play dialogues. New directions for child development* (Vol. 25, pp. 5–22). San Francisco: Jossey-Bass.

Göncü, A. and Kessel, F.S. (1988). Preschooler's collaborative construction in planning and maintaining imaginative play. *International Journal of Behavioral Development*, *11*, 327–344.

Hartup, W.W. (1983). Peer relations. In P. Mussen (Series ed.), E.M. Hetherington (Vol. ed.), *Handbook of child psychology* (Vol. 4, pp. 103–196). (4th ed.) New York: Wiley.

Hay, D.F., Stimson, C.A., and Castle, J. (1991). A meeting of minds in infancy. In D. Frye and C. Moore (Eds), *Children's theories of mind: Mental states and social understanding* (pp. 115–137). Hillsdale NJ: Erlbaum.

Heath, S.B. (1983). *Ways with words: Language, Life, and work in communities and classrooms*. New York: Cambridge University Press.

Howes, C. (1985). Sharing fantasy: Social pretend play in toddlers. *Child Development*, *56*, 1253–1258.

Howes, C. (1987). Peer interaction of young children. *Monographs of the Society of Research in Child Development*, *53* (Series no. 217).

Howes, C., Unger, O., and Seidner, L. (1989). Social pretend play in toddlers: Parallels with social play and solitary pretend. *Child Development*, *60*, 77–84.

Kaye, K. (1982). *The mental and social life of babies*. Chicago: University of Chicago Press.

Kaye, K. and Charney, R. (1980). How mothers maintain 'dialogue' with two-year-olds. In D.R. Olson (Ed.), *The social foundations of language and thought: Essays in honor of Jerome S. Bruner* (pp. 211–230). New York: Norton.

Kessel, F. and Göncü, A. (Eds) (1984). *Analyzing children's play dialogues. New directions for child development*. (Vol. 25). San Francisco: Jossey-Bass.

Miller, P. and Garvey, C. (1984). Mother–baby role play: Its origins in social support. In I. Bretherton (Ed.), *Symbolic play: The development of social understanding* (pp. 101–130). New York: Academic Press.

Nelson, C. and Seidman, S. (1984). Playing with scripts. In I. Bretherton (Ed.), *Symbolic play: The development of social understanding* (pp. 45–72). New York: Academic Press.

Newson, J. (1977). An intersubjective approach to the systematic description of mother–infant interaction. In H.R. Schaffer (Ed.), *Studies in mother–infant interaction* (pp. 47–61). New York: Academic Press.

Newson, J. (1978). Dialogue and development. In A. Lock (Ed.), *Action, gesture and symbol: The emergence of language* (pp. 31–42). London: Academic Press.

Olson, D.R. (Ed.) (1980). *The social foundations of language and thought: Essays in honor of Jerome S. Bruner*. New York: Norton.

Parten, M.B. (1932). Social participation among preschool children. *Journal of Abnormal Psychology*, *27*, 243–269.

Piaget, J. (1962). *Play, dreams and imitation in childhood*. New York: Norton. (Originally published in 1946).

Radke-Yarrow, M., Zahn-Waxler, C. and Chapman, M. (1983). Children's prosocial dispositions and behavior. In P. Mussen (Series ed.), E.D. Hetherington (Vol. ed.), *Handbook of child psychology* (Vol. 4, pp. 469–545). (4th ed.). New York: Wiley.

Rogoff, B. (1982). Integrating context and cognitive development. In M. Lamb and A. Brown (Eds), *Developmental psychology: An advanced textbook* (pp. 125–170). (1st ed.). Hillsdale NJ: Erlbaum.

Rogoff, B. (1990). *Apprenticeship in thinking*. New York: Oxford University Press.

Rogoff, B. and Gauvain, M. (1986). A method for the analysis of patterns illustrated with data on mother–child instructional interaction. In J. Valsiner (Ed.), *The role of individual subject in scientific psychology*. New York: Plenum.

Rogoff, B., Malkin, C. and Gilbride, K. (1984). Interaction with babies as guidance in development. In B. Rogoff and J.V. Wertsch (Eds), *Children's learning in the zone of proximal development. New directions for child development* (Vol. 23). San Francisco: Jossey-Bass.

Rommetveit, R. (1979). On the architecture of intersubjectivity. In R. Rommetveit and R.M. Blaker (Eds), *Studies of language, thought, and verbal communication* (pp. 147–161). New York: Academic Press.

Rommetveit, R. (1985). Language acquisition as increasing linguistic structuring of experience and symbolic behavior control. In J. Wertsch (Ed.), *Culture, communication, and cognition: Vygotskyan perspectives* (pp. 183–204). New York: Cambridge University Press.

Rosenberg, D.M. (1983). The quality and content of preschool fantasy play: Correlates in social-personality functioning and early mother–child attachment relationship. Unpublished Ph. D. dissertation, University of Minnesota.

Rubin, K.H. and Krasnor, L.R. (1980). Changes in the play behaviors of preschoolers: A short-term longitudinal investigation. *Canadian Journal of Behavioural Science*, *12*, 278–282.

Rubin, K.H., Maioni, T.L. and Hornung, M. (1976). Free play behaviors in middle and lower class preschoolers: Parten and Piaget revisited. *Child Development*, *47*, 414–419.

Rubin, K.H., Watson, K. and Jambor, T. (1978). Free play behaviors in preschool and kindergarten children. *Child Development*, *49*, 534–536.

Rubin, K.H., Fein, G. and Vandenberg, B. (1983). Play. In P. Mussen (Series ed.), E.M. Hetherington (Vol. ed.), *Handbook of child psychology* (Vol. 4, pp. 693–774). (4th ed.). New York: Wiley.

Sachs, J., Goldman, J. and Chaille, C. (1984). Planning in pretend play: Using language to coordinate narrative development. In A.D. Pellergrini and T.D. Yawkey (Eds), *The development of oral and written language in social contexts* (pp. 119–128). Norwood NJ: Ablex.

Schwartzman, H. (1978). *Transformations: The anthropology of children's play*. New York: Plenum.

Stone, A. (1993). What's missing in the metaphor of scaffolding? In E. Forman, N. Minick, and A. Stone (Eds), *Contexts for learning: Sociocultural dynamics in children's development* (pp. 169–183). New York: Oxford University Press.

Stone, A. and Wertsch, J.V. (1984). A social interactional analysis of learning disabilities remediation. *Journal of Learning Disabilities*, *17*, 194–199.

Sutton-Smith, B. (1980). A sportive theory of play. In H.B. Schwartzman (Ed.), *Play and culture* (pp. 10–19). West Point NY: Leisure Press.

Torrance, N. and Olson, D.R. (1985). Oral and literate competencies in the early school years. In D. Olsen, N. Torrance, and A. Hildyard (Eds), *Literacy, language, and learning* (pp. 256–284). Cambridge: Cambridge University Press.

Trevarthen, C. (1979). Communication and cooperation in early infancy: A description of primary intersubjectivity. In M. Bullowa (Ed.), *Before speech: The beginning of human communication* (pp. 321–347). Cambridge: Cambridge University Press.

Trevarthen, C. (1988). Universal cooperative motives: How infants begin to know the language and culture of their parents. In G. Jahoda and I.M. Lewis (Eds), *Acquiring culture: Cross-cultural studies in child development*. London: Croom Helm.

Trevarthen, C. (1989). Origins and directions for the concept of infant intersubjectivity. In B. Rogoff (Ed.), *Society for Research in Child Development Newsletter* (pp. 1–4). Chicago: University of Chicago Press.

Trevarthen, C. and Hubley, P. (1978). Secondary intersubjectivity: Confidence, confiding and acts of meaning in the first year. In A. Lock (Ed.), *Action, gesture and symbol: The emergence of language* (pp. 183–229). London: Academic Press.

Tudge, J. and Rogoff, B. (1989). Peer influences on cognitive development: Piagetian and Vygotskyan perspectives. In M. Bornstein and J.S. Bruner (Eds), *Interaction in human development*. Hillsdale NJ: Erlbaum.

Vygotsky, L.S. (1978). *Mind in society: The development of higher mental processes*. Cambridge MA: Harvard University Press.

Wertsch, J. (1984). The zone of proximal development: Some conceptual issues. In B. Rogoff and J.V. Wertsch (Eds), *Children's learning in the 'zone of proximal development'. New directions for child development* (Vol. 23, pp. 7–18). San Francisco: Jossey-Bass.

Wertsch, J. (1985). *Vygotsky and the social formation of mind*. Cambridge MA: Harvard University Press.

Wertsch, J.V., McNamee, G.D., McLane, J.G., and Budwig, N.A. (1980). The adult–child dyad as a problem solving system. *Child Development*, *51*, 1215–1221.

Wolf, D. (1984). Shared information in play episodes: Beyond a single-minded theory of human activity. Paper presented at the annual meeting of the American Psychological Association, Toronto.

Chapter 8

Cultural knowledge and social competence within a preschool peer-culture group*

Rebecca Kantor, Peggy M. Elgas and David E. Fernie

Introduction

Children's play and their developing social abilities are related emphases in early childhood classrooms, both currently and historically (Weber, 1984). Yet, even in, and perhaps as a result of, the preschool experience, we see children's uneven social success and abilities. Some children are very adept socially, participating in the creation and maintenance of group play smoothly, as in the following example:

> *Example 1*
>
> Bob is sitting in the bottom of the climber playing with a magnet on a string. Lisa "flies" over, modeling her Batman cape for Bob, and then crawls into the climber next to him. Lisa says to John who is standing nearby: "Wanna be in our Batman house?" John: "I got a cape." He enters and the three of them sit next to each other laughing and playing with their Lego guns. Lisa stands up: "We're the bad guys. Let's go." They all fly off together.

In such instances, we are impressed with the ongoing flow of players' "reciprocal involvement" (Mandell, 1986) as they construct play that reflects shared definitions of the situation.

Corsaro (1985) introduced the concept of "peer culture," a culture constructed and maintained entirely by children, as a wider framework for understanding such shared definitions that underlie children's play and friendships within an ongoing group. From the "inside" perspective gained through ethnographic participant observation, Corsaro saw the communal production and sharing of social activities among peers as patterned around a "common set of activities or routines, artifacts, values, concerns, and attitudes" (p. 171).

* This is an edited version of an article that appeared in *Early Childhood Research Quarterly*, 8(2), 1993.

In sharp contrast to reciprocal involvement, other children are repeatedly unsuccessful in their attempts to participate in the play of an ongoing peer culture group and to create shared and non-conflictual grounds for social play. In the next example, William tries to join in with some of the very same children from the previous example:

Example 2

Bob and Paul are on the climber and shooting with hand-made Lego guns. William rides back and forth on a large wooden tractor. William: "What are you doing?" They ignore him. William leaves and returns with a plastic camera. Ken and Jack: "You can't touch anything." William: "Cheese! Cheese!" They ignore him.

Corsaro (1985) would interpret the rejection seen in Example 2 as linked to the fragile and shifting nature of play and friendships in the busy, crowded life of the early childhood classroom. In other words, he sees children trying to control and protect their "interactive space" and their communal activities from others because these activities are so vulnerable to disruption. Thus, inclusion, exclusion, and status are common themes within the social dynamics and social organization of the broad peer culture of the classroom.

The ethnographic analysis presented in this article is framed within Corsaro's (1985) notion of a preschool peer culture. But unlike Corsaro, who described the construction of peer culture at the whole-classroom level, we found several distinct, stable, and enduring friendship groups in this classroom, each with its own locally constructed peer culture patterns documented in earlier analyses (Elgas, 1988; Elgas, Klein, Kantor, and Fernie, 1988; Meyer, 1989).

In the preceding examples, Lisa, Bob, and John's easy involvement with each other reflects their collective membership in one such ongoing and stable friendship group found within this classroom. In turn, the challenge that William fails to meet is not that of joining the spontaneous play of a temporary group of children, but of trying to gain membership in such a cohesive group. The purposes of the analysis to be presented in this chapter are twofold: (1) to understand how the ongoing life of this preschool peer culture friendship group is defined and maintained, and (2) to understand the experiences of three individuals in relation to this group – two who have membership and one who seeks and fails to attain it.

In the next section, three different theoretical-research perspectives for understanding children's involvement with each other in play will be contrasted, each with distinctive implications for children's social competence.

Three approaches to examining children's social experiences

A sociometric approach

One traditional approach for examining such social acceptance issues in children is sociometrics. In this approach, social assessments are elicited in which children make judgments about peers in a social group. Different methodologies are used in sociometric work, but all rely on classmates' assessments of one another. In sociometric peer nominations, for example, children select their preferred play or work partners. In peer ratings, class members might be asked to place each other along continua such as attraction–rejection, or to rate each other according to Likert-type scales. Social status is determined by the ranking scores received on those assessments. Such social status may then be related to child characteristics or behaviors. Elements examined may vary from study to study, for example the language skills of popular children (Hops, 1983) or the characteristic ways in which they enter, maintain, and cope with conflict during play (Asher and Renshaw, 1981).

According to the sociometric literature, when children are repeatedly unsuccessful in accessing appropriate play experiences with others, these "outsiders" (or "isolated," "rejected," or "stigmatized" children) may be at risk for difficulties both in the classroom and beyond (Garnica, 1981; Hatch, 1987; Peery, 1979; Scott, 1991). Teachers are often concerned that such children will become dependent on them, will exhibit inappropriate social behaviors, and/or will have difficulty engaging in any type of play. In fact, future problems have been identified for such children, with negative peer status in childhood linked to a variety of maladaptive outcomes in adolescence and adulthood (Cowen, Pederson, Babigian, Izzo, and Trost, 1973; Roff, Sells, and Golen, 1972).

An underlying assumption of this body of research is that social success or failure resides with the individual child, his or her assessed status, enduring traits, and typical behavior. In reviewing this work, McConnell and Odom (1986) defined this overall profile of an individual child as social competence, a "summative measure of children's social performance with peers and across situations as evaluated by significant social agents (teacher, peers)" (p. 219). Sociometrics provides a view of children's social competence as evaluated by others, not one seen in the specific accomplishment or the "doing" of social interactions.

A social interactional perspective

A second view comes from observational research in which researchers look directly at the quality of social interactions among peers and interpret social competence in terms of it (McDermott and Church, 1976; Monighan-

Nourot, Scales, Van Hoorn, and Almy, 1987; Ross, 1985). Ross, for example, found that kindergarten-aged children used a variety of social interaction strategies during free play. However, social success was not related to the number or variety of social strategies used, nor to using a high proportion of cooperative strategies. Rather, children's effectiveness and social competence were related to their ability to match appropriate behavior with particular contexts.

In a similar fashion, McDermott and Church (1976) and Monighan-Nourot *et al.* (1987) investigated children's ability to negotiate play inter-actions. McDermott and Church concluded that, as a guide to one's social actions, children need to take the perspective of others in order to predict their responses appropriately. Monighan-Nourot *et al.* emphasized the importance of children's communication strategies for introducing and expanding play themes, for coordinating their ideas with others, and for producing situationally appropriate verbal and non-verbal behavior. The loner, or rejected child, was "out of tune" with others in relation to one or more aspects of this sociocommunicative repertoire.

Collectively, these studies define and examine social competence interactionally. They focus on the skills needed to enter interactions successfully and to be "in tune" with the doing of social interaction (e.g., reading situational cues, monitoring one's behavior in anticipation of others' reactions, and coordinating one's ideas with those of others). Conversely, unsuccessful children's difficulties may be characterized by a lack of communicative and social–cognitive abilities and an inability to "read" and respond appropriately to the complexities of play interactions. This body of literature focuses on the "match" between individual children's actions and their peer social contexts, with a focus on the individual children and their generic strategies. Missing from this literature is a conceptual framework for understanding the construction of context in cultural terms. In the sociocultural perspective taken in this study and described in the next section, such a framework is provided.

A sociocultural perspective

Researchers who examine issues related to children's play, friendship, and social relations from a sociocultural perspective (or the compatible social-constructionist perspective) employ interpretive analysis procedures in order to understand the meanings of such processes for the participants of particular settings (Corsaro, 1985; Elgas *et al.*, 1988; Hatch, 1987; Rizzo, 1989; Rizzo, Corsaro, and Bates, 1992). Sociocultural researchers seek to understand different types of context (as do social interactionists), but distinctively define contexts as cultures; consequently, social interactions are viewed as having cultural meanings and, in turn, the group culture is seen as framing ongoing interactions.

With respect to educational settings, sociocultural researchers seek to understand the locally constructed meanings of peer interactions and events, over time, in particular settings, and from the participants' viewpoints, and to study their "logic-in-action" (Rizzo *et al.*, 1992, p. 114). Thus, the distinction between the study of classrooms in social interactional versus sociocultural terms is the latter's emphasis on interpreting classroom social actions over time and in light of the *social–cultural world* that classroom participants construct and maintain.

These social worlds are accessed by the researcher through a systematic examination of the daily life of participants, which is patterned and socially constructed as members interact and react to each other (Bloome, 1987; Fernie, Kantor, Klein, Meyer, and Elgas, 1988; Green and Meyer, 1991; Gumperz, 1981). As cultural routines and rituals are established, so too are common expectations, language, and patterned ways of behaving (Bloome and Theodorou, 1988; Kantor, Elgas, and Fernie, 1989; Wallat and Green, 1979). Within this view, the experiences of individuals can be examined in relation to the group, with an understanding of the group's culture a necessary component to a fuller interpretation of social behavior.

[. . .]

By adopting a situated perspective, each aspect of social competence is examined in relationship to the larger fabric of the classroom. Social participation, whether in school events or within the peer world of the classroom, is not examined as something separate from the flow of everyday life: rather, it is viewed as part of the social history of the group, and as practiced in the ways of the group.

In this study, a preschool peer culture friendship group and the experiences of several individuals in relation to it are examined from this situated perspective. After the data are interpreted for their local meanings, a final section will draw implications of this perspective for understanding aspects of social competence, and integrate these implications with those of the two more traditional perspectives.

The study

This study is part of the larger ethnography outlined above and thus benefits from the overall understanding of the classroom gained from the multiple analyses just described. The analysis to be described, however, flows most directly from Elgas (1988). Elgas described a salient play group within the peer culture of the preschool, the group presented in Examples 1 and 2. Although there were several stable friendship groups in this classroom, this salient group was dubbed the "core group" because of its great cohesion, salience, and influence in the wider peer culture of the classroom. Indeed, it seemed at the center or core of the peer social world in this classroom.

These characteristics were evident in the distinctive ways in which this group used objects. With respect to group cohesion, certain objects (red rhythm sticks) were used as social markers that signaled membership within, and identification with, this group. These coveted objects, endowed with social value by the core group, were hoarded and protected by its members. In seeking to identify with this influential group, non-core group members sought possession of these sticks. Other more scarce objects, for example superhero capes, were used as entry vehicles by the core group to control inclusion in, and exclusion from, the group.

Whereas this popular group and its socially constructed "currency" were pursued by other children, only a few non-core group members were able to possess these objects and then only for short durations. Occasionally, some non-core group members were able to participate in the play of the core group by obtaining these objects, but others were not able to participate despite their possession of the objects (in 53 play episodes sampled across the year, 40 unsuccessful and only 13 successful participations were recorded when non-core group members possessed such group objects).

In documenting and discussing this finding with the research team, it became apparent that ongoing membership in the group involved something beyond object possession. In other words, looking like a member was a neces-sary but not sufficient criterion for membership. This led to the obvious question: What more is required for membership in the core group?

This study was undertaken to address this question. As ethnographers, we knew that in this preschool core group, as with any cultural group, objects are only part of the shared cultural meaning constructed by the group and held by its members. We also knew that our task resembled that of the children who desired membership in this group, that is, we needed both to access and to understand this cultural knowledge.

Methodology

Setting

This study was conducted in a university child care center. The program was staffed by two lead teachers, one of whom was a faculty member and the other a graduate student. Undergraduate students also staffed the program by par-ticipating in the classroom once a week for one quarter in a practicum teach-ing course. Children were enrolled in the program 4 days per week, 3 hours per day.

The philosophy of the program is based upon social-constructionist and constructivist theories. Children are encouraged to investigate, create, prob-lem solve, and question through planned (school culture) and play (peer culture) experiences. The daily curriculum is generated, negotiated, and con-structed by all members (children and teachers). A strong sense of community pervades the classroom, and "Working from the Ideas of Children" is its explicit motto.

In this classroom, the general peer culture is sanctioned and supported by the lead and assistant teachers in several ways. Peer culture interaction is supported by providing large blocks of time for free play, one beginning 45-min outdoor period and one 45 to 60-min indoor period. In addition to the provision of large blocks of play time, teachers value children's play and interactions with each other. They demonstrate this by encouraging and facilitating children's interactions and social problem solving by sanctioning and preserving their play through polaroid pictures and various written forms (signs, notes, children-dictated books), and by accepting, promoting, and extending children's ideas for play.

Furthermore, the teachers also accept and work with children's superhero/power themes – popular themes with the core group from a peer culture perspective. Thus, children's pretend "shooting," their interest in constructing various pretend weapons, and their general bravado are interpreted as linked to peer culture themes of power, control, and status. The teachers accept Corsaro's (1985) suggestion that children create opposition to adults in order to redress the imbalance of power that exists between generations. The teachers are deliberate in their setting of limits and parameters for such play, maintaining physical and emotional safety for all at all times (e.g., no one can pretend shoot at a child who isn't interested in being involved). Last, the teachers use the content of peer culture superhero play to help support their overall program goals, for example to support material and social problem solving, divergent use of materials, and collaborative effort.

The research strategy

The strategy we designed to explore our questions about the core group, and individuals' relative success in relation to the group, was to trace the participation of three children, each of whom had differing success and involvement within this core group. The choice of these particular children was strategic: the first, Bob, was the leader of the core group and thus seemed a productive choice to learn more about the workings of this group; the second, Lisa, was the only girl to have membership in the group, and thus achieved success despite her gender; and the third, William, sought membership in the group but was continually rejected.

Lisa's and William's contrasting experiences evolved despite some seemingly important background similarities. Both children entered school at approximately the same age (3 years, 3 months for William and 3 years, 6 months for Lisa). Both were the youngest children of older parents, with siblings in their 20s who did not reside at home. Thus, both children resided in "adult" homes with no peer interaction. Also, the parents of each child reported that television watching was not a primary source of recreation. This factor becomes important because the majority of the core group's themes were about superheroes and derived directly from television and movie viewing. Thus, accessing such themes comes second hand, as an interpretation of themes that are socially constructed by peers during play. At the time of school entry, both sets of parents reported that their child did not have established neighborhood play partners or peer groups. Thus, interpretation of their relative success logically rested with their direct experiences with the core group.

With this in mind, the purposes of this study are to make visible the implicit norms and actions that make up the shared cultural knowledge of this group and to see what distinguishes members from non-members.

Procedures

A variety of strategies and techniques were employed to gather data during the first year of ethnographic investigation. Extensive videotaping, daily field-note taking, and teacher retrospective notes were used. The second and third authors, as well as two other members of the research team, became participant observers in the classroom for the school year. The roles of the participant observers were modeled after Corsaro's (1985) "reactive participant" role. Our participant observers were adults who avoided teacherlike behavior whenever possible. Furthermore, whereas they reacted to children's overtures, they did not initiate interaction with them.

[. . .]

Findings and interpretation

Figure 8.1 displays the elements of commonly held knowledge (norms and expectations) among members that were identified and organized into a taxonomy. These were aspects of interaction seen frequently among members of the core group. Aspects of interaction that were not consistent across members of the core group or not seen frequently were not included in the taxonomy.

Table 8.1 Common elements in core group play

---

1 The possession of certain objects (core group objects are sticks and capes).
2 The use of objects in certain ways (as pretend weapons and other aggressive uses or as a marker to signify group membership).
3 Certain pretend roles (superhero, ghostbuster, firefighter).
4 Certain kinds of language use ("I'm a bad guy. I can fly away").
5 The excluding of teachers verbally or physically (a sign that says "No teachers allowed").
6 The mock intimidation of teachers verbally or by using objects ("We're gonna cut you with our sword").

Child profiles

After the six common elements in core group play were identified, the participation of each of the three focus children was examined in relation to those elements. Table 8.1 shows a tally by target child of how many times each child displayed each element across the total number of episodes he or she appeared in. From this individual data, the following profiles were developed to characterize each child's experience with the group.

Bob: acknowledged leader of the core group

Bob, as the acknowledged leader of the core group, provides a metric against which to judge the relative success of others. As Table 8.1 shows, Bob shows the most in-tune behaviors. This characterization follows from the fact that Bob introduced and/or engineered many of the core group's themes, routines, and objects, but as illustrated in the following, he did so in a subtle way that belied his power and status within the group.

Example 3

"Ta da! I'm Superman." Paul twirls around showing his cape to Bob. Bob nods and jumps on and off the climber several times. Paul and Bob run to the shelves and make guns for themselves out of bristle blocks. They both have red rhythm sticks in their belt loops. They shoot each other and laugh and then turn their guns on William who has just entered the block area. "Get out of here," Bob says to William. "Bang! Bang! Get out of here. You're dead." John enters wearing a cape and climbs up the climber shooting his gun. "If you get in here we'll shoot you. I have super power. You don't."

Example 4

Ken, Paul, Bob, and Dennis are building a block structure. They are all carrying sticks and Lego guns. Dennis and Ken are wearing capes. "This is our house. It has everything. Our house has lots of guns and swords." Alan is standing close by, watching. "Get away." They throw a Lego brick at him. "This is our Batman house – only Batmen can get in." A student teacher asks if she can help. "No teachers allowed – only Batman." Don tries to enter the block structure. "He'll kill you. This is ours," Paul yells. Bob replies, "Yeah, you need a cape. Get a gun." Ken, Bob, and Paul run around the block structure shooting Don and everyone else in close range.

Bob always used some of the play elements that demonstrated and defined the core group's cultural knowledge: object possession, object use, role play, and

Table 8.2 Elements of core group play by target child

	Possession of object		Object use		Role		Language		Exclusion of teachers		Mock intimidation of teachers		Total no. of play episodes
	No.	%	No.	%	No.	%	No.	%	No.	%	No.	%	
William	14	46.7	14	46.7	9	28.0	3	10.0	0	0	0	9.0	30
Lisa	22	100.0	22	100.0	22	100.0	22	100.0	12	54.0	7	31.8	22
Bob	49	100.0	49	100.0	49	100.0	49	100.0	26	53.0	24	49.0	49

Note: No. = number of occurrences; % = percentage of total.

appropriate language use (100 percent of the episodes). In many instances, Bob's leadership and modeling created what became accepted within the core group. For example, the red rhythm sticks (used as social markers) are Bob's "invention." In Example 4, Bob makes clear the object requirements of an episode ("Yeah, you need a cape. Get a gun."). His remarks to adults are also typical: he excluded teachers (53.1 percent) and mock-intimidated teachers (49 percent) frequently, protecting the play as a peer-dominated arena.

Lisa: the only female core group member

Lisa exhibits a profile of activity within the core group that is much like Bob's, as well as some unique personal characteristics that result in membership and successful participation in the core group, despite her gender. Lisa was observed exhibiting actions in tune with the core group peers 100 percent of the time for the four categories of object possession, object use, role play, and appropriate language use. She excluded teachers from play 54.5 percent of the time and used objects to mock-intimidate teachers 31.8 percent of the time (see Table 8.1). Her in-tune style of play within the core group is illustrated in the following anecdote.

Example 5

Bob, Paul, and Lisa are running through the block area shooting with Lego-made guns. Ken enters and says "You gotta get a weapon." "I have a weapon." Paul shows his gun. "I have one, too," says Lisa. Bob and Lisa run to the climber. "This is our house," Lisa says to Bob. They have a box of red rhythm sticks on the floor of the climber and several in their pockets. "Yeah, but c'mon. Let's get more weapons." They fly away together to another part of the room.

In this example, Lisa assertively claims her right to the group by demonstrating that she possesses a core group object that she uses as a weapon. She also uses the sticks as a social marker by wearing several in her pockets and bringing a box of sticks to the climber.

In the next example, Lisa extends typical core group play in the absence of its members, sharing this cultural knowledge with a non-core group member in order to create common action.

Example 6

Beckoning to one of the younger female members of the classroom, Lisa asks: "Wanna come to my house?" Anne nods in acceptance. "Good, this is our Batman house. We need guns. We need a cape. I'll get you one." She leaves and returns with two scarves that she ties like a cape around

Anne's neck. Lisa hands her a stick and then puts her hands on her hips. "We're bad. Stay out. This is our house."

In Example 6, Lisa adopts a core group role, plays with core group objects, and uses core group language. Lisa often used the climber, a frequent site for play of the core group, as her Batman house. She often wore a cape and carried sticks, alone and with core group members and other peers. In Example 7, she communicates a superhero persona typical of the core group's play to an adult play partner.

Example 7

Lisa, while inviting one of the participant observers to play, informed her that she needed a cape. "Play bad guys . . . have to get guns and capes . . . guns and swords . . . have to be bad." This statement was repeated again with more emphasis, accompanied by furrowed eyebrows and a very serious look. She then picked out two hollow rods taped together and a rhythm stick she offered to her playmate.

In each of the preceding examples, Lisa not only *looked like* a member, but, more importantly, she *acted like* a member, demonstrating her full membership with a broad mastery of play themes, routines, and even attitudes valued by the core group. She was able to identify the group's social expectations, to participate in the group's constructed activities, and to apply this knowledge by reproducing those behaviors in other contexts.

Lisa's success reflects not only her cultural knowledge, but the history that she shares with the group, and her personality as well. Undoubtedly, her alliance as a play partner with Bob during the first few days of school set a tone for her continued involvement. Moreover, her easy disposition and tendency toward what Mandell (1986) called "social adjustment" played into this successful play history, as we shall further demonstrate in the Discussion section.

William: an outsider to the core group

William's style of interaction was problematic from the very beginning, setting up a negative social history with future members of the core group, as evidenced in Example 8.

Example 8

Ken is playing alone at the sandbox with trucks and dinosaurs. William enters: "I have a big shovel," but Ken ignores him. Lisa walks up to the sandbox too, pulls up a chair, and begins to play quietly. William offers a small dinosaur to Ken and he accepts it, but doesn't say anything.

William: "I am a sand monster and I'm going to eat you up," he says to Lisa who ignores him. William: "I'm going. Don't you take my dinosaur." But he doesn't leave and he then sticks his dinosaur in front of Lisa who briefly feeds it. William: "My lion is going to eat her dinosaur." Ken ignores him. William then has his lion "eat" Ken's. Ken: "Don't." William pulls away but continues to make noises. Lisa tries the same idea, pulls her animal back when Ken shouts, and then plays quietly.

This scenario around the sandbox on the first day of school reveals many of the differences in the personal styles of Lisa and William. First, there is the difference in how each enters the play: Lisa pulls up a chair and quietly fits in, whereas William loudly announces his arrival. Second, as the interaction unfolds, Lisa appears to know that Ken is not interested in playing together and so she plays in a parallel fashion across from him. William, however, repeatedly tries to engage both Ken and Lisa in play. More than just trying to engage them in play, William intrudes in several ways: he chatters inappropriately, he grabs toys, he invades their physical space, and he uses provocative and confrontational language. Most of all, William never gives up; he never reads the cues of his peers who are clearly not interested in his bids. This is in contrast to Lisa, who shows her accommodating nature in several ways: she ignores William's provocations, she feeds William's dinosaur when he is insistent, and she immediately retreats when Ken protests.

In his interactions with the core group, William failed to change the early course of this history because he rarely acted in tune with the group's concerns and activities during play. In Example 9, he fails to assume an appropriate role: attempting to participate in a superhero episode, he assumes a firefighter role that contradicts the group's ongoing activity and results in his rejection by them.

Example 9

Bob and Paul are sitting on top of the climber pointing sticks at children walking by their area. Bob and Paul: "Bang! Bang! Gotcha!" as they point their sticks at William. William watches this and then holds up the stick he is carrying. William: "Wissshhh," spraying it like a firehose. "I put the fire out." Both Bob and Paul respond by shooting at him. William: "Don't do that." He walks away.

As Example 9 demonstrates (and Table 8.1 corroborates), William's out-of-tune behavior prevented him from acting like a member with any consistency. He adopted roles appropriate to the group only 29 percent of the time and used appropriate language even less frequently (10 percent). His typical language consisted of gun and firefighter noises, often invoked for the wrong themes. Furthermore, he persisted in his ways even when questioned or corrected by core group members. His participation lacked other necessary components: he failed to verbalize superhero roles, or to exclude or mock-intimidate teachers with pretend weapons. Over the year, in fact, he increasingly relied upon teachers (rather than peers) to help him accomplish social play. Despite his ability to look like a member at times, both obtaining and using objects as weapons (46.5 percent of the time), this analysis reveals that William did not act like a member, lacking the group's broader cultural knowledge.

Apparently, without the ability to access the group's cultural knowledge, William could not determine the group's social expectations to position himself successfully or to adapt his behavior to fit a particular situation. He failed to determine the social expectations of each specific situation, and to take the group's perspective in order to modify his actions. These failures often disrupted the flow of the play, precluding a joint line of action that included him because he was out of tune. William's misinterpretations of play themes were rejected by the core group, and so fostered his exclusion.

William also tried to use teachers to enter the play. As we confirmed in this analysis, this particular core group tried to exclude teachers from play or, in some instances, they tried to mock-intimidate teachers by their use of weapons. Therefore, using a teacher to try to gain access was an inappropriate strategy in this setting. Not only had William aligned himself physically with teachers, he was asking them for information regarding participation and entry strategies. Whereas the teacher would, of course, be able to identify the theme and describe some of the roles, she could not identify the participation demands because she was not a member, and therefore did not have access to them. In addition, even if she could identify some of the ground rules for participation, it would be difficult ethically for a teacher to recommend shooting other playmates or excluding teachers.

One of William's limitations was that he saw only one part of the picture – the importance of acquiring particular objects in order to participate in the core group's play. He lacked the insight that a combination of elements comprised the cultural knowledge that had to be shared and produced in order to be a successful core group member.
[. . .]
He seemed unable to take the perspective of others, to predict their responses appropriately, to adapt his behavior to shifting standards, or to negotiate common meanings with the core group in play.

Discussion

Comparing William and Lisa

A comparison of William and Lisa's behavior supported the hypothesis that object possession is necessary but not sufficient for group membership. Lisa exhibited a complex of cultural behaviors and knowledge shared with other core group members such as Bob. In contrast, William produced only discrete parts of the group's shared knowledge; thus, although carrying the same objects allowed him to *look* like a member, without the accompanying language and social action he did not *act* like a member.

William and Lisa were different, not only in the knowledge they each possessed, but also in their abilities to reproduce that knowledge, and to do so at the appropriate time and place. It is one thing to know that intimidating teachers is part of a group's cultural repertoire; it is another to produce the intimidation with your language and social action. In other words, an individual must have the social and communicative repertoire to enact that cultural element.

Furthermore, cultural knowledge has to be applied to fit the moment and dynamics of any particular play episode or situation. As children play, a "flow" (Mandell, 1986) is created that must be protected and maintained even as children enter and leave, create and shift topics, negotiate and renegotiate roles, and appropriate and distribute space and materials. Thus, for example, producing an intimidating response to a teacher might not be appropriately timed when one's peers are actually soliciting a teacher's help to create a sign for their play, or protect a spaceship from intruders.

The contrast between Lisa and William, with respect to having, producing, and applying cultural knowledge, is all the more striking given that both William and Lisa had limited opportunities for peer interaction in their homes and neighborhoods. It seems unlikely that Lisa could have learned to be in-tune with peers through her interactions with adults.

Whereas William and Lisa's opportunities for accessing cultural knowledge at home and at school were similar, their personal styles were very different. Lisa had an accommodating interpersonal style, consistent with her in-tune behaviors, whereas, conversely, William's personality was problematic. In the sandbox example that occurred early in the school year, Lisa's interactional style could be characterized as flexible and adaptive, which is in direct contrast to William's rigid and confrontational style.

There was a synchrony between the personal styles of these children and their relative success as they sought to position themselves across other contexts of the classroom. For example, Lisa's adaptable, accommodating personality positioned her successfully with different groups in the classroom, allowing her easy entry not only to the core group, but to other peer groups and to events planned by teachers. Lisa positioned herself in the core group through oppositional, assertive behavior (using a stick as a weapon) as easily as she participated in a teacher-facilitated group time through accommodating behavior (sharing materials). William, in contrast, was somewhat rigid and inflexible in his participation strategies (using the same theme and language to participate in all play episodes), though he was able to sustain interactions with teachers, and eventually to participate successfully in the more structured events of the school culture.

As both children positioned themselves in everyday life in the classroom, a social history of these two players in relation to the group was also constructed. Cumulatively, this social history has its own impact, for better and for worse, on the experiences of William and Lisa and on the expectations the core group held for them. Retrospectively we came to view the sandbox example as foreshadowing Lisa's success and William's failure in participating in core group play.

Toward a multifaceted and integrated view of social competence

This study was conducted as part of a larger ethnography, in order to understand better how children construct their membership within a preschool friendship group. A guiding assumption in our work is that such phenomena are most fully accessed and interpreted as a part of the common culture constructed by the members of the classroom in their daily life. This sociocultural perspective implies taking a wide look at any phenomenon, for example situating it across contexts, relating one phenomenon to another, and, in this case, viewing the experiences of individuals in juxtaposition with the experiences of a group of friends. This perspective also implies taking a long look – an over-time look at a group's daily interactions – in order to make visible the cultural patterns characteristic of their social life.

In this final section, we will show the unique contribution of the sociocultural perspective to our overall understanding of children's social competence (and incompetence), and relate this understanding to the extant sociometric and social interactional literature on children's social competence in peer interactions.

In our own data, we see interacting aspects of a child's social competence, all of which have unique cultural interpretations, and all of which may contribute to social success or lack of success within peer group play: children's personality and behavior position them in various ways, influencing the construction of their social experience with others; their ability to access, interpret, and be part of the construction of the cultural knowledge of a group; their ability to produce and reproduce this cultural knowledge through interactional strategies from their sociocommunicative repertoire; and, last, their place within the ongoing social history in a classroom, which further supports or constrains their chances of achieving social success. Each of these elements belongs in a multifaceted and integrated notion of social competence as discussed in the following.

To begin, this analysis has revealed the complex and locally constructed cultural knowledge held by a group of peer players, and thus the challenge for any individual child to contribute to, understand, and access this knowledge. Moreover, it demonstrates that partial knowledge (such as looking like a member), or knowledge reproduced inaccurately (shooting with bwam bwam sounds when the group shoots with boom, boom) will not support a child's participation in the group. If one is to be successful, he or she must fully understand the specific nature of what is valued: in this case, specific roles, themes, and objects, produced through particular attitudes, language, and social action.

Socially competent behavior, both here and in general, is, in part, defined situationally and accomplished in the doing. What counts as socially competent behavior in a particular situation cannot be entirely known *a priori* but, rather, must become known as the cultural patterns of a social group are constructed. Thus, neither the children nor the researchers in this setting could have accurately predicted the particulars of the cultural knowledge that was to be constructed here. We argue that an understanding of the evolving group culture is more than background: it is essential to an understanding of individuals' experiences as they seek social efficacy. Furthermore, it is the central feature that distinguishes this approach from the social interactional and sociometric perspectives on social competence.

In part, what we have found here supports much of what social interactional researchers have argued with respect to social competence. For example, at a general level, William's strategies for participating with the core group resemble those of children described in interactional terms as generally socially unsuccessful: his communication is poor and poorly timed; his initiation and entry strategies are ineffective; and he overused particular strategies, persisting even when they do not fit with the ongoing play (Corsaro, 1985; Monighan-Nourot *et al.*, 1987; Ross, 1985).

The sociocultural perspective we have taken, however, gives us a different picture of the inadequacies of William's strategies. With this perspective, we shift from viewing social strategies as general and as either appropriate or inappropriate across all interactional contexts, toward viewing social strategies as context-specific and dynamic syntheses of strategies with cultural knowledge. So, whereas offering objects might be a common child strategy for entering play, we contend that it will succeed only if the child understands the culturally defined values and uses of such objects. Importantly, the child must also have the abilities within his or her sociocommunicative repertoire to produce and/or reproduce the socially constructed and ongoing cultural "text." Thus, William would have needed to identify the red sticks as of value to the group, to use those objects as objects of intimidation, and to use the appropriate gesture, tone, and language to enact intimidation.

Thus, we share several corroborative themes with social interactionists but maintain important theoretical distinctions. We share a belief that children's social competence should be seen in the doing. For social interactionists, the focus is on the accomplishment of the moment or episode of interaction. In taking our long look, however, we also see how these moments and episodes contribute to, and reflect, the evolving peer culture of a group of peers. Both perspectives hold that children must read the ongoing social reality in order to guide successful participation. Interactionists see the successful child as having to read the moment (and the context) and then to apply the right general strategy to fit in. In our view, however, the child has to read (and contribute to) the wider cultural knowledge created by the group over time, and then he or she must apply that knowledge dynamically, fitted with the moment's instantiation and version of cultural knowledge. Finally, we share a belief that children need and evidence many sociocommunicative abilities in accomplishing successful interactions. But, we see such abilities as useful only to the extent that children can use them as they produce the right cultural knowledge.

We also agree with the traditional view that children's personality and behavior influence their social success and status. Lisa's observant, flexible, accommodating style gets her close to the action, where she is positioned well to access the group's cultural knowledge. Conversely, William's loud, insistent, confrontational style keeps him from being a part of the group's activities. This distance subsequently makes it difficult for him to access the ongoing cultural knowledge, because it develops in sustained interactions and is an evolving social construction that comes to have meaning for the group. Thus, although this analysis supports the link between social success and personality and behavior – a major thesis in the sociometric literature – it casts this relationship in social and cultural terms: personality and behavior will bear on, but not determine, one's relative ability to share and participate in diverse aspects of a constructed social world.

Last, we see evidenced in these data a central tenet of the sociocultural perspective, that is, interactions become patterned and those patterns frame the expectations that individuals hold for each other. Thus, from the interactions William and Lisa had with the core group emerged a social history of success or failure that, in turn, became part of the group's expectations for each of them. Lisa's membership became part of the group's cultural life together, just as attempts to resist William became part of their routines.

Although all three of the socioculturally defined aspects of social competence discussed here interact to produce a child's place within a group, it seems likely that different elements have salience at different points in time. At the beginning of the year, for example, disposition and personality probably contributed most to Lisa's success and William's failure as we saw it in the sandbox example. Over time, however, as the group established its patterned culture and Lisa enjoyed continued success as a participant in the group, she established the *right* to join their play, and becoming a member ceased to be an issue at all. Likewise, over time, the group constructed its *rites* to exclude various children, including William. Overall, these positive or negative social histories either supported or constrained all subsequent interactions.

By looking at the specific context of particular play events, we have seen that peer group membership and participation in group play is a complex process that requires children to possess sophisticated social abilities. Successful participation requires children to access and to display cultural knowledge, to determine implicit rules for membership, and subsequently to adapt their behavior to fit the existing theme and social context. Moreover, social acceptance in play involves more than producing the elements that fit with the ongoing play episode. Complicating this social difficulty is the complexity of the social reality in this classroom, that is, one in which play groups construct and enforce complex multilevel membership and status criteria that frame specific play events.

At the same time, there is reason not to be overly pessimistic about William's future relationships. In a 2-year ethnographic piece, Massoulos (1988) described a child who was rejected like William within a peer group during Year 1, but then was very successful during the 2-year with a different group of peers (when the Year 1 group had graduated from the program). Groups such as these are dynamic entities and children are in a period of rapid development and growth. Thus, the group norms may change over time, William may become more socially adept, and different configurations of peers will develop as William continues in his schooling (and might produce more accessible dynamics for William). Also, children like William, who are rejected, might find effective coping strategies. This happened later in the year for William when he learned to adjust in this classroom by becoming more of a "teacher player," by creating his own solitary pretend play, and by seeking out others who were not part of a cohesive peer group.

Although the particulars of what counts as socially competent must be seen locally, successful participation in play groups generally is dependent on accessing the cultural knowledge of a specific group. This includes reading and interpreting group expectations and subsequently being able to produce appropriate behaviors suggested by these group norms within the existing context of these play groups. Future work could include comparing the core group to other peer groups in this classroom and exploring multiple groups in other classrooms. By doing such a comparison, specific aspects of local construction (e.g., mock-intimidation) could be distinguished from more general elements of peer culture play that appear across groups (e.g., object use, language play).

A move away from an emphasis on determining personality characteristics or status labels (such as "unpopular" or "popular" children) suggests a move away from teaching or telling unsuccessful children how to be successful. Rather, it suggests facilitating numerous interactions with a variety of groups across contexts. It also suggests sanctioning creative gender positioning, helping children learn to be adaptable and flexible in social interactions, and to learn to read social cues and to access the cultural knowledge of specific groups. This could be approached in a way similar to the cognitive problem-solving approach found in many preschool classrooms, but with the emphasis here on facilitating social development.

The view we present in this chapter signals a shift from viewing social competence as a static set of abilities, bounded by particular contexts, to a more complex, fluid, and dynamic interpretation. Social competence is conceptualized as a dynamic process in which children are active and competent in interpreting subject positions, reading social cues, and accessing cultural knowledge over time and across contexts. Socially competent children are viewed as having a multiple and fluid approach to being, in and across diverse settings (including the classroom), as children become gendered persons, students, and peers. We do not claim that the sociocultural view presented in this chapter can identify all facets of social competence, but we do argue the need for a multifaceted definition of social competence to be developed in the literature across perspectives and across contexts. In this chapter, those aspects of social competence related to participation in ongoing peer culture group play have been explored from a perspective uniquely constructed to examine such issues.

References

Asher, S. and Renshaw, P.   (1981). Children without friends: Social knowledge and social skill training. In S.R. Asher and J.M. Gottman (Eds), *The development of children's friendships* (pp. 207–241). Cambridge: Cambridge University Press.

Bloome, D. (1987). *Literacy and schooling.* Norwood, NJ: Ablex.

Bloome, D. and Theodorou, E. (1988). Analyzing teacher–student and student–student discourse. In J. Green and J. Harker (Eds), *Multiple perspective analysis of classroom discourse* (pp. 217–248). Norwood, NJ: Ablex.

Corsaro, W.A. (1985). *Friendships and peer culture in the early years.* Norwood, NJ: Ablex.

Cowen, E.L., Pederson, A., Babigian, M., Izzo, L.D., and Trost, M.R. (1973). Long-term follow up of early detected vulnerable children. *Journal of Consulting and Clinical Psychology, 41*, 438–446.

Elgas. P.M. (1988). The construction of a preschool peer culture: The role of objects and play styles. Unpublished doctoral dissertation, The Ohio State University, Columbus.

Elgas, P., Klein, E., Kantor, R., and Fernie, D. (1988). Play and the peer culture: Play styles and object use. *Journal of Research in Childhood Education, 3*, 142–153.

Fernie, D.E., Kantor, R., Klein, E., Meyer, C., and Elgas, P. (1988). Becoming students and becoming ethnographers in a preschool. *Journal of Research in Childhood Education, 3*(2), 132–141.

Garnica, O. (1981). Social dominance and conversational interaction – the Omega child in the classroom. In J.L. Green and C. Wallat (Eds), *Ethnography and language in educational settings* (pp. 229–252). Norwood, NJ: Ablex.

Green, J.L. and Meyer, L. (1991). The embeddedness of reading in classroom life: Reading as a situated process. In C. Baker and A. Luke (Eds), *Toward critical sociology of reading* (pp. 86–106). Pedagogy, PA: John Benjamin.

Gumperz, J. (1981). Conversational inference and classroom learning. In J.L. Green and C. Wallat (Eds), *Ethnography and language in educational settings* (pp. 3–24). Norwood, NJ: Ablex.

Hatch, A. (1987). Status and social power in a kindergarten peer group. *The Elementary School Journal, 88,* 79–93.

Hops, H. (1983). Children's social competence and skill: Current research practices and future directions. *Behavior Therapy, 14,* 3–18.

Kantor, R., Elgas, P., and Fernie, D. (1989). First the look and then the sound. Creating conversations at circle time. *Early Childhood Research Quarterly, 4,* 443–448.

McConnell, R. and Odom, S.L. (1986). Sociometrics: Peer referenced measures and the assessment of social competence. In P. Strain, J. Guralnick, and H. Walker (Eds), *Children's social behavior.* Orlando, FL: Academic.

McDermott, R.P. and Church, J. (1976). Making sense and feeling good: The ethnography of communication and identity work. *Communication, 2,* 121–142.

Mandell, N. (1986). Peer interaction in day-care settings: Implications for social cognition. *Sociological Studies of Child Development, 1,* 55–79.

Massoulos, C.G. (1988). Acceptance and rejection of friendships in peer culture within an early childhood setting: An observational study approach. Unpublished doctoral dissertation, The Ohio State University, Columbus, OH.

Meyer, C. (1989). The role of peer relationships in the socialization of children to preschool: A Korean example. Unpublished doctoral dissertation, The Ohio State University, Columbus.

Monighan-Nourot, P., Scales, B., Van Hoorn, J. and Almy, M. (1987). *Looking at children: A bridge between theory and practice.* New York: Teacher's College Press.

Peery, J.C. (1979). Popular, amiable, isolated, rejected: A reconceptualization of sociometric status in preschool children. *Child Development, 50,* 1231–1234.

Rizzo, T. (1989). *Friendship development among children in school.* Norwood, NJ: Ablex.

Rizzo, T., Corsaro, W., and Bates, J.E. (1992). Ethnographic methods and interpretive analysis: Expanding the methodological options of psychologists. *Developmental Review, 12,* 101–123.

Roff, M., Sells, S.B., and Golen, M.M. (1972). *Social adjustment and personality development in children.* Minneapolis: University of Minnesota Press.

Ross, D. (1985, April). Social competence in kindergarten: Applications of symbolic interaction theory. Paper presented at the annual meeting of the American Educational Research Association, Chicago.

Scott, J. (1991). The social construction of "outsiders'" status in preschool. Unpublished doctoral dissertation, The Ohio State University, Columbus.

Wallat, C. and Green, J. (1979). Social roles and communication contexts in kindergarten. *Theory Into Practice, 18,* 275–284.

Weber, L. (1984). *Ideas influencing early childhood education.* New York: Teacher's College Press.

Part III

Relationships and learning

Chapter 9

Aspects of teaching and learning*

David Wood

Introduction: images of the learner and reflections on the teacher

Teaching is a complex, difficult and often subtle activity. Although I will be arguing that a great deal of teaching is spontaneous, 'natural' and effective, deliberate teaching of groups of children in formally contrived contexts is an intellectually demanding occupation. It is also a relatively new one. Compulsory formal education for all has a short history, and the technologies and consequences it has spawned, both material and mental, are still poorly understood and the subject of political and academic debate.

Some years ago, Greenfield and Bruner (1969) argued that the invention and widespread availability of schooling has had dramatic effects on the nature of human knowledge, creating not simply wider dissemination of facts but fundamental changes in the nature of thinking itself. Although ensuing studies of the impact of schooling on the human intellect have shown that the effects are somewhat less general than this hypothesis suggested (e.g. Cole and Scribner, 1974), they have shown that schooling, in company with other technologies (notably literacy), has marked effects on various intellectual 'skills'. Donaldson (1978), in a critical examination of Piagetian theory, argues that schooling does help to create certain varieties of human reasoning, particularly a capacity to deploy powers of reasoning to solve problems that involve abstract hypothetical entities. In such contexts, thinking out problems and understanding what is implied by them demands attention to the formal structure of the problem and cannot be achieved by appeals to common sense or plausible inferences. Thus, Donaldson concludes that schooling is the source of special ways of thinking about and operating upon the world.

One implication of this view is that teachers (broadly rather than narrowly conceived) are responsible for inculcating certain ways of thinking in children. They pass on not only facts and information about things but also ways

* This chapter first appeared in Richards, M. and Light, P. (eds) *Children of Social Worlds*, Cambridge: Polity Press, 1986, pp. 191–212.

of conceptualizing and reasoning. Where they succeed, teachers recreate their own ways of thinking in their pupils; where they fail, they may inhibit or prevent a child's access to power within his or her own society.

Our knowledge of the 'psychology of teaching' is derived from several sources. The first and most obvious is from theories and studies of learning and development. Theorists of human development, notably Bruner, Vygotsky and Piaget, offer not only radically different views of what children are like, what *knowledge* is and how it develops; they also sketch out radically different images of the teacher. In this chapter we will examine some of the major features of these theories in relation to the issue of what teaching *is*.

A second source of information about teaching stems from the now numerous attempts to describe and analyse teaching as it occurs in classrooms. Unfortunately, many such studies are largely atheoretical and even idiosyncratic, so it is seldom possible to utilize the data they provide to inform our arguments about theories of what teaching is. One possible reason for this is that teachers do not actually do what any of the theories dictate they should do, either because teachers are ignorant of theories or because theorists are ignorant of teaching. One view is that theories developed out of psychological research cannot be used to develop categories to describe what goes on in classrooms because their relevance is limited to what happens in laboratories. There has been a good deal of debate in recent years about the status and relevance of theories about children based largely on experimental psychological research. For example, Cole and his colleagues (1979) observed children in home-like contexts and reported that they seldom found evidence of the sorts of demands, tasks and interactions that cognitive psychologists use in the laboratory to explore learning and development. Thus, psychologists *qua* psychologists are likely to be working with very different raw material in fashioning their theories of children's thinking from that which informs the views of parents and others. Herein, perhaps, lie some reasons for different conceptualizations of the nature of children by psychologists and non-psychologists. Psychologists may be accused of having created 'straw children' and imaginary learners who haunt the psychological laboratory but not the 'real' world.

I shall be arguing, however, that the differences between children's behaviour in different contexts (e.g. laboratory versus home) are of more interest and importance than this interpretation suggests. More specifically, I will be exploring the idea that interactions between adults and children in 'spontaneous' and 'contrived' encounters are different in nature. By contrived, I mean teaching/learning/testing encounters that are deliberately brought about by those with power (e.g. teachers or psychologists), as opposed to those that 'arise' spontaneously out of adult–child contacts. I shall also work on the assumption (not totally without evidence) that most interactions at home are spontaneous and child-initiated, and those in schools or psychological laboratories are usually contrived and adult-controlled. I also suggest that when adults and children in the two different contexts appear to be working on the 'same' tasks or doing superficially similar things, the processes involved are dissimilar. The interactions follow different 'ground rules' and create different demands of both the adult and the child, and this explains why children often appear to display varying levels of intellectual or linguistic competence in different situations. We will consider, for example, why children who are inquisitive and loquacious at home may show little initiative in school.

What are 'ground rules'? Mercer and Edwards (1981) have provided some examples in a consideration of classroom interactions, drawing attention to differences between the constraints that operate in classroom and everyday discourse. For example, being able to answer questions such as 'It takes three men six hours to dig a certain sized hole. How long would it take two men to dig the same hole?' demands more than a knowledge of how to apply and execute the sums involved. One must also appreciate what constitutes appropriate and inappropriate answers. Problems demanding similar decisions in everyday life (e.g. working out how long a certain job will take) might legitimately concern issues such as when the ground was last dug over; what tools are to be used; how experienced the men are and so forth. In mathematics lessons, however, such considerations are 'irrelevant'. To know what is relevant, a child has to discover or infer the rules underlying what is a very special form of discourse. Arguments, for example, about making mathematics 'relevant' are likely to founder if they simply choose 'everyday' situations and ignore the fact that the ground rules for solving everyday practical numerical problems and abstract formal mathematical problems are different.

If one accepts that activities occurring across contexts may be governed by different implicit social practices and rules, then what may seem like the 'same' task in different contexts may, to children who have yet to acquire all the rules, appear very different. Several researchers (e.g. Donaldson, 1978) have shown that young children often appear able to do things in some contexts but not others. They possess competence that does not always emerge in their performances. One may seek to understand such discrepancies in the fact that some contexts are more threatening, unfamiliar or less motivating to children; but it is also likely that the apparent similarities between the competences demanded in such situations are misleading. Thus, identifying the reasons why observations of teaching and learning in home, school and laboratory often yield different views of the processes involved is no simple matter. What might seem to be essentially similar tasks and activities in various contexts may well be located in quite different 'rules' of conduct and interpretation.

Another line of evidence relating to the question of what effective teaching is would seem, on first sight, to offer the most direct and compelling way of adjudicating between competing theories. A number of educational programmes have been set up, particularly in the USA, to help provide young children from economically poor homes with a 'Headstart' in their educational life by providing preschool educational experiences (see Woodhead, 1985 for an overview). There have been some successful intervention programmes, but these were inspired by a range of *different* theories of learning and development. No one theory held the day. Weikart (1973), commenting upon the success of his own, neo-Piagetian, programme and those of others who had based their interventions on other theories, concludes that the important common element in success was not the curriculum *per se* nor the material it employed but the commitment and competence of its teachers! The *nature* of such competence remains obscure.

We will examine just a few aspects of what teaching competence might involve. I do not claim, however, to be more than scratching the surface of what is undoubtedly an extremely complex issue.

Learning and development

I will in this part of the chapter be discussing in some detail a series of studies of the teaching–learning process that have employed a common task. The children being taught range from three to five years of age. Left to their own devices, the children would not be able to do the task at hand. Nor do they learn how to do the task if they are taught ineffectively. Given effective instruction, however, they can be taught how to do most or all of it alone (Wood and Middleton, 1975).

Although the task we shall be considering is a specific and concrete one, I shall argue that some aspects of the teaching–learning process it identifies are general ones that are relevant to and implicated in many naturalistic encounters between adults and children. I shall also try, however, to identify some important differences between the nature of interactions observed in such contrived teaching–learning encounters and those found in more spontaneous encounters between adults and children in homes and schools.

The conceptual framework adopted in this chapter is derived from the theorizing of Vygotsky (1978) and Bruner (1968). Vygotsky, for example, contributed the concept of a 'zone of proximal development'. This expression refers to the gap that exists for a given child at a particular time between his level of performance on a given task or activity and his potential level of ability following instruction. Vygotsky offers a conceptualization of intelligence that is radically different from that promoted by either conventional psychometric intelligence tests or Piagetian theory. Vygotsky's theory of intelligence takes the capacity to learn through instruction as central. The intelligence of a species is determined by a capacity not only to learn but also to teach. Furthermore, two children who behave similarly in a given task situation, suggesting similar levels of competence, may in fact be quite different, in that one may prove able to benefit far more from instruction in that task than another.

Underlying this view of the role of instruction in learning are radically different conceptions of the nature of knowledge, development and maturity from those embodied in Piagetian theory. Piaget's child is an epistemologist – a natural seeker after, and architect of, his own understanding. He learns largely through his own activity in the world. He constructs progressively more powerful, abstract and integrated systems of knowing by discovering how his actions affect reality. All a teacher can do is to facilitate that understanding by providing appropriate materials and contexts for the child's actions and by helping the child to discover inconsistencies in his own views. The primary motivator of developmental change for Piaget is 'disequilibration' – a state of conflict between what the child expects as a result of his interactions with the world and what actually transpires. Knowing the stages of development and materials and activities that are likely to be relevant to the activities dictated by each stage, a teacher can facilitate developmental change by helping the child to discover implicit contradictions in his own thinking. Any contradictions must, however, be *latent* in the child's structure of knowledge. They can be activated but not induced. There is no point and may even be harm in confronting the child with hypotheses, demonstrations or explanations that are not 'natural' to his stage of development.

Whilst there is evidence favouring the view that one basis for developmental change or learning is cognitive conflict and contradiction (e.g. Glachan and Light, 1982), I will be arguing that far more is involved in effective teaching than simply providing material for the child to 'digest' or activating competing ideas that are already implicit in his thinking. We will explore the view that adult and child, working together, can construct new schemes through shared interaction. The potential effects of teaching will prove to be far greater than Piagetian theory allows. What the child develops, in this alternative conceptualization, are not mental operations derived from his actions on the world but 'concepts' that are jointly constructed through interaction with those who already embody them, together with ways of doing and thinking that are cultural practices, recreated with children through processes of formal and informal teaching.

The nature of effective instruction: contingent control of learning

We are confronted with two individuals who are in asymmetrical states of knowledge about a problem facing them. The more knowledgeable, the teacher, is attempting to communicate a more informed understanding to the less knowledgeable, the learner. How are practical skills and ideas transferred from one body to the other?

Our task here is to discover an analysis of teaching and learning interactions that will enable us to relate instructional activity to the learning process. If we are successful in identifying the crucial features of effective teaching, then it should be possible to examine a range of different teaching styles or strategies and make testable predictions about their relative effectiveness.

Some years ago we attempted to meet these goals in an analysis of mother–child interactions in an experimental situation (Wood and Middleton, 1975). The children involved were four years old and the task the mothers were asked to teach them was a specially designed construction toy. When a child first encountered the task, he or she saw 21 wooden blocks of varying size and shape. The mother had already been shown how these could be assembled to create a pyramid, but the child had no knowledge of the solution to the problem. The mother was asked to teach the child how to put the blocks together in any way she saw fit. She was also told that when the pyramid had been put together, it would be taken apart and the child asked to assemble it alone.

Each block in the toy is unique and will fit into only one position in the final construction, but the task was designed to incorporate a number of repeated rules of assembly. The pyramid (more accurately, a ziggurat) comprises five square levels, each a different size. The bottom level is approximately nine inches square and is constructed out of four, equally sized, square pieces. Two of these assemble by fitting a peg in one into an equally sized hole in the second. When this pair is assembled in the correct orientation, two half-pegs, one on each block, are brought together. Similarly, two other blocks assemble by a hole and peg arrangement but to bring two half-holes together. When the two pairs are constructed, the peg and hole formed can be fitted together to produce a level of the pyramid. This rule of assembly is repeated with sets of blocks of diminishing size to construct four more levels. The assembly of each set of four also creates connectives to enable them to be piled on top of each other. On the 'top' of each block is a quarter section of a round peg. When each level is assembled correctly, these come together to form a peg which fits into a circular depression in the base of the level above, which is similarly created from four quarter depressions in each block. Thus, the levels can be piled to form a rigid structure. The assembly is completed by placing a single block with a depression in its base on the top level.

The blocks were designed so that any peg would fit into any hole and any level could fit onto any other. Thus, the task presents many possibilities for 'incorrect' assembly. Left to their own devices, four-year-olds cannot do the task, but given effective instruction they can. What, however, does effective instruction look like? How are we to describe the maternal attempts to teach children?

Imagine we are watching a mother and child in a teaching–learning encounter with these blocks. The mother has just given an instruction. First, we determine how much *control* the instruction implicitly exerts over what happens next. Five categories are listed in Table 9.1 which, we have found in a number of studies, can accommodate any instruction a teacher might make in this situation. These vary in terms of degree of control.

The first category, general verbal prompts, includes instructions that demand activity but do not specify how the child should proceed to meet such demands. Specific verbal instructions give the child information about features of the task that need to be borne in mind as he or she makes the next move. If the teacher not only tells the child what to attend to in making his or her next move but also shows him or her what is referred to by pointing at or picking out relevant material, then the instruction is classified as Level 3. If the teacher not only identifies material but goes on to prepare it for assembly, then the child is simply left with the problem of how to complete the operation in question. Finally, if the teacher demonstrates, he or she takes full control of the next step in the construction while the child, hopefully, looks on and learns.

As we come down the list, then, the instructions become more controlling, with the teacher implicitly taking more, and offering the child correspondingly less, scope for initiative.

Mothers vary enormously in the way in which they attempt to teach their young children how to do this task, and children also vary widely in their ability to do the task alone after instruction. Does the style of teaching affect what is learned? It does. Mothers whose children do well after instruction are those who are most likely to act in accordance with two 'rules' of teaching. The first dictates that any failure by a child to bring off an action after a given level of help should be met by an immediate increase in help or control. Thus, if the teacher, say, had provided the child with a specific verbal instruction and then found that the child did not succeed in complying with it, the appropriate response is to give more help either by indicating the material implicated in the previous instruction or by preparing it for assembly.

The second rule concerns what should happen when a child succeeds in complying with an instruction. This dictates that any subsequent instruction should offer less help than that which pre-dated success. In other words, after success the teacher should give the child more space for success (and error).

The pattern of responses by the teacher to a child's momentary successes

Table 9.1 Levels of control

Level	Example
1 General verbal prompts	'Now you make something'
2 Specific verbal instructions	'Get four big blocks'
3 Indicates materials	Points to block(s) needed
4 Prepares for assembly	Orients pairs so hole faces peg
5 Demonstrates	Assembles two pairs

and failures *judged in relation to the instructions that pre-dated them* is the basis for our evaluation. Every time a teacher acts in accordance with the rules, she is deemed to have made a *contingent* response. Every time she does something different (e.g. fails to provide an instruction immediately after a child fails or gives one at an inappropriate level), the instruction is non-contingent. What we find is that the more frequently contingent a teacher is, the more the child can do alone after instruction.

Stated simply and boldly, the rules of contingent teaching sound easy. However, even in our experimental situation involving a practical task with a single solution, it is difficult to teach all children contingently all the time. Indeed, when we trained an experimenter to teach children according to different rules, we found that she was able to follow the contingency rules only about 85 per cent of the time (Wood, Wood and Middleton, 1978). Monitoring children's activity, remembering what one had said or done to prompt that activity, and responding quickly to their efforts at an appropriate level is a demanding intellectual feat. Effective teaching is as difficult as the learning it seeks to promote.

Scaffolding the learning process

We have defined the *process* of effective instruction as the contingent control of learning. Elsewhere, using the metaphor of 'scaffolding', we have identified some of the *functions* that instruction may fulfil for the learner (Wood, Bruner and Ross, 1976). Since this notion has been extended beyond laboratory studies to help describe more naturalistic teaching–learning processes, it is necessary to explore the characteristics of scaffolding and its relationship to control and contingency before moving on to consider more general aspects of teaching and learning.

One of the most influential approaches to the study of human intelligence stems from a view of a human being as a 'limited information processor'. Individuals can take in only so much information about their situation at any moment in time, so they must organize their activities over time (develop a plan) in order to assimilate and operate within that situation. The development of knowledge and skill involves the discovery of what is best paid attention to, borne in mind and acted upon in an appropriate (goal-achieving) sequence.

At the heart of this conception of human abilities is the notion of 'uncertainty'. When we find ourselves needing to act in a very unfamiliar situation, uncertainty is high and our capacity to attend to and remember objects, features and events within the situation is limited. Observation, practice, trial and error, the growing appreciation of regularities and learning, involve the progressive reduction of that uncertainty. Accompanying its reduction are increased accuracy of perception and powers of memory. Thus, experts in a task are able to observe, take in and remember more of what they experience (within the task situation) than novices.

Children, being novices of life in general, are potentially confronted with more uncertainty than the more mature, and, hence, their abilities to select, remember and plan are limited in proportion. Without help in organizing their attention and activity, children may be overwhelmed by uncertainty. The more knowledgeable can assist them in organizing their activities, by reducing uncertainty, breaking down a complex task into more manageable steps or stages. As children learn, their uncertainty is reduced and they are able to pay attention to and learn about more of the task at hand.

Such assisted learning, however, presupposes that the children are actively involved in trying to achieve task-relevant goals. Clearly, what individuals attend to and remember in a given context is dictated by their purposes and goals; relevance is relative to the purpose in mind. Children may perceive a situation differently from an adult because they face greater uncertainty and/or because they may be entertaining different ideas about the opportunities for activity offered by the task situation.

Where a child is already involved in the pursuit of a goal or the fulfilment of an intention, then provided that the would-be teacher is able to discover or infer what that goal is, the child may be helped to bring it off. In formal or contrived situations, where the teacher decides what purpose the child must pursue, *task induction* becomes a primary scaffolding function and a *sine qua non* for effective learning. Children also face additional problems in contrived encounters because, given that they are compliant, they have to discover what their intentions are supposed to be.

How does one invoke intentions or a sense of goal directedness in the young child? More specifically, can demonstrations or verbal instructions be used effectively to invoke relevant activity? Clearly, showing children things or asking them to perform activities that they are currently unable to do will be successful only if the child understands enough of what was said or shown to lead to relevant, if not fully successful, task activity. Instruction must, to use Vygotsky's term, operate within the learner's 'zone of proximal development'. For such a concept to be useful, perception must, in some way, help to lead or constrain action and understanding.

I suggest that young children often think they understand and are capable of doing what an adult shows or tells them when, in fact, they do not. Young children, in short, often overestimate their own abilities. However, children's beliefs about their own competence lead to intentional activity and trap them in problem-solving: in trying to do what they think they can do. Provided that effective help is forthcoming, the child may be led to construct new skills. These, in turn, accompany modified perceptions of what is seen and heard. The learner comes closer to mature understanding. Put another way, both demonstrations and verbal instructions can be used to define problem spaces within which adult and child can work co-operatively and contingently to promote learning. Perhaps a few examples will illustrate this argument.

In the experimental situation already outlined we found that three-year-old children showed signs of *recognizing* what was an appropriate task goal before they were able to *achieve* that goal. For instance, they appreciated the fact that four dissimilar blocks could be put together to create a single and more parsimonious *Gestalt*. They would usually attempt to reproduce such a configuration after a demonstration. When their attempted constructions did not look similar to that demonstrated, they would usually take them apart and try again. However, they almost never took apart a construction that did look like the model – evidence both that they possessed some sense of what was task-relevant and that their activities were goal-directed.

Although purely verbal instruction proved an ineffective teaching strategy, every child so taught did begin by attempting to do what was requested. We suggest that the young child possesses sufficient linguistic competence to derive plans from verbal instructions that are partially but not fully understood. Thus, when told to 'Put the four biggest ones together', they never selected the smallest blocks and usually attempted to fit pegs into holes. Although they did not realize, early in the instructional session, all the constraints that were implicated in such general verbal instructions, they understood enough of what they implied to lead them into task-relevant activity.

Even when children do not fully understand what we show them or ask of them, they may believe that they understand, and understand enough to lead them into task-relevant, if initially unsuccessful, action. We suggest, then, that a learner's *incomplete* understanding of what he or she is shown and told (what is perceived) is a vital basis for learning through instruction. Perhaps incomplete but relevant understanding of what children see adults doing and hear them saying is at the heart of what Vygotsky termed the 'zone of proximal development'.

Once the learner is involved in task-relevant activity, other scaffolding functions become operative. I have already said that young children, like all of us, are limited in how much they can attend to and remember in problematic situations. There is also evidence that, left to their own devices, they are unlikely to realize whether or not they have actually examined a situation 'fully' (Vurpillot, 1976). Preschool children do not search exhaustively or systematically for evidence that might be relevant to what they are trying to do; they tend to make up their minds on the basis of a limited inspection of the situation at hand (in contrived problem situations, at least).

There is also evidence, again from contrived situations, that young children are unlikely to 'rehearse' what they are trying to remember. Thus, their powers of memory may be limited not only by an uncertain world but also because they have yet to learn (or to be taught) how best to remember what they seek to retain.

Given children's propensity to attend to a limited range of features of problematic situations and, perhaps, their immature strategies for deliberate memorization, a teacher will often have to scaffold their immediate actions.

They may, for example, *highlight* crucial features of the task situation that have been ignored or forgotten. In so doing, they also help the child to *analyse* the task. They may act as an external source of memory and planning for the child, either by prompting recall of a previous activity or, more subtly, by holding constant the fruits of past activities while the child concentrates his or her limited resources on another domain. For example, children in our task situation would often put together two pieces and then try to add a third one. The blocks are so designed that it is extremely difficult to put together four pieces without first constructing the two pairs. By directing the child's attention away from the first-assembled pair or by keeping hold of it while the child attempted to assemble the second pair, the instructor helped the child by breaking down a goal into a series of less complex sub-goals.

Scaffolding functions effectively support and augment learners' limited cognitive resources, enabling them to concentrate upon and master manageable aspects of the task. With experience, such elements of the task become familiar and the child is able to consider further related task elements. Contingent control helps to ensure that the demands placed on the child are likely to be neither too complex, producing defeat, nor too simple, generating boredom or distraction.

Teaching: natural and contrived

So far, we have been exploring the concepts of scaffolding, control and contingency in contrived encounters between adults and children in laboratory settings. We have also been dealing with very specific short-term learning outcomes in a well-structured, concrete task with a specific 'right' answer. Are such concepts useful in more naturalistic situations? Are the effects of contingent teaching task-specific or does it engender more general effects?

In this section, I will explore some attempts to extend the concepts of scaffolding and contingency to adult–child interactions in studies of language acquisition to see how far their use in this, more naturalistic, research involves more than a metaphorical relationship with their use in more formal specific contexts.

Bruner's (1983) account of the development of the pre-verbal foundations of language acquisition extends the concept of scaffolding to the analysis of mother–child interactions. He argues that the development of early linguistic competence in the child depends upon the (informal) teaching roles played by the adult. The development of the infant's communication abilities takes place within frequently recurring 'formats' of interaction. Initially, such formats (families of interactions such as simple games, feeding sessions, nappy changing etc., which take on a predictable pattern) are largely regulated by the adult and are the basis of what Bruner terms 'Language Acquisition Support Systems'. The frequent repetition of formats provides infants with opportunities to discover and exploit regularities in their experiences. Adults, however, play the major role in initiating and structuring the early interactional formats. Bruner writes:

> If the 'teacher' in such a 'system' were to have a motto, it would surely be 'where before there was a spectator, let there now be a participant'. One sets the game, provides a scaffold to assure that the child's ineptitudes can be rescued by appropriate intervention, and then removes the scaffold part by part as the reciprocal structure can stand on its own.
>
> (Bruner, 1983: 60)

Whilst he sees adults taking the leading role in the construction of such systems of support, it seems that what is involved is not so much a process of *directing* the child but one more akin to 'leading by following'. Once the child's involvement has been gained and he is inducted into activity that can be orchestrated into an emerging system of interaction, adults tend to make what they do contingent upon their interpretation of what is likely to be the current focus of interest or relevance to the child. Thus, 'it becomes feasible for the adult partner to highlight those features of the world that are already salient to the child and that have a basic or simple grammatical form'. To the extent that adults make where they look and what they do and say contingent upon their interpretation of the child's current interest, what they are likely to be putting into words is relevant to what is in the child's mind. Thus, adults help to bring the infant's experience of the world and linguistic communication about that world into contact.

Bruner's use of the concepts of scaffolding and contingency shares formal similarities with the processes described in the analysis of contrived teaching. The task of inducting the infant into what is to become a predictable format of interaction; supplementing and orchestrating the child's role in the inter-action by actions designed to highlight critical features of the joint task or activity; reducing degrees of freedom for action (buffering from distraction) to encourage the infant to focus on critical aspects of the situation; trying to hand over increasing responsibility for the execution of actions that have been constructed with the child; attempting to perform such functions in a manner that is contingent upon the child's activities, are important features of the teaching process, whether natural or contrived. Whilst I would argue, how-ever, that the scaffolding functions are common to both types of activity with children of very different ages, the means whereby such functions are achieved change with the developing competence of the infant. Induction, for example, changes from a process that we might term 'capture' to one of 'recruitment'. This change occurs in response to the (co-ordinated) development of planning and self-consciousness in the child.

For example, in the early encounters described by Bruner and others, what might initially be a 'chance' or unintentional act by the child may be high-lighted and responded to by the adult 'as if' it were an intended component of an envisaged performance. Such highlighting can be achieved by the adult performing a marked, exaggerated action or *display* that is contingent upon and follows closely in time behind the infant's activity. To the extent that this display captures the infant's attention and interest, it may evoke a repetition of the child's initial activity. Initially spontaneous, unpremeditated movements by the baby may thus form the basis for the emergence of intentional acts of communication.

A number of studies have highlighted the degree of 'fit' between both the content and timing of events that are likely to grasp the infant's attention and the 'natural' or spontaneous displays of adults (or even very young children) *en face* with the infant (e.g. Brazelton, 1982). The adult achieves induction of the infant by *capturing* his attention.

With older children, induction is easier in some contexts and more difficult in others. Once attention and interest can be solicited by verbal invitations or demonstrations, the teacher may evoke intentional action towards a goal from the child. As early as nine to 18 months, young children also display some knowledge of the fact that the adult can be *recruited* to help them in an activity that they are unable to bring off alone (Geppert and Kuster, 1983). By 30 months, teaching–learning encounters may be solicited by either party. Around the same age, however, infants also show evidence of wishing, at some times, to maintain the independence of their own actions, of wanting to 'do it myself'.

Although, as we have seen, it is possible to induce the preschooler into joint problem-solving, evidence from naturalistic observations in the home indicates that most encounters between young children and their parents are of the children's own choosing. In short, they tend to solicit rather than be inducted into most exchanges with parents.

The evidence comes from Wells (1979) who found, from audio-taped recordings of exchanges between parents and their three-year-olds at home, that 70 per cent of interactions were initiated by the child. Thus, what adults and child are likely to be working on, attending to and talking about is still largely determined by the *child's* interests.

Wells's analyses also indicate that parents who respond contingently to the child's utterances by elaborating, developing and negotiating about what they mean are more likely to engender conditions for establishing mutual understanding and the development of linguistic competence in the child. Although his analyses do not make explicit use of concepts such as scaffolding and control, he does employ the term contingency in a similar way. I suggest that his findings are consistent with the view that effective scaffolding and control are factors that influence the development of linguistic competence in children. To extend this argument, however, I need to make reference to other research in which the notions of control and contingency have been exploited to study the effects of different styles of talking to children on the child's performances in school contexts.

Asking and telling: who is contingent upon whom?

We are studying two complex systems that know things: teacher and child. We believe that these two systems are in asymmetrical states, in that the teacher knows more than the child and has responsibility for transferring that knowledge. The asymmetry is not entirely one-sided, however: the child also knows things about the world and himself that the teacher does not know. The desire to make teaching 'relevant', 'learner centred', to 'start where the learner is at' or to be contingent upon their attempts to learn is implicated in most theories of learning and development (Wood, 1980b). Thus, teachers must also seek to understand what the child knows if they are to help develop, extend, clarify and integrate that knowledge.

Wells's studies, in company with research by Tizard and her colleagues (Tizard and Hughes, 1984), suggest that preschool children tend to initiate interactions, ask questions and seek information more readily at home than at school. Much of their 'epistemic' activity is directed towards achieving explanations about facts of everyday life and is occasioned by happenings in the local culture. The parent tends to be in a privileged position in relation to these requests and demands, being a *part* of that culture. Their practices and talk are embedded in what it is that the child seeks to know. Further, their privileged access to the child's history provides a basis for intersubjectivity. Their implicit hypotheses about what is likely to have motivated an epistemic act from the child; what the child is already likely to have experienced in relation to it, to know, think and feel about it, are more likely than those of strangers to prove workable or enactable.

Thus, the conditions that promote the quest for knowledge from the child are often present in the home, and the needs of the child are most likely to be interpretable to those who know them. Conditions for the generation of a contingent learning environment are more likely to be endemic to the home or local culture in a way that they are not to school. Thus, the preschool child at nursery or school is less likely to be prompted to wonder about the 'whys' and 'wherefores' of what is going on, which is perhaps why their discourse often centres on the happenings of the moment and thus seems 'context-dependent'. When children *do* talk about things outside the classroom, not surprisingly it tends to be to mention significant others in their daily life (relatives), or the events, happenings, promises and surprises that occur at home (Wood, McMahon and Cranstoun, 1980).

Children, then, 'present' themselves differently at home and at school. Even when teachers set out to work with individual children, they face considerable difficulties in establishing a contingent interaction because children generally give them relatively few epistemic offerings to be contingent upon. Thus, task induction becomes a more demanding activity for the teacher than the parent (and, by the same token, for a psychologist in a laboratory setting: Wood, 1983). Other factors also operate against the establishment of child-initiated adult-contingent encounters. One is group size. At home, the presence of a third person, particularly a younger sibling, is likely to promote talk between parent and child about the actions, needs and morality of another (Dunn and Kendrick, 1982). Children, in their second year of life, begin to wonder about the nature of other people. At school, however, surrounded by numbers of relative strangers, observations by children about the 'psychology' of other people around are relatively rare (Wood *et al.*, 1980). Faced with groups of children, the teacher encounters purely numerical difficulties in any effort to promote and sustain productive encounters with individuals. Management of self, time and resources becomes an important feature of the teaching role. Any attempts to instruct or inform are thus embedded within a wider set of roles and objectives.

The common teacher response to these difficulties is to initiate and sustain interactions not by showing or telling but by demanding and asking. Both demands and questions are exercises in *control*. In a number of different studies, several classroom observers have noted the very high frequency of teacher questions. Such studies range from preschoolers to children about to leave school (Wood and Wood, 1985). Furthermore, teacher questions tend to display a number of 'special' characteristics. They are often specific, demanding a narrow range of possible 'right' answers (e.g. MacLure and French, 1981; Tizard, Philips and Plewis, 1976; Wood *et al.*, 1980). Teachers often know the answers to the questions they ask, and children, by four years of age, possess the ability to recognize this fact, in some contexts at least (Wood and Cooper, 1980). Furthermore, the readiness of children to talk about what they know is likely to be inhibited by such questions.

Several reasons have been given for the frequency and nature of teacher questions. Questioning groups is one strategy whereby (at best) the minds of all involved can be focused on the same idea or topic. Questions are one tactic for the achievement of 'group intersubjectivity'. When a child is not forthcoming with numerous spontaneous epistemic acts, then questions will usually achieve a response and, therefore, may be used as tactics for initiating and, perhaps, modelling epistemic inquiry. Speculating further, it might be the case that the use of questioning represents a historical reaction to 'talk and chalk' or 'didactic' methods of education. Questioning may be seen as a tactic designed to engage the child actively in the teaching–learning process. Rather than 'passively' sitting and listening to the teacher's declarations, the child should be enjoined, through questions, to wonder and think about the topic at hand.

Whatever the rationale or 'cause' of frequent questioning by teachers, I would argue that the strategy is counter-productive.

If we accept the fact that, particularly with young children, what we seek to show them and tell them demands a knowledge of what they can already do and what and how they think about the task at hand, how are we to encourage them to display their knowledge? Focusing for the moment on mainly verbal exchanges, I suggest the following 'operationalized' definition of knowledge display. Children will ask questions about the topic, revealing their uncertainty and what they seek to know. They will take up openings to contribute to and comment upon the topic at hand. They may go beyond a direct answer to the teacher's questions to add additional information, ideas or observations that they consider supplement or qualify their answers. Further, if, as Wells argues, adult and child need to negotiate their perspectives on and objectives in a given domain, we may find that a child responds to the teacher's questions with requests for clarification or to negotiate the conditions under which they are prepared to answer.

These aspects of children's discourse define a set of conditions in which the teacher can gain access to the *child's* thoughts and uncertainties about opinions and attitudes towards the topic at hand.

These conditions are inhibited to the extent that teachers manage the interaction through questions. The more they question, the less children say. Children's contributions (even when an opportunity is given) become rarer and more terse, the more questions are asked (e.g. Wood and Wood, 1983). Children are only likely to go beyond the force of teachers' questions to give additional ideas and explanations if questions are relatively infrequent. In some contexts at least, they are less likely to seek information through questions themselves when the teacher is asking a lot of questions.

Pupils tend to take single 'moves' in dialogue with the teacher. Whereas teachers display a number of offerings in their turns (e.g. accepting what a child has said, offering a contribution to the discourse and immediately asking a question), pupils are most likely to make a single type of move. Thus, if the teacher terminates his or her utterance with a contribution (i.e. statement, opinion, speculation), children are likely to respond with a contribution of their own, more so if the teacher's contributions are frequent. Similarly, if a teacher accepts or acknowledges what a child says but offers no further question or observation, the child is likely to continue with the topic at hand. There are also a number of second-order effects of teaching style. The less a teacher interrogates children, the more likely they are to listen to, make contributions about and ask questions of what the other children say (Griffiths, 1983; Wood and Wood, 1983). Such findings occur as correlations between teaching style and pupil responses in natural classroom discourse, and can be brought about in experimentally contrived encounters in which teachers vary their style of responding to groups of children (Wood and Wood, 1983, 1984).

The extent to which a child reveals his or her own ideas and seeks information is thus inversely proportional to the frequency of teacher questions – and this finding embraces studies of preschool children through to 16-year-olds, deaf children and children acquiring English as a second language.

Some of the teachers who have participated in experimentally contrived classroom sessions, in which they have modified their style of talking to children by asking fewer questions, becoming less controlling and giving more of their own views and opinions, have commented that they found out things about the children's experiences, views and ideas that they did not know and would not have thought to ask questions about (Lees, 1981). Questions may solicit the information demanded by the teacher and serve as specific probes and checks for retention of information or of a child's capacity to draw inferences. As tools for finding out things that a child thinks or knows but that are not already anticipated or known by the teacher, however, they are ineffective, at least when used in excess. If it is a teacher's goal to discover 'where the child is at' in order to respond contingently to their ideas and thoughts, the established 'register' of the classroom is generally ineffective in achieving this goal. Teachers can, however, engender sessions in which children show more initiative, if they are prepared to ask fewer questions and say more about their own ideas and views. Just as effective teaching of practical skills demands a contingent combination of showing and telling, so the extension of children's understanding through discourse demands an integration of the declarative and interrogative voice.

There is now an extensive and growing literature on the 'effective use of questioning' (e.g. Blank, Rose and Berlin, 1978). Although the issue of what constitutes a 'good' and timely question is not resolved, and the literature on the effects and effectiveness of questions has produced somewhat equivocal results, a few general points and reasonable speculations are emerging from the literature. First, as we saw above, several researchers have concluded that too many teacher questions are 'closed' and lead children to search for specific right answers rather than into processes of reasoning and weighing evidence. Second, teachers tend to leave relatively short pauses after their questions before taking back control of the interaction. When they are helped to extend these pauses (from one to three seconds), the frequency and level of student response increase (Rowe, 1974; Swift and Gooding, 1983). It seems that pupils usually need more time to think about their answers to teacher questions than teachers normally allow. Questions to which the teacher already knows the answer are also common. Thus, the implicit theory of learning involved is one in which the teacher knows all the answers and the child's task is simply to find them. Sigel and his colleagues (Sigel and McGillicuddy-Delisi, 1988), analysing discourse between parents and children, have shown, for example, that more open-ended demanding parental questions (which, in Sigel's terms 'distance' the child from and encourage him to reflect upon his immediate experiences and concerns) are positively correlated with various measures of the child's intellectual development, whereas more closed questions are not. Similarly, Redfield and Rousseau (1981), in a review of questioning, concluded that the use of questions high in 'cognitive demand' by teachers has a positive effect on student achievement.

Unfortunately, however, studies in this area usually concentrate on comparisons of different types of questions and fail to explore any effects of different levels of teacher contributions of statements. In a small-scale study (Wood and Wood, 1983), we found that where a teacher offers contributions that are high in level of presentation (e.g. speculations, opinions, reasoning, etc.), children are likely to respond in kind. Questions high in cognitive demand (similar to the definitions of Blank *et al.*, 1978) also solicit high cognitive responses from children, but at the cost of inhibiting follow-through, elaboration or spontaneous comments from them. Where teachers, in one sense, answer their own putative questions to provide possible answers, opinions and so on, children as young as four years of age reciprocate by adopting a similar cognitive–linguistic stance and remain relatively active and forthcoming at the same time.

High control of interactions by teachers in natural or contrived encounters, in laboratory, home or school, are likely to inhibit overt epistemic activity from children. Furthermore, the fact that children are not contributing ideas, asking questions or elaborating on their answers to the teacher's questions, but spending the vast majority of their time in complying or answering questions means that their thinking (unless they 'drop out' of the interaction) is almost entirely contingent upon the demands of the teacher. If teachers are not gaining knowledge from the children, then they have few opportunities for making any questions, comments or ideas that they have contingent upon the children's own thoughts, for these are simply not revealed or displayed.

The role played by children in teaching–learning encounters is fundamentally constrained by the way in which teachers manipulate control. If a child is not active, forthcoming and curious about the task at hand, the main cause of this inactivity may lie not in some 'inner resource' lacked by the child, but in the level of control and ensuing lack of opportunity for contingent instruction determined by the manner in which the teacher orchestrates the interaction.

Teaching as epistemic inquiry

Teaching is usually defined as the *transmission* of knowledge and the inculcation of skills and understanding. Such definitions seem reasonable but are inadequate and even misleading. Teaching also involves learning; it provides opportunities for the acquisition of knowledge. It is epistemic activity. Furthermore, the knowledge obtained from acts of teaching informs the process of effective teaching.

Piaget has characterized the child as a 'natural' epistemologist. We have not rejected this basic stance but have argued that the epistemological activity of the child is, and often must be, enveloped within that of a teacher. Piaget has also demonstrated how the study of the systematic and 'universal' errors that children make can be exploited to investigate the nature and development of knowledge. Similarly, I have suggested that the study of 'errors after instructions' is a primary basis for learning about the learner, learning, what is being learned and teaching. An instruction from a teacher is, potentially, an epistemic probe as well as an attempt to prompt epistemic activity in the child. If it is treated as a hypothesis about the child's 'zone of proximal development', for example, then a failure to comply by the child suggests that the hypothesis may be invalid and that he or she needs more help. Conversely, success serves as a signal to the teacher to update her hypothesis about where the child is 'at' and, hence, to revise future instruction or, in Bruner's economic metaphor, to 'up the ante'. Teachers may utilize the fate of their own instructions as a basis for learning and revising their 'theory' of the child and what he or she is learning. The tremendous difficulties in doing this in school environments, however, often preclude such contingent instruction, and demand, essentially, that it is the child who must make his or her thinking contingent upon that of the teacher. If children are able and willing to be contingent upon the thought processes and actions of another, then learning may proceed. If they are not, then it seems unlikely that learning will follow.

Although we have been stressing the importance of teaching and exploring the complex questions of what effective instruction involves, this does not imply that effective teaching is a sufficient or always a necessary condition for learning. We have not been advocating a return to classical learning theory nor rejecting the now extensive evidence that shows that young children form hypotheses, infer and generalize rules to make creative and productive use of their experiences. What we have tried to identify are some factors in natural and contrived encounters that serve to facilitate or inhibit such epistemic activities by the young child. Such a view leads us, for example, to attribute failure or lack of progress by a learner not simply to factors located 'in' the child but to constraints that arise as an emergent property of teacher–learner interactions. These, in turn, are tightly constrained by the nature of the institutions that we have invented to bring teachers and learners together. If we find ourselves dissatisfied with the interactions that take place in such institutions, measured against what we take to be the optimum contexts for learning, then we must question not simply the teacher's 'skills' but the form of the institution within which we expect these to be deployed.

References and further reading

Blank, M., Rose. S. A. and Berlin, L. J. (1978) *The Language of Learning: the Preschool Years*, New York: Grune & Stratton.

Brazelton, T. B. (1982) 'Joint regulation of neonate–parent behavior', in E. Z. Tronick (ed.) *Social Interchange in Infancy: Affect, Cognition and Communication*, Baltimore, MD: University Park Press.

Bruner, J. S. (1968) *Toward a Theory of Instruction*, New York: Norton.

Bruner, J. S. (1973) 'The organisation of early skilled action', *Child Development* 44: 1–11.

Bruner, J. S. (1983) *Child's Talk: Learning to Use Language*, Oxford: Oxford University Press.

Cole, M. and Scribner, S. (1974) *Culture and Thought: a Psychological Introduction*, New York: Wiley.

Cole, M., Hood, L. and McDermott, R. (1979) *Ecological Niche Picking*, New York: Rockefeller University Monographs.

Donaldson, M. (1978) *Children's Minds*, London: Fontana.

Dunn, J. and Kendrick, C. (1982) *Siblings: Love, Envy and Understanding*, London: Grant McIntyre.

Geppert, U. and Kuster, U. (1983) 'The emergence of "wanting to do it oneself": a precursor of achievement motivation', *International Journal of Behavioral Development* 6: 355–70.

Glachan, M. and Light, P. (1982) 'Peer interaction and learning: can two wrongs make a right?', in G. Butterworth and P. Light (eds) *Social Cognition: Studies of the Development of Understanding*, Brighton: Harvester.

Greenfield, P. M. and Bruner, J. S. (1969) 'Culture and cognitive growth', in D. A. Goslin (ed.) *Handbook of Socialisation Theory and Research*, New York: Rand McNally.

Griffiths, A. J. (1983) 'The linguistic competence of deaf primary school children', Ph.D. thesis, University of Nottingham.

Lees, J. M. (1981) 'Conversational strategies with deaf children', M.Phil. thesis, University of Nottingham.

MacLure, M. and French, P. (1981) 'A comparison of talk at home and school', in G. Wells (ed.) *Learning Through Interaction: the Study of Language Development*, London: Cambridge University Press.

Mercer, N. and Edwards, D. (1981) 'Ground rules for mutual understanding', in N. Mercer (ed.) *Language in School and Community*, London: Edward Arnold.

Murphy, C. M. and Wood, D. J. (1981) 'Learning from pictures: the use of pictorial information by young children', *Journal of Experimental Child Psychology* 32: 279–97.

Piaget, J. and Inhelder, B. (1969) *The Psychology of the Child*, London: Routledge & Kegan Paul.

Redfield. D. L. and Rousseau, E. W. (1981) 'A meta-analysis of experimental research on teacher questioning behavior', *Review of Educational Research* 51: 237–45.

Rowe, M. B. (1974) 'Wait-time and rewards as instructional variables, their influence on language, logic and fate control. I. Wait time', *Journal of Research in Science Teaching* 11: 81–94.

Sigel. I. and McGillicuddy-Delisi, I. (1988) 'Parents as teachers to their children', in A. Pellegrini and T. Yawkey (eds) *The Development of Oral and Written Language*, Norwood, NJ: Ablex.

Swift, J. N. and Gooding, C. T. (1983) 'Interaction of wait time, feedback and questioning instruction on middle school science teaching', *Journal of Research in Science Teaching* 20: 721–30.

Tizard. B. and Hughes, M. (1984) *Young Children Learning: Talking and Thinking at Home and School*, London: Fontana.

Tizard, B., Philips, J. and Plewis, I. (1976) 'Staff behaviour in pre-school centres', *Journal of Child Psychology and Psychiatry* 17: 251–64.

Vurpillot. E. (1976) *The Visual World of the Child*, London: George Allen & Unwin.

Vygotsky, L. S. (1978) *Mind in Society: the Development of Higher Psychological Processes*, Cambridge, Mass.: Harvard University Press.

Walkerdine, V. (1982) 'From context to text: a psychosemiotic approach to abstract thought', in M. Beveridge (ed.) *Children Thinking Through Language*, London: Arnold.

Weikart, D. P. (1973) Cited in Brainerd, C. J. (1983) 'Modifiability of cognitive development', in S. Meadows (ed.) *Developing Thinking: Approaches to Children's Cognitive Development*, London and New York: Methuen.

Wells, G. (1979) 'Variation in child language', in P. Fletcher and M. Garman (eds) *Language Acquisition*, Cambridge: Cambridge University Press.

Wood, D. J. (1980a) 'Teaching the young child: some relationships between social interaction, language and thought', in D. Olson (ed.) *Social Foundations of Language and Cognition: Essays in Honor of J. S. Bruner*, New York: Norton.

Wood, D. J. (1980b) 'Models of childhood', in A. J. Chapman and D. M. Jones (eds) *Models of Man*, London: The British Psychological Society.

Wood, D. J. (1983) 'Teaching: natural and contrived', *Child Development Society Newsletter*, no. 32, London: Institute of Education.

Wood, D. J. and Cooper, P. J. (1980) 'Maternal facilitation of 4–5 year old children's memory for recent events', *Proceedings of the XXIInd International Congress of Psychology*, Leipzig, East Germany: International Union of Psychological Science.

Wood, D. J. and Middleton, D. J. (1975) 'A study of assisted problem solving', *British Journal of Psychology* 66: 181–91.

Wood, D. J. and Wood, H. A. (1985) 'Teacher questions and pupil initiative', paper to the American Educational Research Association, Chicago, USA.

Wood, D. J., Bruner, J. S. and Ross, G. (1976) 'The role of tutoring in problem solving', *Journal of Child Psychology and Psychiatry* 17: 89–100.

Wood, D. J., Wood, H. A. and Middleton, D. J. (1978) 'An experimental evaluation of four face-to-face teaching strategies', *International Journal of Behavioral Development* 1: 131–47.

Wood, D. J., McMahon, L. and Cranstoun, Y. (1980) *Working with Under-fives*, London: Grant McIntyre.

Wood, D. J., Wood, H. A., Griffiths, A. J., Howarth, P. and Howarth, C. I. (1982) 'The structure of conversations with 6- to 10-year-old deaf children', *Journal of Child Psychology and Psychiatry* 23: 295–308.

Wood, H. A. and Wood, D. J. (1983) 'Questioning the pre-school child', *Educational Review* 35: Special Issue (15), 149–62.

Wood, H. A. and Wood, D. J. (1984) 'An experimental evaluation of five styles of teacher conversations on the language of hearing-impaired children', *Journal of Child Psychology and Psychiatry* 25: 45–62.

Woodhead, M. (1985) 'Pre-school education has long effects: but can they be generalized?', *Oxford Review of Education* 11: 133–55.

Chapter 10

Adult–child interaction, joint problem solving and the structure of cooperation*

Mariëtte Hoogsteder, Robert Maier and Ed Elbers

Introduction

A mother helps her 4-year-old daughter to do a task. They are building a tower with Duplo blocks according to a model that we had provided (cf., Elbers, Maier, Hoekstra and Hoogsteder, 1992). Although the child is fairly competent, the mother intervenes regularly in order to correct errors and to make suggestions. Halfway through the task, the mother goes to the kitchen for a moment. During this interval, about one and a half minutes, the child goes on building the tower. She succeeds in completing part of the tower all by herself, by comparing the tower with the model and selecting and placing the pieces correctly. As soon as the mother comes back, the child stops working and asks "What next?"

This observation illustrates the issues we will be concerned with in this chapter. The dyad organized its cooperation according to two distinct patterns of interaction: a pattern in which the mother regulates the building of the tower, and a pattern in which the child controls the building on her own with the mother only present in the background. Moreover, in addition to building the tower, the parent and the child have to build their interaction. With her question "What next?", the child invites her mother to renegotiate the division of roles between them. The child does not only acquire competence in the construction of a tower according to a model, the task is also an "exercise in collectivity" for her (Bruner, 1986, p. 132): it involves negotiating and disagreeing, exchanging and sharing information, knowing when to follow the adult's instructions and when not to.

Many studies on problem solving by adult–child dyads have concentrated on the process of teaching and learning. They rarely focused on interaction patterns, on the way in which adult and child negotiate and reach an agreement about how to cooperate. Researchers assumed that the conditions of cooperation could be taken for granted. The assumption was that adult and

* This is an edited version of an article that appeared in *Learning and Instruction*, 6(4), 1996.

child would engage in an instructive interaction, with the former in a teaching and the latter in a learning role. However, these conditions do not occur as a matter of course: they are constructed, they are the subject of negotiation and change. Each interaction is a construction, to which the participants bring their experiences, repertoires and the previous history of their relationship (cf., Minuchin, 1985). The outcome can certainly be didactic interaction, but a diversity of other interaction patterns is also available to the dyad.

In the first part of this chapter, we will discuss the modes of interaction (cf., Elbers *et al.*, 1992) that dyads use to mould their cooperation. What are the characteristics of these modes and how can they be recognized by an observer? In the second part, we will discuss a case-study of an interaction within a didactic mode of interaction. We will concentrate on the negotiations during the interaction and show how actively the child is involved in the construction and maintenance of the cooperation.

Some assumptions about adult–child interaction

A major problem in the field is that many studies have implicitly adopted a unidirectional approach. The focus is on how adults direct and control the interaction, while there is a conspicuous lack of interest in children's contribution. A transfer view on learning is at the basis of this account on adult–child interaction. The adult's regulation and management of the problem solving are thought to be transmitted to the child. In the course of time, the child learns to do the task independently, using the regulative strategies that the adult has taught in the past. The adult is the architect of the collaboration; the child only carries out the adult's instructions.

Instead of focusing the attention solely on the adult, we prefer to study the way in which the participants influence one another (cf., Stafford and Bayer, 1993) and the way in which they shape their cooperation. We regard children as actively involved in task situations in which they need assistance from an adult. They do not necessarily have a subordinate position, and they negotiate with the adult about how to proceed. The process of doing a task is not dominated by an adult, but jointly regulated by adult and child.

A related problem is that researchers of adult–child interaction tend to connect the child's learning in an interaction rigidly to the instructive behaviour of the adult. The origin of this view is, we think, their educational interest in how educators can most effectively stimulate a child's development. Research was designed in order to explore which kind of instruction is the most useful for children, what levels of abstraction adults may employ, and how effective communication can be brought about (for example, Wood, Bruner and Ross, 1976; Wood, Wood and Middleton, 1978).

However, there is more to children's learning than following the adult's lead. From the view on learning we adopt, a child's persistence in following his or her own way is not necessarily unconstructive. Rather, those kinds of actions can often be considered as genuine attempts to contribute to a solution of a task, even if they are clearly wrong or in disagreement with the adult's suggestions. Therefore, we argue for studying adult–child interaction from the assumption that the child's learning does not necessarily depend on the adult's correct and proper way of intervening.

A third problem is connected to comparative research of adult–child interaction. This research has convincingly shown that there is no universal format for instruction (e.g., Greenfield and Lave, 1982; Wertsch, Minick and Arns, 1984). Rogoff (1990) distinguishes between two cultural patterns for learning through adult–child interaction. In Western middle-class communities, situations are adapted to children. In many non-Western cultures, however, children are adapted to situations; they are involved by adults in the life of the community, first as close observers and gradually as participants.

The danger here is that culture is taken as an independent variable for explaining the observed interactions that are taken as dependent variables. We would rather take a more constructivist stance: there is a variety of cultural options open to an adult–child dyad. Every culture provides adults and children with a repertoire of interaction formats or patterns. Although these patterns certainly borrow their meaning from the wider sociocultural context, there is no one-to-one relationship between culture and adult–child interaction.

To summarize, we wish to contribute to the field by emphasizing the construction of adult–child interaction. In particular, we want to study how adult and child shape their cooperation and how the child learns, not only about the task at hand, but also about problem solving as a joint enterprise. With Jerome Bruner, we believe that

> we shall be able to interpret meanings and meaning-making in a principled manner only in the degree to which we are able to specify the structure and coherence of the larger contexts in which specific meanings are created and transmitted.
>
> (Bruner, 1991, pp. 64–65)

In order to write this chapter, we have drawn from our observations in two adult–child interaction studies, involving various problem-solving tasks – construction tasks – and including children from 3 to 5 years old (Elbers *et al.*, 1992; Maier, Elbers and Hoekstra, 1992; Hoogsteder and Elbers, 1994; Hoogsteder, 1995). The adults were the children's parents (or other caregivers) and all interactions were videotaped at their homes. Parents were told that our interest was in investigating how children can solve a practical task with possible assistance by the parent. They were asked to assist the child in their own way and whenever they thought it necessary.

The variety of interactions we observed is partly dependent on the arrangements made with the parents. They participated on a voluntary basis, and appointments were made to come to their homes. It was up to them to prepare their child. Once we arrived, the parent set the scene by indicating a working-space (table, couch or floor) and by getting the attention of the child in question. Other children present were occupied with something else, and the participation of the adult meant that usual household tasks were ignored and that adults dedicated their time to joint problem solving with the child. This whole scene probably also meant that adults (re)presented themselves as "good" parents, discarding, for example, fights or arguments.

Modes of adult–child interaction: status and types

A mode of interaction is a certain type of interaction, a genre, with a typical dynamic. It is the framework giving meaning to the overall activity of the participants, comparable to Leont'ev's activity (1981) as, for example, investigated by Wertsch *et al.* (1984). On the basis of an analysis of 25 parent–child dyads, we distinguished three modes of interaction. We will first give a brief provisional description, and discuss them more systematically later.

A *playful mode of interaction*. Adult and child played together. The aim of constructing a tower was not altogether ignored, but was rather secondary to the aim of maintaining a pleasurable relationship between the participants. In one case, for example, the quality of "togetherness", a kind of playful, almost sensuous, interaction between a father and daughter, governed the entire interaction. The daughter followed eagerly and in delight any hint given by her father, and was rewarded with kisses and other emotional back-channels.

An *economic and efficient mode*. Some dyads were mainly concerned with the correct and rapid execution of the task, avoiding conflicts or troubles between them or with the task as much as possible. If the child was not competent enough for an efficient completion of the task, the adult gave a minimum of instructions or commands to enable the task to be carried out, or she took over the entire responsibility for the task.

A *didactic mode of interaction*. Quite a few parents left a lot of space and time for explorations by the child, which could lead to errors and (self-)corrections. Those errors were seized as opportunity, for example, for explaining the rules of the task by the adult. Adults intervened when asked by the child or in order to clarify errors, or in order to evaluate the procedure followed.

Characteristics

What kind of criteria can be used for distinguishing and classifying the various types of interactions as belonging to one mode or another? How can modes be recognized by an observer? Although the modes of interaction are typified globally, they need to be justified and can be recognized by a combination of significant local elements. A mode of interaction can be specified by the following characteristics:

1   the role distribution between adult and child;
2   the instruments at their disposal, and in particular the forms of communication between adult and child;
3   the aim(s) pursued.

Role distribution concerns the symmetrical or asymmetrical constellation of responsibilities for the participants. Symmetry is an essential characteristic of play, so in a playful mode the participants have, in principle, equal opportunities. In efficient and economic interactions, the most competent participant (the adult) controls and dominates the other (the child) at all times in order to reach the goal either rapidly, or with a minimum of effort and fuss. The role distribution is asymmetrical. In didactic interactions, the expert will monitor the contributions of the child, and the child will have numerous opportunities to explore and to make mistakes. Therefore, with regard to responsibilities, a didactic mode has a layered structure. This means that the adult will not control each specific action of the child, but will keep an eye on the various actions of the child with regard to her understanding of the task and with regard to a satisfying solution. On the one hand, the participants have asymmetrical roles – the adult monitoring the actions of the child – but on the other hand, there is a specific form of symmetry, because adult and child attempt to reach a common understanding.

A role distribution also involves a particular *kind of identity* for the participants. In a playful mode, the participants adopt fictional identities belonging to the kind of play agreed on. In an efficient mode, the adult or expert will strictly control the procedure for reaching the goal in a minimum of time or effort, which reduces the child to a role of sole executor of those parts of the task that she can do correctly. The adult has an identity as manager and performer of all other aspects of the task. In a didactic mode of interaction, the identities of the participants are more subtle: the adult will monitor the activities of the child, and in this sense adopts an identity as manager, but the child has, at the same time, an identity of competent participant and one who can work on specific aspects of non-competence through participation.

The *instruments* at the disposal of the participants are mainly communicative instruments, such as demands, requests, orders, but also postures, gestures and other body-language conveying agreement or doubt. In play, we encounter role-playing and the associated forms of communication that are all of the register of adopted identities. In efficient interactions, communication is governed by a means–end rationality that is characteristic for this mode of interaction and often has the form of (indirect) commands, either with words or with gestures. In the didactic mode of interaction, one can encounter a great variety of communicative means, for example advice or encouragement, illustrations, explanations, suggestions, evaluative remarks, but also proposals by both parties to review what has been achieved up to now at a meta-level.

The *aims* pursued are of two kinds. Firstly, there are practical aims concerning the manner of proceeding with the task. For example, in the efficient and economic mode, the result-oriented production of the task is the aim, and therefore errors are prevented as much as possible. Secondly, there are aims concerning the participants. In play, an aim can be to seek pleasure and delight. In a didactic interaction, the aim is to transform the non-competent participant (the child) – as far as his or her knowledge on a specific point is concerned – into a competent one, and thus to transform the relationship between the participants. Errors are not prevented but seized as learning or teaching opportunities. A mode of interaction not observed in our studies, but present in many experimental studies in which an adult experimenter interacts with a child, is a test mode (e.g., Elbers and Kelderman, 1994; for an overview see Schubauer-Leoni and Grossen, 1993). Here the aim is that one participant evaluates the capability of the other in performing a task without any assistance.

In addition to the three characteristics of modes, observations about the order in and closure of a certain mode may help to recognize a mode.

First, participants systematically distinguish between what is *usual* and what is *exceptional* within an ongoing interaction. Parents and their children seem to be quite competent – when interacting in a specific mode – to discriminate between the ordinary and the unconventional. What is usual and belongs to the interaction is more or less self-evident, whereas the exceptional is easily identified as not acceptable within that particular mode. Let us illustrate with some examples.

In a playful interaction between a father and his daughter, the play was that the daughter followed any suggestion of her father without any autonomous initiative, for which she was rewarded every time. At some moments, she did something that was in some sense outside the agreed play – an autonomous selection of a block for the tower – but she spontaneously stopped with these initiatives, being apparently aware of the fact that these actions belonged to another game, in which she would have a different role.

An efficient or economic mode has a result-oriented agenda, and any disruption of this procedure, for example by making a mistake or by playing with the blocks without a task-relevant result, is immediately identified.

Didactic interactions are a rather particular case. Within this mode of interaction, a great variety of actions may occur, because of the combination of symmetrical and asymmetrical role distributions. However, all these actions will be coordinated at some phase of the interaction. This coordination establishes a shared understanding of the task and will finally lead to a correct execution of the task, although probably preceded by many errors. So a block that is selected correctly by the child but not put exactly on the right place may be left there for a while. This typically happens when the child is busy with part of the task and focusing her efforts on some aspect while neglecting others. In this sense, an error is perfectly normal and usual for a didactic interaction. However, in the long run, this incorrect placement will be taken up at some moment, for example when the child recognizes a similar error with another block. The child herself may go back to the former block and correct the error, or the adult may guide the child in doing this. We may state that in a didactic interaction, errors are exceptional only in the long run, because all actions will be linked and coordinated with each other and with the aim of the task in order to increase participation of the child.

This brings us to a second feature, the particular *sequential* order of actions. In a didactic mode, various sequences of corrections, evaluations and explanations are possible, but most steps will be reconsidered in a later phase of the interaction. This means that all particular actions will be integrated in a meaningful whole at some moment. In an efficient mode, however, the management of the procedure for completing the task is taken over completely by the adult. The chosen procedure will then fully determine the order of the actions. Actions will not be reconsidered; for example, the correct placement of a block has its own value, and will not be related to the placement of an earlier block with the same principle. In play, once the "rules of the game" have been established, just about anything can happen as long as it fits into the play agreed on.

To a certain extent, we suppose that modes of interaction are structured totalities, and this view is supported by the function of conflicts. During some interactions, one of the participants (usually the child) stops acting and functioning according to the characteristics of the agreed mode. A conflict arises, a clash between one mode and another. This can be settled only if the participants renegotiate (explicitly or implicitly) and agree on how to proceed further. Sometimes they will adopt another mode of interaction, adjusting their actions accordingly; sometimes they will proceed in the old mode. In the example at the beginning of this chapter, the girl was eager to go back to a didactic mode in which her mother made suggestions for the task, after she had been building part of the tower independently.

We argue that modes of interaction are more or less closed structures, but open to change and applicable to a wide range of practical situations. Trespassing or disrupting a mode may result in a conflict – for example when a child is making mistakes on purpose, or when she asks her mother "what next?" while she has shown to be quite competent on her own – but by conflict one might pass from one mode to another. This pattern of changing modes was found in several dyads. Conflicts are therefore not exclusively disruptive, but also constructive; it is by conflict that switches from one mode to another can be realized.

As a preliminary conclusion, modes of interaction – classified globally and characterized locally – can be powerful frameworks for participants, although they may not be aware in which mode they interact and how this affects their (inter)actions. We will now have a closer look at how participants in a concrete interaction realize their cooperation.

The structure of cooperation in a didactic mode of interaction: a case-study

In order to illustrate the way in which a parent and a child cooperate, a case-study of one dyad interacting in a didactic mode will be presented. The choice of a case-study as a methodological procedure for presenting data and making argumentative claims may need clarification. Analogous to the claims made by studies on conversation and discourse analysis, case-studies on adult–child interaction serve to support certain types of claim (see Jackson, 1986; Jacobs, 1986). None of these claims is of a quantitative nature – about what frequently or usually happens – because such claims need evidence different from the evidence in a case-study. Case-studies serve other functions. First, a case-study may be evidence for something that had, until then, been unnoticed. A single case suffices to show the contrary, provided that readers regard the case as recognizable. Second, a case-study may serve as support for analysing the organization or structure of an interaction. Structures, simple or complex, cannot be explained with discrete, quantifiable data. Third, a case-study has an heuristic function. A well-done analysis has a demonstrative power that may generate new relevant questions and hypotheses concerning adult–child interaction.

The aim of the following case-study is to show how parent and child, interacting in a didactic mode, structure their cooperation with regard to a task. In line with this structure, their responsibility for acting, and hence the child's participation and learning, is distributed accordingly.

The dyad consists of a girl aged 3 years 7 months and her mother. The girl will be called Claire (C) and her mother Amy (A). Their case is drawn from a study with 15 caregivers and their 3-year-old children (Hoogsteder, 1995). The task was to build a tower of 13 wooden blocks (see Figure 10.1).

Episodes

In order to manage the problem of building a tower, the dyad has to divide the task into manageable steps. We called these steps *episodes*, a series of meaningful actions that form the interaction. An episode can be seen as a structural equivalent of a textual paragraph. The structure of both text and adult–child interaction can be marked by an author or by the interacting participants respectively by means of various instruments. For example, texts can be structured by punctuation marks, blank lines, choice of adverbs or topic shifts (Brown and Yule, 1983). Interactions can be structured by actions, pauses, regulations or goal-setting. We took goal-directed acting as a criterion for identifying episodes. An episode in an interaction is defined as a series of meaningful actions in which a *goal* is set by the dyad, implicitly or explicitly agreed on, performed and (sometimes) evaluated (See also Elbers *et al.*, 1992). Pauses, gestures and

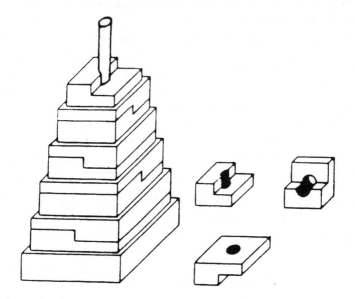

Figure 10.1 Construction task used with mothers

other acts or utterances can support the marcation of one episode from another.

How episodes structure an interaction

The transcription in Figure 10.2 presents the first 2 minutes and 45 seconds and starts after the introduction of the task by the researcher.

In each episode, the verbal formulation of the goal that is central for that specific part of the interaction is in *italics*. In the first episode (from line 1 to line 5), the dyad is concerned with the seriation aspect of the task; their searching for the biggest block. Claire selects the big yellow block (line 2), her mother explicitly states their goal of searching for the biggest one (lines 4–5). Claire again selects the yellow block as the biggest one (line 8), her mother disagrees with her choice and suggests looking for another big block (lines 10–12). Claire takes another block, checks her choice by comparing the blue block with the black base of the tower, and then places the blue one on the spindle (lines 12–13). Her mother evaluates with "right" (line 14). These series of actions form the first episode.

Then a new problem arises, it is not the selection of the blue block that is questioned, but its placement on the spindle. This problem is explained by Amy (lines 16–20) and verified by Claire. Amy then suggests a new goal; the blue block does "need another one" (line 22). She formulates the goal in terms

A: 1 Now, we'll have a try then (.) it is quite a
very difficult high tower, isn't it?

             C takes a big yellow block
             and

What do you think? (.) *the biggest one is*
  5 *always down under,* uh? (.) You should first
look for the biggest one

             puts it on the stick

C: [whispering] This one

             C points to the yellow one on the stick

A: 10 That one? (.) you could take another one
that's very big (.) and have a look which
one is the biggest

             C takes off the yellow one from the stick,
             takes big blue one, compares it to the
             black base, puts it on the stick upside
             down

     right

I

Hey (.) There is something strange, isn't
there (.) do you see? (.) What do you see
here? (.) That wasn't quite like this when
Mariëtte had the tower (.) Then it fitted
  20 nicely (.) How is that possible?

             A points to 'hole' under the blue block,
             C watches

Would it need another one?

             C nods, puts yellow one down and takes
             little blue one

  25 You should first (.) yes (.) wait a moment
II

             A takes off big blue one, C lays down little
             blue one

Do you know what you should do first? (.)
We have this one (.) that's the biggest one,
but there is *another one, that is as big*

  30

             C points to yellow one, looks at other
             blocks on the table, takes big red one

Is that one as big?
III   That one is as big, isn't it? (.)
So suppose you place that one on top of it
  35

             C places red block upside down on blue

No (.) No it doesn't fit yet (.) And when
you turn it

             block, on table

             C turns around red one, places it with
             thick side on thick side of blue block

  40 Look (.) No, it isn't yet *one block* (.) *How
will it become one block?*

continued

		C brings red one to the stick
	No. (.) Look carefully (.) If you turn it like this	A constructs red and blue block together, red on top of blue one
	45 Hey (.) do you see this? (.) you should have a look at this side (.) Now it has become	
IV	one big block, hasn't it? (.)	A turns the block and points to the side
	Now it can be put on the tower	
		C laughs and takes the big pair of blocks
	50 Yes	together as pair
C:	51 It is going to break down	C brings pair to the stick and tries to put it on the stick
A:	Yes, it slips apart a little bit (.) Could you do them both together? (.) Just hold them	
	55 real tight	
C:	It won't work	C stands up to have more strength and places the pair of blocks on the stick
A:	It works very well (.) really good	
V		C takes the big yellow one and wants to
C:	[whispering] Now this one	place it on the stick
A:	Hey no, again you should look for *two that belong together* (.) Which ones are equally	
	65 big?	C takes the big green one
	Yes, I think so too	
C:	I don't know that tower	C tries to fit yellow and green one, constructs a pair and places them on the
A:	70 Just try (.) watch the piece carefully (.) turning, very good	stick
		C turns the blocks on the stick a little, places them neatly and looks at the tower
	Really good sweetheart (.) Beautiful, isn't it, with all those colours together (.) wonderful	
VI		

Figure 10.2 Transcribed excerpt of interaction between Amy and Claire

Notes: A = Adult (Amy); C = Child (Claire, 3.7 years); (.) = small pause; blank line = longer pause; ___ = end marcation of episode. The formulation of a new goal is marked by *italics*.

of belonging. Claire nods and searches for a corresponding block; she selects a small blue one, implicitly defining the question of belonging in terms of colour. This is the second episode, concerning the selection of a block related to the big blue one, in order to make it fit.

Her mother then formulates a new goal, because the block needed should not be selected in terms of colour, but in terms of size. She formulates the goal explicitly, "another one, that is as big" (line 29). This is the goal for the third episode. Claire searches for a block as big as the blue one, selects a red block (lines 30–31) and now holds the two biggest blocks, so this goal has been performed, which is acknowledged by Amy (line 33).

The fourth episode concerns yet another aspect of the task, the construction of a pair out of the two biggest blocks. This is formulated by Amy in lines 34 and in 40–41. Claire tries a few times, but eventually it is Amy who performs the goal, by placing the two blocks on top of each other, so they become "one big block" (lines 43–47).

The fifth episode involves placing the pair on the stick. Claire marks her recognition of the new goal by a smile and she supports her understanding of this and the previous goal (line 51); the two blocks form one pair, but by holding them in her small hands, the pair nearly breaks apart. She eventually places the pair of blocks on the stick.

Altogether, this part of the interaction is divided into five episodes, each one with a distinct goal. The dyad needs these five episodes before the two biggest blocks are put together on the stick as a pair. The fact that the goals of episodes IV and V – the construction and placement of a pair of blocks respectively – involve a *pair* of blocks and not two separated blocks, is illustrative of the rest of the building process. During the part of the inter- action in the sixth episode, the goal involves the selection and placement of one pair of blocks. This goal is formulated again by Amy (lines 63–64), but the separate goals of construction and placement are no longer explicitly formulated, because these are performed automatically together (lines 68– 70). After that (not shown in the excerpt), the dyad finishes the whole tower within two more episodes: one episode for the third pair of blocks, and another episode for the smallest three pairs and the final block-on-top, which are placed successively without any new goals being explicitly set.

During the entire interaction, the number of blocks placed in one episode increases. The first pair of blocks is placed during episodes I–V, the second pair of blocks is placed in episode VI, the third pair of blocks is placed in episode VII, and the fourth to sixth pairs and the block-on-top are placed in episode VIII. This means that the terms in which Claire and Amy set goals change. The excerpt in Figure 10.2 indicates that in episode I the goal con- cerns the size of one block, while in episode VI the goal is to select, construct and place one pair of blocks. In episode VIII (not in Figure 10.2) the goal is to finish the tower, the rules governing its construction now having become self-evident. Claire's participation in episode VI is built on the dyad's way of setting goals. She now understands and performs a goal that is formulated not in terms of separate blocks (as was the case in episodes I, II and III), but in terms of pairs of blocks. So, one way of learning during the course of this interaction is exemplified in the *kinds* of goal the dyad sets and performs in the successive episodes. Claire's understanding improves in terms of the goals she can handle. She has learned through participating in the earlier episodes (although her responsibility was low), as appears from her ability to deal with goal formulations in terms of pairs of blocks in the later episodes. This is an improvement compared to the start of the interaction, where the goals were formulated and performed in terms of the selection or placement of one block.

In the case of Claire and Amy, it is clearly shown how a kind of symmetry can be found in their interaction. This symmetry was not found in dyads interacting in an efficient mode, because the parents set the goals for an efficient construction of the tower, which meant that the child participated under the conditions of the parent.

It is important to realize that any adult and child have to construct their goals for acting on the spot. The goals emerge out of the dyad's interaction itself, specifically for the purpose of this problem-solving situation, and there is no predefined way of doing this. In the case of Amy and Claire, it might seem that Amy is responsible for the construction of goals. But although Claire's participation in the construction of goals is peripheral, especially in the first half of the interaction, it is the dyad who should be held responsible for the construction of goals. Amy and Claire have to negotiate the construction of a goal that can be agreed upon by both of them. For example, the goal in episode III, the selection of the two biggest blocks, can be seen as the outcome of such negotiations. This goal was first formulated as a selection of two blocks that belong together (in episode II), but Claire looked for a combination in the same colour. This made her mother formulate a new goal that explicitly mentions an important rule of the tower: the fact that the blocks should be selected by size and not by colour. Claire's participation, and hence her negotiations, are primarily in the sphere of operations with the blocks and not in the sphere of speech. Still, it is important that the goal is agreed on by both of them. The fact that it has become a *joint* goal is confirmed in episode VI, where the goal is set in lines 63–64, and Claire selects and constructs a new pair of blocks without much help from her mother. Amy does not intervene after the goal has been formulated, neither does she make suggestions. No further negotiations are necessary, because the goal has become intersubjective and silently agreed upon.

A layered structure

As has been argued before, a typical characteristic of a didactic mode of interaction is its layered structure of symmetrical and asymmetrical responsibilities.

We will illustrate a way in which this becomes manifest with an example from the same dyad.

After the completion of the task by the dyad, Claire spontaneously – without the researcher or her mother asking or encouraging her to do so – started to take the tower apart with the aim of building it again. Although she is now more familiar with the tower, the situation remains a tutoring interaction in a didactic mode. In the beginning of this second building process, it seems that the joint goal-directed procedure of selecting two blocks, making them into a pair and placing them on the stick, has become intersubjective and implicit. This goal is formulated either in a very abbreviated form or not at all.

While placing the third pair of blocks, however, something strange happened. The two blocks came apart and fell down on the stick one after the other. Amy says: "You can do it like this as well, did you see that?", so that Claire realizes that their procedure of placing pairs could be replaced by a procedure of placing blocks one after the other. This incident has consequences for the interaction in the next episode, in which the dyad started renegotiating the procedure of constructing and placing pairs. Claire selects the correct blocks, constructs them into a pair on the table, and then tries to place the blocks on the stick one after the other. She needs five attempts before the blocks are placed correctly (see Figure 10.3)

In the end, she decides to do it the old way because "it is not possible like this". In her fifth and last attempt, she constructs the pair on the table and places them on the stick as a pair. Apparently, it was very difficult for her to

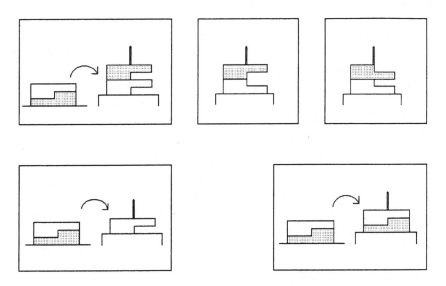

Figure 10.3 The child's incorrect and correct attempts within one episode

see that the position of the yellow block on *top of* the green one, as constructed on the table, is *not* the same as its position on the stick if placed as the *bottom* block of the pair. This is a problem she had not yet met, because in the old procedure, she placed both blocks on the stick as a pair instead of one by one. As a result of this problem, a break-down in the way the agreed goal is performed, the structure of the interaction becomes more complex. Four attempts result in incorrect placement of the blocks. It is not the goal itself that is brought up for discussion, but the (incorrect) result due to the way in which the goal is carried out. The *performance* of the goal becomes the focus of attention, resulting in a series of temporary subgoals. These subgoals within an episode lead to a layered structure of the interaction. The two layers in the structure of the interaction that can be discerned are (1) the agreed-on overall goal (placing a constructed pair of two blocks of the same size on the stick; this goal no longer needs negotiation) and (2) the temporary subgoals that are negotiated and performed, each with the intention of performing the overall goal, but four of them failing to do so.

Conclusions

The interaction between Claire and her mother is typical of a didactic mode. They take time to work on all the problems they come across (size, pair construction, placement on the stick), neither adult nor child wants to get a quick result, and mistakes are not immediately corrected but explored by the child, verbally mediated by the adult. In other words, a didactic mode is oriented towards the process of increasing the child's competence, not towards the product of the task (cf., Renshaw and Gardner, 1990). As will be clear, it is not just the adult having a didactic role, the child also participates in this didactic mode. She takes her time, listens to her mother, explores new ways of doing things. In other words, she knows to separate this kind of problem-solving from activities in another mode, such as play (which would have resulted in a fantasy construction with the blocks) or efficient productive activity. Amy and Claire combine symmetrical and asymmetrical role distribution, as shown while Claire explored her mistakes on her own, as long as she kept sharing the agreed overall goal.

The problem-solving interactions we analysed can be seen as *episodic* (cf., Valsiner, 1987), an emergent structure of goal-directed acting. The dyad as a problem-solving entity is responsible for these episodes. This means that although a child cannot perform the task alone, she is able to conceive and participate in the interaction as a problem-solving situation that needs goal-directed acting.

A structural analysis of adult–child problem-solving in terms of modes and episodes calls for an idea of control that is different from the idea displayed in most studies. An adult does not control a child on a moment-by-moment basis, as is implied by the notion of *contingency* (Wood *et al.*, 1976; Wood,

1989). On the contrary, a dyad constructs their interaction in accordance with a mode, and their cooperation is realized by a negotiated procedure that becomes manifest in episodes.

The variety of types of interaction we encountered can be systematized into modes of interaction. We can conclude that, even within the limited set-up of a problem-solving task, adults and children have diverse repertoires of interaction at their disposal. In some cases, adult and child initiated a certain mode of interaction, and this mode governed the whole session, as in the case of Claire and Amy. In other cases, there was quite some conflict, misunderstanding and (re)negotiation, because each participant tried to interact in a different mode to begin with.

The case-study showed that the child's learning does not depend solely on the adult's correct way of intervening. By taking initiatives on how to proceed and by participating in the interaction, Claire contributed substantially to her own learning.

How can instruction and learning be defined within the framework of the modes of interaction we could distinguish? Are there specific modes where learning and instruction take place, or is learning an opportunity in all modes of interaction? There is no single or simple answer to these questions.

To begin with, children have to learn to recognize the various modes of interaction and to function adequately within them. Therefore, the first answer is that learning and instruction always precede a given mode of interaction. Second, as each of the modes of interaction offers a rich field of experience, the second answer is that any mode of interaction offers ample opportunities for learning and instruction. Third, the didactic mode of interaction is a crystallization of a distinctive expert–novice relationship. This mode is a cultural invention, presupposing a social division of labour and considered as the ultimate educational activity in our culture. The third answer is that – at least in our Western history – a particular mode of interaction came into being as a very specific social organization of instruction and learning. However, learning and instruction as organized in a didactic mode can function only if embedded in other forms of learning and instruction; and, as shown by our case-study, learning should not be viewed only as the result of instruction.

We conclude that, on the one hand, learning and instruction are a specialized set of (inter)actions developed and constructed jointly by adult and child in a social history, but on the other hand, learning and instruction can never be reduced to these specialized (inter)actions. Learning and learning to learn are not the same.

References

Brown, G. and Yule. G. (1983). *Discourse analysis*. Cambridge: Cambridge University Press.

Bruner, J. (1986). *Actual minds, possible worlds*. Cambridge, MA: Harvard University Press.

Bruner, J. (1991). *Acts of meaning*. Cambridge, MA: Harvard University Press.

Elbers, E., Maier. R., Hoekstra. T. and Hoogsteder, M. (1992). Internalization and adult–child interaction. *Learning & Instruction, 2*, 101–118.

Elbers, E. and Kelderman, A. (1994). Ground rules for testing: Expectations and misunderstandings in test situations. *European Journal of Psychology of Education, 9*, 111–120.

Greenfield, P. and Lave, J. (1982). Cognitive aspects of informal education. In D. A. Wagner and H. W. Stevenson (Eds), *Cultural perspectives on child development* (pp. 181–207). San-Francisco: Freeman.

Hoogsteder, M. (1995). Learning through participation. The communication between young children and their caregivers in informal tutoring situations. Unpublished doctoral dissertation, Utrecht University, The Netherlands.

Hoogsteder, M. and Elbers, E. (1994, July). Children's and adults' roles in tutoring interactions. Paper presented at the XIIIth Biennial Meeting of the ISSBD, Amsterdam.

Jackson, S. (1986). Building a case for claims about discourse structure. In D. G. Ellis and W. A. Donohue (Eds), *Contemporary issues in language and discourse processes* (pp. 129–148). Hillsdale, NJ: Lawrence Erlbaum.

Jacobs, S. (1986). How to make an argument from example in discourse analysis. In D. G. Ellis and W. A. Donohue (Eds), *Contemporary issues in language and discourse processes* (pp. 149–168). Hillsdale, NJ: Lawrence Erlbaum.

Leont'ev, A. N. (1981). The problem of activity in Soviet psychology. In J. V. Wertsch (Ed.), *The concept of activity in Soviet psychology* (pp. 37–71). Armonk, NY: Sharpe.

Maier, R., Elbers, E. and Hoekstra, T. (1992). Wertsch's puzzle. A case study. *Cultural Dynamics, 5*(1), 25–42.

Minuchin, P. (1985). Families and individual development. Provocations from the field of family therapy. *Child Development, 56*, 289–302.

Renshaw, P. D. and Gardner, R. (1990). Process versus product task interpretation and parental teaching practices. *International Journal of Behavioral Development, 13*, 489–505.

Rogoff, B. (1990). *Apprenticeship in thinking. Cognitive development in social context*. New York: Oxford University Press.

Schubauer-Leoni, M. L. and Grossen, M. (1993). Negotiating the meaning of questions in didactic and experimental contracts. *European Journal of Psychology of Education, 8*, 451–471.

Stafford, L. and Bayer, C. L. (1993). *Interaction between parents and children*. Newbury Park, CA: Sage Publications.

Valsiner, J. (1987). *Culture and the development of children's action*. Chichester: John Wiley.

Wertsch, J. V., Minick, N. and Arns, F. J. (1984). The creation of context in joint problem-solving. In B. Rogoff and J. Lave (Eds), *Everyday cognition. Its development in social context* (pp. 151–171). Cambridge, MA: Harvard University Press.

Wood, D. J. (1989). Social interaction as tutoring. In M. H. Bornstein and J. S. Bruner (Eds), *Interaction in human development* (pp. 59–80). Hillsdale, NJ: Lawrence Erlbaum.

Wood, D. J., Bruner, J. and Ross, G. (1976). The role of tutoring in problem-solving. *Journal of Child Psychology and Psychiatry*, *17*, 89–100.

Wood, D. J., Wood, H. A. and Middleton, D. (1978). An experimental evaluation of four face-to-face teaching strategies. *International Journal of Behavioral Development*, *1*, 131–147.

Chapter 11

Collaborations among toddler peers

Individual contributions to social contexts*

Celia A. Brownell and Michael Sean Carriger

The idea that much of what children know and understand about the world is acquired in social contexts has gained increasing currency among developmental psychologists, fueled in particular by the rediscovery of Vygotsky's work (Wertsch, 1985). Although this perspective has long historical roots within developmental psychology (cf. Brownell, 1989), its impact was eroded in the last few decades by interest in more traditional Cartesian questions of what develops within the individual mind as a function of solitary activity in the world. Now development again is coming to be viewed as an interpersonal process as well as an intrapersonal one. Researchers have begun to realize that not only are knowledge, strategies, and skills used in social contexts, they are also acquired during social commerce.

Social processes of knowing
[. . .]
Relationships and Development

Social relationships are the contexts in which knowledge and expertise are acquired and consolidated (Hartup, 1986; Hinde, Perret-Clermont, and Stevenson-Hinde, 1985). Hartup (1989) has distinguished two broad classes of relationships that are presumably culturally universal: vertical (between individuals of differing knowledge and social power) and horizontal (between individuals of similar knowledge and social power). These two kinds of relationship have consistently been shown to serve different functions in children's development.

Although some psychologists equate Vygotskian notions with vertical relationships and Piagetian notions with horizontal relationships (cf. Musatti, 1986), many important questions are hybrids of these theoretical stances. For example, we would like to know what kinds of cognitive conflict might be engendered in the *expert* who apprentices, scaffolds, or guides the skill

---

* This is an edited version of a chapter that appeared in *Perspectives on Socially Shared Cognition*, Washington: American Psychological Association, 1991.

acquisition of the novice. How does a mother's knowledge change by participating in her child's development? On the other hand, we would also like to know how two novices jointly solving a problem scaffold one another (cf. Brown and Palincsar, 1989; Ellis and Rogoff, 1986). Seldom, if ever, do two learners know precisely the same thing at the same time, even in horizontal relationships. How do children monitor, support, and challenge one another in their respective momentary zones of competence when they work and play together? Although vertical and horizontal relationships contribute differently to development, the social processes that affect change are not given by the form of the relationship alone. Children themselves contribute differently to both vertical and horizontal relationships as they develop. In so doing, they systematically change the contexts or the relationships in which they participate.

Likewise, individual differences among children at a given developmental point can affect the relationships in which these children grow. For example, whereas all children may be generally "tutor-prone" (Bruner, 1972), there are also individual differences in children's willingness and ability to participate as "tutees" (e.g., Matas, Arend, and Sroufe, 1978: Strayer and Moss, 1987). This variability, in turn, results in different sets of dynamics in children's vertical relationships and no doubt also in their horizontal relationships (Hartup and Brownell, 1988). This goes beyond the notion that adults provide different scaffolds in reaction to a child's changing competence. The argument here is that relationships are mutually influenced by both partners. Children actively manage and shape the very relationships that also shape them (cf. Hinde and Stevenson-Hinde, 1987; Rogoff, 1989; Valsiner, 1987).

Thus, our position is that children participate in a variety of structurally different relationships that have different effects on development because of the different interactional processes characterizing them. At the same time, children bring their own developmental and individual characteristics to these relationships. Hence, the processes that are presumably universal within horizontal or vertical relationships, by virtue of the structural features of these relationships, also possess unique variation contributed by the children themselves who participate. It is these individual contributions to social contexts on which we focus in this chapter.

Peer collaborations

The particular relationship context we have chosen to study is peer relationships, and within these relationships we focus on collaboration. From the perspective of contextual influences on development, peer relationships are not studied as often as parent–child relationships. Several scholars have, nevertheless, recently argued that peer contexts are central to the child's social construction of reality (Azmitia and Perlmutter, 1989; Damon and Phelps, 1989; Mueller and Cooper, 1986).

Peer collaborations capture well the emphasis on the bidirectional nature of social and cognitive processes in development. On the one hand, children's collaborations are fundamentally *social* in nature. They encompass motivational and affective factors. They are founded on a repertoire of particular social behaviors, including expressive behavior and communicative behavior. They depend on two or more people interacting with one another dynamically, mutually regulating behaviors that possess meaning in the context of the social exchange. For example, my taking a puzzle piece from your pile is an act with a different meaning when we are cooperating at putting the puzzle together than when we are not. At the same time, collaboration is also fundamentally *cognitive* in nature. It requires goal recognition or definition, planning of behavior around the goal, adopting effective goal-related strategies, monitoring and changing goal-directed behavior, and so on.

Collaborations also include *bidirectional* influences between social and cognitive processes. First and most simply, the cognitive elements of problem solving have to be coordinated with another person through social means. The planning, monitoring, motivating, and regulating of behavior have to happen on the interpersonal plane as well as through intrapersonal processes. Second, the actual processes of coordination – the dynamics of social interaction – are often hypothesized to change the nature of the cognitive events in social problem solving as compared with solitary learning (Rogoff, 1983; see Azmitia and Perlmutter, 1989, for a review of peer collaborations). Concomitantly, the knowledge and skills brought by each of the participants to the collaboration will affect the processes of coordination.

The focus of this chapter is on the earliest social collaborations among peers. If social interaction "creates the mind," as Mead, Vygotsky, and others have argued, then early interactions in horizontal relationships should contribute as much as those that occur in vertical relationships. Nevertheless, the sharing of knowledge among young peers must be a different event, governed by different social processes, than collaborations between parents and young children.

Most of the research on collaborative problem solving in young children has emphasized adult–child interaction among preschoolers (Azmitia and Perlmutter, 1989). The assumption seems to be that young children cannot jointly regulate the planning and strategy formation that are necessary for effective problem solving, and, therefore, they depend on "other-regulation." But there is a small literature on early peer interaction that suggests that between 18 and 24 months, a transition may occur in children's social competencies to permit cooperation and the establishment of "shared meanings" with each other (Brenner and Mueller, 1982; Eckerman, Didow, and Davis, 1989; Eckerman and Stein, 1982; Goldman and Ross, 1978: Ross and Lollis, 1987). Thus, rather than studying socially skilled individuals who possess a wide repertoire of interactional skills, including how to coordinate behavior with someone else, where the question is how these two skilled individuals coordinate their knowledge through language and skilled interaction, we are exploring the genesis and early development of these skills of coordination, largely through non-verbal means.

Our data address two specific questions. First, when do children become able to collaborate to solve a problem together, and what do these early collaborations look like? Second, what do developmental differences in social understanding contribute to these early collaborative efforts? We pursued these questions using dyads of children aged between 12 and 30 months, children who are just beginning to show interest and some rudimentary skills in peer interaction. One reason for examining these ages for the origins of collaboration is that peer interaction is just emerging in the second year. But another – and perhaps more interesting and compelling – reason to look at the second year is that this is the time when the young child begins to differentiate *self* from *other* as independent causal agents and to form complex relations among events.

How do these changes relate to the origins of collaboration? If we think of collaboration as establishing joint goals and referents and adjusting one's own behavior to fit or coordinate with another's toward a joint goal, it becomes difficult to conceive of true collaboration without recognition of both self and other as causal agents, as autonomous initiators and controllers of behavior. In other words, although the very young infant can participate in social inter-action under the direction of a parent, he or she is not truly a contributor, we would argue, until able to join planfully and intentionally in the interactions of another, actively affecting the other's behavior and the course and outcome of the interaction and, thereby, the collaborative process of knowledge acqui-sition. Individuals who do not recognize that another person can cause things to happen autonomously cannot join their efforts intentionally to reach a common, shared goal. Although some scholars of infant development claim that the youngest infants are capable of intersubjectivity between minds of interactants, there is much controversy on this matter. Many other scholars of early social development argue that the appearance of intersubjectivity in young infants is a convenient social construction by parents and adults who must interact with the socially naive infant (e.g., Dunn, 1982; Kaye, 1982; Schaffer, 1984). Regardless of the disposition of this controversy among scholars of infant–adult interaction, however, the evidence on early peer interaction supports the emergence of intersubjectivity during the second year.

How toddlers collaborate

We will report data from a study of collaborative problem solving in 12-, 18-, 24-, and 30-month-olds that focused on the relationship between col-laboration and the development of self–other differentiation, or decentration.

We paired 16 children at each age, who were unfamiliar with one another, in dyads to solve a simple cooperation problem. The children were also individually administered a pretend-play task that indexed their ability to represent the causal autonomy of animate replicas (i.e., their ability to pretend that a doll or stuffed animal could control its own actions). This task is a well-established means of estimating early self–other differentiation.

There were three cooperation problems, all similar in operation. Each dyad received one problem and had 7 minutes in which to solve it. Each problem required one child to push a piston (or lever or rotating handle) through a clear plexiglass box to get access to some small animals placed in a cup attached to the end of the handle (or piston or lever). However, by the strategic placement of springs and plexiglass barriers, the child's access was blocked as he or she operated the handle. Furthermore, if the child released pressure on the piston (or lever or rotator), it would slip back inside the box. This apparatus, therefore, required a second child to retrieve the animals. To do so, the second child had to position himself or herself opposite the first and reach for the animals as the first child made them available. The problems thus required the coordinated action of two children for solution. The children had to adopt complementary roles spatially by positioning themselves opposite one another at the apparatus, and they also had to adopt complementary roles temporally, with one child pushing the handle and holding it extended while the second child retrieved the animals. Once children solved the problem, they were permitted to play with the animals briefly, whereupon the apparatus was reloaded, and they were asked to solve it again.

The pretend-play task to index self–other differentiation involved experimenter modeling of five short scenarios with dolls or stuffed animals as the actors (e.g., going to bed, eating breakfast), after which the child was asked to imitate the experimenter's actions. As with the elicited imitation procedure used in language development research, children will typically imitate at their highest level of competence, even if it is lower than that represented in the modeled scenario. We coded four levels of children's imitations, as previously established in the literature. At Level 1, the lowest level, the child cannot pretend with animate replicas at all and instead pretends that he himself is the agent. For example, if the experimenter models giving the doll a drink of juice, the child imitates by pretending to drink juice himself or herself. At Level 2, the child can represent another as a recipient of her actions but does not pretend that others can control their own behavior (e.g., the child gives the doll a drink, but cannot pretend that the doll holds the cup and drinks by itself). At Level 3, the child represents others as active agents of their own behavior (e.g., puts the cup in the hands of the doll for the doll to drink by itself). At this point, one can infer that the child is able to represent other people as initiators and controllers of behavior and events in the world, independent of the child's own actions, desires, or interests. At Level 4, the child can represent two dolls autonomously interacting with one another (e.g. one doll gives another doll a drink).

We derived two measures: (a) the highest level imitated by the child across scenarios, and (b) a composite decentration score, which was the number of different actions imitated at each level (e.g., two actions imitated at Level 1 and one action imitated at Level 2 sums to a score of 4; two actions at Level 2 and one at Level 3 sums to a score of 7).

From the cooperative problem-solving tasks, we coded several behaviors that were meant to index attempts to coordinate behavior with a partner. We counted the number of solutions to the problems and latency to solution. We also coded (a) the children's movements around the apparatus, both to the same side as the partner and to the opposite side from the partner; (b) the frequency with which a child manipulated the handle with a pause for the partner versus manipulations without a pause; (c) the frequency with which one child anticipated the appearance of the animals as the partner operated the handle; (d) commands; (e) compliance versus resistance; (f) displacement by one child of the partner; and (g) simple exploration. We then created a composite coordination score by summing the variables of manipulate – pause, anticipate animals, commands, and compliance with command, and dividing the sum by all on-task behavior.

We conducted analyses in three steps. The first step was a fairly global description of the cooperative problem-solving behavior of the children (paired in dyads). The second step was a more detailed analysis of particular kinds of behaviors and intercoordinations of behavior that might, together, describe the collaborative process more convincingly. The final step was an assessment of relations between collaboration and decentration.

Collaborative solutions

When we consider children's ability to solve the problem collaboratively, we see clear age differences, both in their success rates and in the means by which they achieved success (see Table 11.1). No 12-month-olds and only half the 18-month-olds solved the problem, whereas all of the 24- and 30-month-olds solved it. In fact, most of the older dyads solved the problem multiple times. In contrast, those 18-month-olds who managed to solve the problem once were never able to re-achieve the solution, suggesting, perhaps, that their initial solutions were accidental. We should note that all dyads engaged in problem-solving behavior, and all manipulated the apparatus in such a way as to have been able to achieve an individual solution had the springs and barriers not prevented it. What this suggests, then, is that the difficulty for the younger children was in figuring out how to work together to a common end. As will become evident, there were differences among the older children as well in the degree to which they were able to coordinate their behavior. That is, although children older than 12 months

Table 11.1 Solution characteristics as a function of age

Solution characteristics	Age			
	12 months	18 months	24 months	30 months
Number of solutions per dyad	.00	.50	4.80	4.50
Coordinated behavior (proportion)	.03	.20	.38	.33
Type 1 solutions (proportion)	—	.80	.18	.05
Type 2 solutions	—	.20	.52	.40
Type 3 solutions	—	.00	.30	.55

solved the problem together, the particular solutions they used were more or less collaborative.

Except for the 12-month-olds, there were no age differences in movements around the task, either to the same side (e.g., to join, displace, or imitate the partner) or to the opposite side (e.g., to complement the partner's behavior). However, there were differences for the proportion of problem-solving behavior that was coordinated with the partner's behavior. Children in the two older age groups (24 and 30 months) coordinated their behavior with one another a much greater proportion of the time than did children in the two younger age groups. There were no differences in proportion of coordinated behavior, however, between 18-month-olds who solved the problem and 18-month-olds who failed to do so. Once more, this suggests that the 18-month-olds solved the problem by accident, not by actively coordinating their behavior.

We decided to examine the children's collaborations in more detail, partly because it was possible to solve the problems accidentally and partly because we wished to understand what was happening socially during these problem-solving attempts. We focused on several specific aspects of the collaborative process: solution styles, solution times, monitoring one another's task-related behavior, attempts to influence one another's goal-directed behavior, and responses to violations by the partner of appropriate goal-directed sequences.

Solution styles

Consider the following example of a solution. Child A pushes the handle and holds it in its extended position, looks at the animals as they appear in the hole on the other side of the plexiglass barrier, tries to reach through the plexiglass to get them, and then, while still holding the handle, looks away, distracted by something else happening in the room. Child B, meanwhile, has ignored Child A's activity on the task and is busy exploring the screws that hold things together; moments earlier, he had tried to reach through the hole to get the animals but was unsuccessful. Now he looks up from his exploration, notices that the animals are at the opening, and runs over to get them. As B exclaims his delight, A returns attention to the task, joins B, and they share the animals. This would have been counted as a solution, and technically it is cooperative, because two children did together what one child could not do alone. It is not really collaborative, however, because these children worked independently of each other. There is little sense here of joint regulation of behavior, of trying to coordinate two separate roles, or of sharing any kind of knowledge.

On the basis of exchanges such as these, we determined the major ways in which children actually solved the problem. There were three main ways, and these differed in their apparent planfulness or intentionality. Type 1 solutions involved simply reaching into the box (through the small hole in the end or the top), without any consideration of what the partner was doing. This was a sort of independent exploration of the problem and an attempt to solve it alone. In fact, the child could not get the animals this way. But if the partner pushed the handle, also independently exploring the problem, and this happened to put the first child in contact with the animals, he could remove them. Type 2 solutions occurred when a child retrieved the animals *after* the partner manipulated the handle and held it. Again, still opportunistically, the second child simply noticed that the animals were available and got them out. Type 3 solutions involved anticipating the partner's action with the handle. In this case, one child stood next to the hole where the animals would become available and clearly waited for the partner to push the handle; the child placed his or her hand, head, or body in an expectant position, such as holding his or her hand next to the hole where the animals would appear, and did so when the partner was about to push the handle.

There are clear changes with age in the children's use of these solution styles. As Table 11.1 shows, 80 percent of 18-month-olds' solutions were of the direct reaching, accidental variety (Type 1), and none of their solutions was of the anticipatory variety (Type 3). By 30 months, only 5 percent of solutions resulted from reaching directly into the hole (Type 1), and 55 percent included anticipation of the partner's behavior (Type 3). The 24-month-olds were in between. They anticipated the partner's behavior some of the time (30 percent) (Type 3), but mostly they were doing solutions that were more opportunistic (Type 2). This suggests, again, that 18-month-olds' solutions were almost entirely accidental; 24-month-olds' solutions were anticipatory some of the time and were seldom a simple by-product of reaching directly through the hole for the animals; and not until 30 months were children regularly aware of and likely to consider the activities of the other child.

Solution times

For joint and collaborative problem solving, most writers have suggested that the partners in the collaboration have to establish, either implicitly or explicitly, a common problem-solving space, or a mutual agreement about how the problem is to be approached and defined. If mutual agreement is established early in a dyad's encounters with the problem, we would expect to see a decline in solution times for successive solutions, and indeed we do for those dyads that achieve multiple solutions.

For both 24- and 30-month-olds, the time it took to solve the problem decreased over successive solutions, suggesting that some sort of mutual agreement had been established in the first solution. This implies that, even if the first solution was opportunistic for these young children, subsequent solutions probably were not. Presumably, the children used the first solution to establish agreement about how to solve the problem, and they figured out how to coordinate their behavior relative to one another as well as relative to the goal.

However, there may be alternative explanations for a decrease in solution time. For example, each child could have figured out individually which behavior worked and then simply have repeated that behavior in later solutions. Without the trial-and-error characteristic of the first solution attempt, solution times would decrease. That would be different from what we mean by joint agreement here: that both children understand that their efforts are independently directed to the same reference point, and that they make some effort to coordinate their actions. In communication, for example, speakers establish a common reference point and check with each other to be sure they are referring to the same shared "space," unless shared reference is assumed to be based on common experience or memory. If speakers discover that reference has not been shared, one of them stops to repair the problem.

In this study, we did not have the luxury of explicit verbalizations about the child's own or the partner's behavior that would have revealed the children's thinking about their relations, as we do with older children and adults. Therefore, we were forced to use more indirect means to infer that the children were indeed collaborating or, alternatively, that we could not be certain that they were. Furthermore, we can seldom be certain that a single pattern decisively reveals real collaboration in this age group. Rather, we must seek a converging pattern of results. Other interactive processes, then, must be examined to determine if these young children were collaborating with one another and to provide insights into the processes of collaboration.

Monitoring partner

If children are aware of one another as actors, as we contend they must be if they are engaging in truly collaborative efforts, then they should look at each other to monitor the other's behavior as it relates to their joint efforts. In fact, they do monitor each other, but the frequency of looking at each other does not change with age (see Table 11.2).

Looking at each other can, however, serve many functions besides monitoring task-relevant behavior. In particular, it can serve purely social functions. One way in which we began to tease apart these two functions was to separate looking at one another, when both children are on task, from looking at each other when only one child is on task and the other child is playing off task or is conversing with another person in the room. As shown in Table 11.2, it becomes clear that with age the children are more likely to monitor one another when they are both working on the task than when one is off task. This suggests that the older children are attempting to establish or monitor joint task-related efforts, whereas the younger children are more likely to be monitoring one another for social reasons.

To make this conclusion stronger, we narrowed down the circumstances under which we would expect monitoring to be functional for coordinated activity and determined whether older children's gazes at each other were more likely to occur in that context. Specifically, we determined whether monitoring the partner was more likely to occur when the partner was manipulating and holding the handle. The pattern in Table 11.2 makes it clear that older children were more likely to engage in this problem-related sort of monitoring of each other than were younger children.

Influence attempts

A still more direct collaborative process is that of attempting to influence the activity of one's partner as it relates to the common goal. We identified three types of influence that are progressively more directive. A *gesture* was any goal-directed gesture, such as pointing to or waving at the apparatus or animals inside. This behavior can serve at least two different purposes. It may simply reflect the child's efforts to direct his or her own attention, as a

Table 11.2 Extent to which toddlers monitored partner during solution attempts

Monitoring	Age		
	18 months	24 months	30 months
Monitor peer	10.90	10.50	10.20
Monitor/both on task	6.30	7.40	8.30
Monitor/one on task	4.70	3.40	1.70
Monitor peer/hold handle (proportion)	.04	.11	.19

slightly more public version of Vygotsky's private speech, or it may be intended to direct the partner's attention to some part of the apparatus or to direct the partner to act on some part of the apparatus. For example, older children would sometimes combine a command such as "Do it! Do it!" with a wave at the other child to move over to the other side of the task and perform the appropriate action. An *indirect verbalization* was a task-related verbalization directed to the other child but not an explicit request or command for action (e.g., "I see it"; "Here it comes"). Thus, as with gestures, this might be interpreted by the other child as a directive but need not be interpreted in this way. A *direct verbalization* was an explicit request or command to the other child to perform a task-relevant behavior (e.g., "Look!"; "Get it!"; or "Do it!").

The data show that there was no change with age in the absolute frequency of influence attempts (see Table 11.3). Rather, the form of influence attempts changed with age, from less direct to more direct. That is, by 30 months, almost one third of the children's attempts to influence one another were by commands and requests for goal-directed action.

Although it might be argued that these findings are confounded with language development more generally, such reasoning cannot be applied to the 24-month-olds. Normally developing 2-year-olds are very capable of saying things such as "Go there," or "Get it." In fact, both 18- and 24-month-olds used indirect verbalizations. Hence, although the 18-month-olds' lack of direct influence attempts may be language related, the transition between 24 and 30 months must certainly be due to something else. It seems that the 30-month-olds were trying to influence the operation of the task *through* influencing their partner's behavior. They were explicitly trying to coordinate their own goal-directed behavior with their partner by altering their partner's behavior as well as their own. The younger children verbalized about the task, but they did not attempt to influence the partner to act. We would speculate that the 30-month-olds were more aware of the relations between their own

Table 11.3 Attempts to influence partner's behavior

Influence attempts	Age		
	18 months	24 months	30 months
Frequency of influence	83	98	77
Gesture to other (proportion)	.70	.64	.31
Indirect verbalization to other (proportion)	.30	.31	.21
Direct verbalization to other (proportion)	.00	.05	.31

and their partner's behavior, and were purposefully attempting to coordinate those relations in the service of a common goal.

Response to violations by partner

Finally, we reasoned that children who were trying to coordinate their behavior with each other should react to their partner if the partner violates the appropriate sequence of events for solution. Reacting *to* the partner suggests that the child is aware that the partner has disrupted the joint effort. In contrast, the child who has simply learned the appropriate individual behaviors to get the job done, without regard for the partner's role in the job, should simply try another non-social problem-related behavior if the partner violates the appropriate solution sequence. For this child, the peer is not truly a collaborator in the enterprise.

A violation was identified as the expected event in the solution sequence not occurring when both children were on task, regardless of whether either child appeared to recognize this as a violation. Violations tended to be of two basic types: the child manipulating the handle let go of it after pausing, often as the partner reached for the animals; or the child on the receiving end failed to reach for the animals while the partner was holding the handle and waiting for the animals to be retrieved.

The pattern of responses and their relation to age are quite striking. Data were not analyzed for 18-month-olds, because of their low frequency of violations. First, 30-month-olds were far more likely to look at the partner when she or he violated the sequence of events; 80 percent of 30-month-olds, but only 20 percent of 24-month-olds, looked at their partners at least once following a violation by the partner. In Table 11.4 the data are presented as a proportion of all violations that elicited a look at the partner, and there are clear age differences. These differences are not due to lower base rates in younger children of either violations or gazes at partners (there were no

Table 11.4 Response to violations by partner of problem-related sequences

Response	Age		
	18 months	24 months	30 months
Violation → Gaze at peer (proportion)	—	.08	.47
Violation → Command (proportion)	—	.01	.11
Violation → Reach for lure through plexiglass (proportion)	—	.33	.03

differences in absolute frequency). Second, although violations were relatively unlikely to elicit a gesture or command, of those commands that were given, more of them were elicited by a prior violation in 30-month-olds than in 24-month-olds. Finally, 24-month-olds were much more likely than 30-month-olds to try to reach the animals directly through the hole or through the plexiglass following a violation – an attempt to solve the problem individually, without regard for the partner. Thus, when the partner did something inappropriate, 24-month-olds did something else to the task, whereas 30-month-olds responded to the partner.

Summary of collaborative solutions

Although 24-month-olds were as successful as 30-month-olds in solving the problem cooperatively, they did not appear, on many counts, to be collaborating to the same degree. On the other hand, they were better able to coordinate their behavior than were 18-month-olds, who either failed to solve the problem altogether or, having solved it, were unable to re-achieve solution. Although 24-month-olds had the task-related spatial and temporal contingencies worked out well enough to produce multiple solutions, they did not appear to be as aware of one another's roles in producing those contingencies as were 30-month-olds. They may, indeed, have simply been learning their own individual roles, failing to take into account the partner's presence and behavior at all. Although there is no single measure that is criterial, the converging evidence from several measures suggests that the 30-month-olds possessed mutual awareness of one another's behavior relative to the outcome, and that their efforts were in part conditioned on their recognition of one another's joint relationship to the goal. Thus, we are provided with an interesting illustration of the potential effects of the child on the social contexts in which development occurs. In this case, we have illustrated developmental effects. Specifically, collaborations, whether in horizontal or vertical relationships, differ as a function of the developmental levels of the participants.

Individual differences within dyads

The collaborations in which children participate also differ as a function of the individual characteristics of the children involved. We have argued that one fundamental contributor to these developments in collaboration is the young child's growing awareness of others as agents of his or her own behavior. Indeed, development of the ability to represent others' behavior symbolically parallels developments in collaboration during the second year. In our study, the numbers of children imitating at Level 3 or Level 4 (the highest levels) increased with age (see Table 11.5). Correspondingly, children's composite scores for self–other differentiation also increased with age. In other words, older children imitated more actions at higher levels. As

Table 11.5 Relation between age and decentration

Age	Decentration			
	Level 1	*Level 2*	*Level 3*	*Level 4*
12 months	5	9	1	0
18 months	0	10	4	1
24 months	0	6	8	2
30 months	0	7	8	1

Note: Values are the number of children for whom a given level of decentration was the highest level represented during imitation.

hypothesized, there were also correspondences between changes in self–other differentiation and children's ability to coordinate their behavior with their peers ($r = .37, p < .01$).

An interesting question, then, is whether differences in self–other differentiation between the children within a dyad affected their collaborations. We can offer only a preliminary answer to this question, partly because these analyses were *post hoc* – we did not assign children to dyads based on their understanding of others as independent agents – and partly because, when we did break things down this way, we were dealing with rather small numbers of observations. Nevertheless, the data are suggestive and point to the need for further inquiry.

We categorized dyads into three types. In the first type, both children failed to represent the other as an active agent. In the second type, one of the children represented the other as an active agent (Level 3 decentration), but the other did not. In the final type, both children represented the other as an active, independent agent. As shown in Table 11.6 it seemed necessary for at least one child to be able to represent the other as an active agent for the dyad to solve the problem more than once. In other words, for the dyad to re-achieve the solution, suggesting that solutions were purposeful and intentionally coordinated, at least one child in the pair had to be able to represent the other as causing his or her own behavior. When we look at how the dyad solved the problem (the type of solution), we see a similar pattern. Dyads in which both children were at Level 2 never solved the problem using the most advanced solution type – anticipating the partner's behavior. Again, having at least one child in the pair at Level 3 appeared to be necessary to achieve this kind of solution. When both children were at Level 3, they seldom used the most primitive solution style. The frequency of coordinated behavior also varied with the makeup of the dyad. Thus, children's differential understanding of self–other relations within a dyad was related to the dyad's performance. Children bring different abilities and understanding to collaborations,

Table 11.6 Solution characteristics as a function of dyad type

Solution characteristics	Dyad type [a]		
	2–2	2–3	3–3
Number of dyads with single solution	5.00	7.00	5.00
Number of dyads with multiple solution	1.00	6.00	4.00
Type 1 solutions (proportion)	.50	.11	.16
Type 2 solutions (proportion)	.50	.59	.42
Type 3 solutions (proportion)	.00	.30	.42
Frequency of coordinated behavior	16.60	24.30	30.30

Notes: a 2–2 = both children at Level 2 decentration (other represented as passive recipient of child's actions): 3–3 = both children at Level 3 (other represented as active agent of its own behavior); 2–3 = one child at Level 2, one at Level 3.

even the very earliest ones, and these differences seem to affect both the processes and the outcomes of collaborative problem solving.

Conclusions

We can offer several conclusions from these data. Most important, children under 3 years old *can* collaborate with one another to solve simple problems. They are neither too egocentric nor too socially unskilled to establish joint goals and to adjust their behavior in the service of these goals. We are led to conclude that peer social contexts may emerge as important influences quite early in children's development.

Nevertheless, there are also clear progressions with age in very young children's ability to collaborate with one another. As they get older, children become better able to comprehend the behavior and intentions of another, as well as better able to affect the other's behavior and to communicate about their own behavior and desires. We are additionally led to conclude, then, that age-related social and cognitive skills contributing to peer collaborations influence what and how children learn from these collaborations.

Finally, within collaborations, individual differences in the collaborators' social and cognitive skills influence the outcomes of the collaborations, even among very young children. Thus, collaborative abilities and collaborative processes *develop*. Our understanding of socially shared cognition must, therefore, depend on our understanding of what develops and how it develops.

We have studied the joint regulation of behavior in a social context in which there is no expert to scaffold or guide the children's skill acquisition. Instead, knowledge or skill must be co-constructed in this context. Children acquire the skills they use in such co-constructions through their participation with others, building understanding by relating. Relatively few principles or mechanisms have been proposed to account for this sort of acquisition. Hence, a major task for future research will be to discover the social processes of knowing, among even the youngest children.

Numerous questions are raised by these data. Because children contribute to the relationships in which they participate, we wonder how differences in social experience, as well as in dominance, sociability, effectance motivation, and similar factors, affect their peer encounters. At this age, perhaps such factors are irrelevant. On the other hand, perhaps they contribute more to these early collaborations than do the age-related skills studied here. The data also raise questions about communicative and collaborative processes themselves, particularly because many of these children are minimally verbal. What social and communicative cues can young children recognize, and to which ones do they respond? How, exactly, do they go about establishing and repairing shared reference and negotiating meaning? And, finally, there are larger, broader questions involved, such as how general such collaborations are, what spontaneous collaborations during freeplay look like at this age, and what the earliest peer collaborations contribute to children's understanding.

It is not unique to speculate that peer exchanges may facilitate the differentiation and understanding of self versus other. However, no one has addressed such questions among the youngest peer collaborators. Nor have researchers addressed how understanding derived from early peer collaborations might contribute to other kinds of collaborations, such as those with siblings or parents. It is also possible that peer collaborations may contribute to only particular aspects of development, or that they may be effective contributors only at particular points in development (cf. Azmitia and Perlmutter, 1989; Damon and Phelps, 1989). It would be worthwhile to explore how and when early peer collaborations serve to enculturate children's thinking, social skills, and relationships.

In conclusion, these data suggest that how children jointly structure peer collaborations and what children take away from these collaborations will differ as a function of what children bring to them. Children's social and cognitive competencies will mediate contextual influences on their development. Our conclusions about social influences on young children's development, then, must take into account both age-related and child-specific contributions to the action of such social influences. The sources of these individual contributions will, of course, themselves be social, cultural, and historical in origin.

Hence, the model of development to be ultimately derived must be multi-causal, reciprocal, and perhaps dialectical. Social contexts do not in any autonomous way create the child, because children themselves shape the action of social contexts at the same time as contexts shape them. Individuals are determined by the relationships in which they participate, and those relationships are simultaneously determined by the participating individuals.

Culture and history create us at the same time that we create them. Simple unidirectional causal models, then, are inadequate and inaccurate. Moreover, individual psychological function cannot be reduced to social processes, and social processes cannot be reduced to the sum of individual psychological functions. The best we can do, within our current conceptual and empirical frameworks, is to select part of this complex network of interwoven processes for investigation. For our part, we have begun to explicate how the toddler contributes to the collaborative enterprise; next we must begin to inquire about what collaborations contribute to toddlers' development.

References

Azmitia, M. and Perlmutter, M. (1989). Social influences on children's cognition: State of the art and future directions. In H. Reese (Ed.), *Advances in child development and behavior: Vol. 22* (pp. 89–144). New York: Academic Press.

Brenner, J. and Mueller, E. (1982). Shared meaning in boy toddlers' peer relations. *Child Development*, 53, 380–391.

Brown, A. L. and Palincsar, A. S. (1989). Guided, cooperative learning and individual knowledge acquisition. In L. B. Resnick (Ed.), *Knowing, learning, and instruction: Essays in honor of Robert Glaser* (pp. 393–453). Hillsdale, NJ: Erlbaum.

Brownell, C. (1989). Socially shared cognition: The role of social context in the construction of knowledge. In L. T. Winegar (Ed.), *Social interaction and the development of children's understanding* (pp. 173–205). Norwood, NJ: Ablex.

Bruner, J. (1972). The nature and uses of immaturity. *American Psychologist*, 27, 1–28.

Damon, W. and Phelps, E. (1989). Strategic uses of peer learning in children's education. In T. Berndt and A. Ladd (Eds), *Peer relationships in child development* (pp. 135–157). New York: Wiley.

Dunn, J. (1982). Comment: Problems and promises in the study of affect and intention. In E. Tronick (Ed.), *Social interchange in infancy* (pp. 97–206). Baltimore: University Park Press.

Eckerman, C., Didow, C. and Davis. L. (1989). Toddlers' emerging ways of achieving social coordinations with a peer. *Child Development*, 60, 440–453.

Eckerman, C. and Stein, M. (1982). The toddler's emerging interactive skills. In K. Rubin and H. Ross (Eds), *Peer relationships and social skills in childhood* (pp. 41–72). New York: Springer-Verlag.

Ellis, S. and Rogoff, B. (1986). Problem solving in children's management of instruction. In E. Mueller and C. Cooper (Eds), *Process and outcome in peer relationships* (pp. 301–345). New York: Academic Press.

Goldman, B. and Ross, H. (1978). Social skills in action: Analysis of early peer games. In J. Glick and A. Clarke-Stewart (Eds), *The development of social understanding* (pp. 177–212). New York: Gardner Press.

Hartup, W. (1986). On relationships and development. In W. Hartup and Z. Rubin (Eds), *Relationships and development* (pp. 1–26). Hillsdale, NJ: Erlbaum.

Hartup, W. (1989). Social relationships and their developmental significance. *American Psychologist*, 44, 120–126.

Hartup, W. and Brownell C. (1988), Early social development: Transitions and concordances, *Eta Evolutiva*, 29, 5–17.

Hinde, R., Perret-Clermont, A. and Stevenson-Hinde, J. (Eds) (1985). *Social relationships and cognitive development*. New York: Oxford University Press.

Hinde, R. and Stevenson-Hinde, J. (1987). Interpersonal relationships and child development. *Developmental Review*, 7, 1–21.

Kaye, K. (1982). *The mental and social life of babies*. Chicago: University of Chicago Press.

Matas, L., Arend, R. and Sroufe, L. (1978). The relationship between quality of attachment and later competence. *Child Development*, 49, 547–556.

Mueller, E. and Cooper, C. (Eds) (1986). *Process and outcome in peer relationships*. New York: Academic Press.

Musatti, T. (1986). Early peer relations: The perspectives of Piaget and Vygotsky. In E. Mueller and C. Cooper (Eds), *Process and outcome in peer relationships* (pp. 25–53). New York: Academic Press.

Rogoff, B. (1983). Thinking and learning in social context. In B. Rogoff and J. Lave (Eds), *Everyday cognition* (pp. 1–18). Cambridge, MA: Harvard University Press.

Rogoff, B. (in press). Joint socialization of development by young children and adults. In M. Lewis and M. Feinman (Eds), *Social influences on behavior*. New York: Plenum Press.

Ross, H. and Lollis, S. (1987). Communication within infant social games. *Developmental Psychology*, 23, 241–248.

Schaffer, H. (1984). *The child's entry into a social world*. London: Academic Press.

Strayer, F. and Moss, E. (Eds) (1987). *Development of social and representational tactics during early childhood*. Montreal: La Maison d'Ethologie de Montreal.

Valsiner, J. (1987). *Culture and the development of children's action*. New York: Wiley.

Wertsch, J. (1985). *Culture, communication and cognition: Vygotskian perspectives*. Cambridge, England: Cambridge University Press.

Chapter 12

Teachers and other adults as talk partners for pupils in nursery and reception classes*

Maureen Hughes and David Westgate

Introduction

What young pupils can do with spoken language (and hence, to a significant extent, how they learn) largely depends on their interaction with others. Talk is, after all, a reciprocal business. Teachers, however, are not usually now the only talk partners available. It is common for a range of adults other than teachers to assist in early-years settings and thus also to act in this role. Frequently they do so with the express intention of fostering language development or supporting the acquisition of new concepts. Nonetheless, research in this area has tended to focus on the talk partner role played by teachers or by other pupils, while neglecting the increasing contribution made by other adults. There has been little monitoring of the success of such adults or of the extent to which pupils' talk experience with them has proved to be enabling.

In a recent study by Hughes (1994), patterns of interaction between pupils and a range of adults in early-years classrooms were analysed and compared. The adults concerned were: nursery nurses, nursery nurse students, parents, auxiliaries, YTS (youth training scheme) helpers, community workers and secondary pupils on work experience – as well as teachers. Certain 'qualitative' aspects of the pupils' talk with adults in each category were established. These were further considered for their effects upon learning and development in the shared contexts.

The study

Audio recordings of adult–pupil talk were collected for the eight categories of adult from five schools, all within one LEA but representing clearly different backgrounds. The recordings sampled children interacting with these adults as a whole class, in large and small groups, and on an individual basis. They covered a wide variety of activities forming part of the normal work in early-

---

* This is an edited version of an article that appeared in *Education 3–13* (1997), March.

years classrooms, also contexts where the adults had clear 'teacherly intentions' and ones where they did not.

The attempt to identify qualitative aspects for analysis grew out of methods used in a previous study by the present authors (Hughes and Westgate, 1990) and drew upon other classroom researchers' treatment of talk data (see Edwards and Westgate's 1994 review of such studies). Experience suggested that coding of the transcripts might focus with particular relevance upon:

1   factors to do with *interaction*: namely the *roles* that pupils play in their talk, indicating for instance the extent to which pupils are being limited to that of responding or being offered a greater diversity (in particular that of initiating topics);
2   factors to do with *discourse*: namely the range of identifiable *discourse functions* that are available to pupils, highlighting the wider or more limited range of pupils' talk purposes associated with particular partners and contexts;
3   factors to do with *cognition* evident in (or behind) the talk: namely such *cognitive functions* as recollecting, making connections, interpreting and speculating – which may be considered as qualitatively significant in various ways.

Notes from observations made at the time of the recordings, as well as interviews with the participating adults and some pupils, provided further and more detailed perspective on the audio-recorded events. Within this complex data-set, however, transcripts, variously coded, remained the prime source.

The picture revealed

Analysis of pupils' *interactional roles* with their teachers and other adults produced some interesting contrasts. When teachers were talking with pupils (either with or without pre-set teaching goals, and with groups or individuals), a form of talk usually predominated from which pupil initiations were largely eliminated and in which pupils were mostly allocated brief response slots. This pattern is demonstrated in the example from a reception class shown in Table 12.1. (The coding used here is based on a form of discourse analysis derived from the work of Sinclair and Coulthard, 1975, at the level of 'Moves'.) The adult directs the topic, asks the questions and evaluates the answers, giving the pupils rather a limited range of possible responses and frequent experience of being evaluated by adult standards as inadequate. The pupils are not given the opportunity to practise a diversity of roles, and the exchanges often contribute little to the development of jointly constructed competence.

This teacherly style of interaction was largely reproduced by parents,

Table 12.1 Interactional roles: pupils with a teacher

		Move
P2	'I've done the sky coming down.'	I
T	'And what's that white above it? The clouds? Right well you need some more sky up there I think and what's in that gap between the sky and the grass? Can you look out of the window and see if there's anything between the sky and the floor. There isn't is there – right so you need to fill that in . . . Right, Kerry, what are you doing here?'	I
P1	'A sheep an an and . . . dog.'	R
T	'You've got four legs and a nose you've done its head . . . What else do sheep dogs have apart from a head a body four legs and a . . . ?'	I
P1	'mmm.'	R
I	'How do you know it's happy? . . . what's a dog do when it's happy?'	I
P1	'Wags its tail.'	R
T	'It wags its tail so what else has it got . . . ? four legs and a head and a . . . ?'	E-re-I
P3	'I need the white.'	I
T	'What does it wag?'	re-I
P3	'I need white.'	I
P1	'I need white an all.'	R
T	'Its tail . . . Do the tail as well.'	E

auxiliaries, YTS helpers and by work experience students, when these were given teaching tasks to perform. This point is illustrated by the excerpt from a number activity with a YTS helper shown in Table 12.2. The strength of the 'intention to teach' appeared to influence the nature and direction of the talk. When nursery nurse students, parents, auxiliaries, YTS helpers and work experience students were engaged in more leisurely conversations with pupils, they characteristically created more space for pupil initiations and provided more opportunities for pupils to share the responsibility for the control of the discourse.

Nursery nurses and community workers, however, consistently used what Wells (1987) has termed a more 'supportive' style of interaction, both in lesson time and in more informal contexts. This is illustrated in the example from a lesson on hatching eggs which is shown in Table 12.3. The pupils are making the initiating moves here and are not merely consigned to a responding role. The conversation appears more meaningful to the pupils.

In terms of *discourse functions*, differences were again found between the various adult talk partners. Teachers, for instance, used a high proportion of eliciting (el) and evaluating (e) acts and replied (rep) infrequently, not only

Table 12.2 Interactional roles: pupils with a YTS helper

		Move
YTS	'Right – so you put a ring round one cat if it's number one or a ring round three cats if it's number three to make the set of three . . . What number's that?'	I
P2	'Three.'	R
YTS	'Number three! Off you go then . . . Let's see what number are you doing now? . . . What number's this?'	E-I
P2	'Two.'	R
YTS	'Yes Two! And then you can colour them in . . . ? What's this number?'	E-I
P2	'One two three.'	
YTS	'Well done! You put a ring round them like this.'	E-I

Table 12.3 Interactional roles: pupils with a community worker

		Move
CW	'Do you know what time it started?'	I
P1	'No cos I wasn't here but Ester and James were here and Ester's dad said how many eggs have you got and he said 35.'	R-I
CW	'Wow!'	R
P2	'But there was 34 and he said 35 see.' (laughs)	I
CW	'That's silly isn't it.'	R
P2	'That's more, isn't it, 35's more.'	I
P1	'I think that one might be smaller than that one because I think one of them hatched later than the other one.'	I
CW	'Oh is that why? Yes it could be.'	R
P1	'One's hatching now look . . . like our tadpoles.'	I
CW	'So everything's changing isn't it from eggs to chicks and from tadpoles to frogs.'	I

during 'lesson time' but in more leisurely contexts too. The nursery class example set out in Table 12.4 shows a teacher retaining control in this way during discussion of a book. (Sinclair and Coulthard's analysis is again employed, at the level of 'Act' this time, to mark discourse functions.) Pupils showed a very limited range of functions in their talk with their teachers. Decisions about the topic (including starting and stopping, digression and return) were the sole prerogative of the teacher. This left few decisions to the pupils, who were thus high on replies, low on elicitations.

Other adults (with the exception of nursery nurses and community workers) also used a high proportion of eliciting acts, again in more informal contexts as well as lesson-time, as in Table 12.5. Here it is an auxiliary who seems to adopt a teacherly style.

The nursery nurses and community workers were exceptional in the

Table 12.4 Discourse functions: pupils with a teacher

		Move	Act
T	'What's happening to the dress?'	I	el
P 1	'On the line.'	R	rep
T	'The line clothes line – why is it hanging on the clothes line? Why do you think it's hanging on the clothes line?'	E-I	e-el
P 1	'Blowing.'	R	rep
T	'Cos it's blowing – Why do you think it's blowing? (silence) 'It's moving yes – why has the mam put it on the line?'	E-I	e-el cl*-el
P2	'Cos it'll dry.'	R	rep
T	'To dry – what's she been doing with it then?'	E-I	e-el
P3	'Hanging it out.'	R	rep
T	'What's she been doing with it?'	I	el
P 1	'To dry.'	R	rep

(*cl = clue)

Table 12.5 Discourse functions: pupils with an auxiliary worker

		Move	Act
Aux	'Do you know why we have an incubator? Because we haven't got a mammy hen – what happens is that when a mammy hen lays the eggs she usually sits on them in the nest to keep them warm so they hatch so we haven't got a mammy hen here so we have to keep them warm in here.'	I	el i*
P 1	'Yes.'	R	rep
Aux	'And there's that nice warm light in – what do you think that does?'	I	i el
P 1	'Keeps them warm.'	R	rep
Aux	'Yes keeps them warm because what would happen if they got cold?'	E-I	e-el
P 1	'They would die.'	R	rep

(*i = inform)

balance they maintained between eliciting, replying and informing, as in the brief extract in Table 12.6.

The nursery nurses and community workers managed much more often to make space for pupils to experience a wider range of functions, especially eliciting and informing acts, and invited the pupils to take more part in the direction of the discourse. The pupils thus had more options available to them and greater responsibilities. They were also, in consequence, provided with greater cognitive as well as linguistic opportunities.

Analysis of the *cognitive functions* identified in the recordings suggests that, when the pupils were talking with their teachers during lesson time, their discourse did not contain the relative richness of thought evident in less formal exchanges. In lesson time with their teachers, pupils displayed a small proportion of 'recollecting' (R) and 'making connection' (MC) between events and experiences but no 'interpreting' (I) or 'speculating' (SP). (These categories are the ones used by the Wiltshire Oracy Project, 1989, for similar purposes.) However, the pupils recollected, made connections and also interpreted more with adults of all categories when engaged with them in more leisurely conversation. The nursery nurse students were nevertheless the only ones to encourage speculation by pupils in these less formal contexts.

Generally, it was the nursery nurses and community workers who were exceptional in encouraging most recollecting, making connections and interpreting. They did so relatively frequently, during lesson time as well as in more informal contexts. There is evidence of some pupil speculation during lesson time with them, too. Examples are given with a community worker (Table 12.7) and then with a nursery nurse (Table 12.8). In such situations, the pupils show an ability to admit alternative possibilities, to interrelate experiences and to formulate meanings. Noticeably, the adults are doing a lot of listening.

Table 12.6 Discourse functions: pupils with a nursery nurse

		Move	Act
P I	'Look at this – what is this? Can you tell me what this is – what's that?'	I	s*-el
NN	'You tell me what it is.'	I	p*
P I	'I don't know I don't know what it is you'll have to tell me.'	R-I	rep-I*
NN	'Eeh John M! It's a train.'	R	i
P I	'Whose is it?'	I	el
NN	'Well it's ours.'	R	rep
P I	'Mine.'	I	el
NN	'It belongs to everyone in the nursery.'	R	i

(*s = starter; p = prompt; I = loop)

Table 12.7 Cognitive functions: pupils with a community worker

		Move	Act	Cognitive function
P I	'That's a small egg.'	I	i	
CW	'For a small chicken.' (laughs)	I	i	
P I	'Dinosaurs come out of an egg.'	I	i	MC
P2	'They'd need a big egg.'	I	i	MC
P I	'A very big egg to fit a dinosaur inside.'	I	i	MC
P2	'Unless they curled up like this . . . if they moved they'd em . . . crack the egg.'	I	i	I
CW	'Bigger animals need bigger eggs than chickens.'	I	i	

Table 12.8 Cognitive functions: pupils with a nursery nurse

		Move	Act	Cognitive function
NN	'Can you see what's happening now?'	I	i	
P I	'Yes they're all sinking down to the bottom.'	R	i	
NN	'mmm'	R	acc*	
P I	'What would happen if you took some of the water out of there?'	I	i	SP

(*acc = accept)

Discussion

On the basis of criteria used in this study, some adults appeared to be providing their young talk partners with more enabling opportunities than others. The teachers' style of interaction, for instance, appeared to be quite consistent but limiting; i.e. in the sense of giving pupils access to relatively few communicative roles other than that of respondent. Thus, too, in teacher-provided contexts, pupils' verbal and cognitive functions were evidently less varied than in those provided by *some* others. A number of other adults (notably work experience students, YTS helpers, auxiliaries and parents) also adopted a teacherly style and seemed similarly limited and limiting as talk partners. On the other hand, nursery nurses and community workers, especially, created more diverse opportunities; so, to a lesser extent, did several other types of adult talk partner, at least when they sensed there was no teaching agenda to transact.

Teachers, of course, work under particularly severe constraints. As well as the pressure to 'get through' National Curriculum content, impinging as this does on time and management skills, there are assessments to be made, and so on. The teachers in this study had the prime responsibility for controlling a large number of pupils at the same time as teaching them, and for ensuring that all would participate in the set activities and that all would get the most out of individual teacher-contact time. These management demands and the concern for specific learning outcomes can all too understandably conflict with, or override, broad educational aims.

Nevertheless, the pupils' interactions with their teachers had a distinctive character which, to some extent, appeared to derive from the teachers' custodial rather than educational role. Indeed, interviews revealed that most of the other adults did not consider they shared this responsibility to the same degree. These perceptions could go some way to explaining why some adults appeared less constrained in interactions with their pupils and thus gave them a wider range of communicative and cognitive options.

Adults' perceptions of their role and status may result in tacit signals being given to pupils about different degrees of approachability. For their part, the pupils revealed quite accurate perceptions concerning the various adults in their classrooms. This was reflected in a greater readiness to initiate topics and to widen the functions of their talk when they were with certain adults but not others. The expectations they had of their teachers (associated with status, rights and obligations) were clearly different from those they had of others; but then some adults chose to act more like teachers. Pupils' perceptions would certainly have assisted them to adjust their talk: i.e. to address some adults directly, to question them, even to interrupt or challenge them, so that the resulting exchanges became in those cases less one-sided.

The significance of these different patterns of interaction lies primarily in their impact upon pupils' development as language users and communicators, but also upon what pupils learn of the world and of themselves in and through such talk with adults. The present study can be seen as accepting, and in its way contributing to, the increasingly accepted view of children as active participants in their own development and learning. That is a view that casts pupils' adult talk partners in a pivotal role: as much more than mere on-lookers but also as much less than total controllers of their shared talk. In this view, young pupils certainly need good (and informed) adult talk models – but ones whose qualities are more similar to those usually thought of as positive in other (non-classroom) contexts, namely a capacity for listening and building upon what others say as well as for making contributions of their own.

[. . .]

References

Edwards, A. D. and Westgate, D. P. G. (1994). *Investigating Classroom Talk* (Second Edition). Falmer Press: London.

Hughes, M. E. (1994). 'Teachers and other adults as talk-partners for pupils in nursery and reception classes', unpublished PhD thesis, University of Newcastle upon Tyne.

Hughes, M. E. and Westgate, D. (1990). 'Activities and the quality of pupil talk', *Education 3–13*, 18(2), 41–7.

Sinclair, J. and Coulthard, M. (1975). *Towards an Analysis of Discourse: The Language of Teachers and Pupils*. Oxford University Press: London.

Wells, G. (1987). *The Meaning Makers: Children Using Language and Using Language to Learn*. Cambridge University Press: Cambridge.

Wiltshire Oracy Project (1989). *Oracy in Action: A Video-based Training Package on Oracy in Secondary Schools*. Wiltshire LEA: Swindon.

Part IV

Cultural perspectives and practices

Chapter 13

Toddlers' guided participation with their caregivers in cultural activity*

Barbara Rogoff, Christine Mosier, Jayanthi Mistry and
Artin Göncü

This chapter focuses on cultural similarities and variations in the guided participation of children in sociocultural activities. Children around the world, including middle-class US children, learn and develop in situations of joint involvement with other people in culturally important activities. Caregivers and companions collaborate with children in deciding the nature of children's activities and their responsibilities for participation. In the process of collaboration, children adapt their knowledge to new situations, structure problem-solving attempts, and regulate their responsibility for managing the process. This guidance and participation includes tacit forms of communication and distal arrangements of children's activities, as well as explicit verbal interaction. The mutual roles played by children and their caregivers rely on both the interest of caregivers in fostering mature roles and skills and children's own eagerness to participate in adult activities and to push their development.

Along with similarities across cultures in children's guided participation in sociocultural activities are important differences in the skills that are valued, the means of communication (e.g., dyadic conversation between adults and children versus action communication with status differences in conversation between adults and children), and the extent to which children enter into adult activity versus adults sharing children's activity. Middle-class children may need didactic instruction, owing to their segregation from opportunities to observe and participate in important cultural activities, whereas children who have the opportunity to participate in the activities of their community may be able to shoulder the responsibility for learning themselves.

These themes are explored with illustrations from preliminary analyses of observations of eight toddlers and their caregivers from a Mayan town in Guatemala and eight toddlers and their caregivers from an urban setting in

* This is an edited version of a chapter that appeared in *Contexts for Learning: Sociocultural Dynamics in Children's Development*, New York: Oxford University Press, 1993.

the United States (Salt Lake City). (The data are from a larger study reported as a monograph, involving 56 toddlers from Guatemala, India, Turkey, and the United States. Rogoff, Mistry, Göncü, and Mosier, 1993.) The toddlers from each setting involved an approximately equal number of boys and girls, first-born and later-born children, and younger (12 to 16 months) and older toddlers (20 to 23 months). Half of the Salt Lake City families were Mormon; half of the Mayan families were Catholic and the remainder Protestant. The Salt Lake City families were much more affluent, with middle-class occupations and high school or college educations; the Mayan families owned relatively little property, with most fathers in farming or labor jobs and most mothers having third-grade schooling or less.

Our observations were videotaped in a home visit involving child-rearing questions and the opportunity to observe the children and their families in everyday problem solving: exploring novel objects (which we supplied), playing social games, handling the feeding implements of their community, being dressed, and treating other people appropriately. In this chapter, we focus on three episodes of interaction in which we asked mothers to get their toddlers to work a wooden nesting doll (like those from the Soviet Union) that comes apart into bottom and top halves, to make a tortilla or hamburger patty out of playdough, and to "take care of" a plastic babydoll. The toddlers interacted with their mothers; in many families, fathers, siblings, and grandparents were involved as well.

The interactions were analyzed in a process of pattern analysis (Rogoff and Gauvain, 1986) that began with close ethnographic transcription of each case, attempting to portray the meanings of the events for the participants in terms that capture local family goals and practices. Then, with the intimate knowledge of the data that develops from such transcription, the team developed specific categories of interaction that we thought portrayed the crucial similarities and differences across communities in terms that could abstract across the specifics of the observations while maintaining the essence. (It was a long process of dialogue across the four researchers, with all representing their knowledge of a different community, which derived from the transcriptions and from either having originated in that community or nation or having spent at least two years in the community.)

The data reported here are based on preliminary application of these analysis categories; they are preliminary in that the definitions are still in the process of being clarified, and we have not examined the extent to which two observers of the same videotape would code the events similarly. Hence we provide the observations as suggestions rather than as final findings, as a start in describing the patterns of guided participation that may be similar and those that may vary in different cultural communities.

This chapter first discusses our conceptual framework deriving from a Vygotskian sociohistorical approach to development and from the concept of guided participation (Rogoff, 1990) that focuses on the tacit and routine arrangements of children's activities and involvements. Using our observations of the eight Mayan and eight Salt Lake City toddlers, we discuss similarities as well as important differences in the children's guided participation in cultural activities. The observations are discussed as they relate to each conceptual issue, with a later section describing two contrasting cases in greater detail.

Sociohistorical approach to development

The influence of the sociohistorical school on conceptions of development has been marked in work on cultural psychology. Scholars interested in cognitive development in cultural context returned from fieldwork believing that views of development that assumed generic and general progress with age were not adequate to their observations that people seemed to vary in their skills according to the cultural familiarity of the context in which they were observed (Laboratory of Comparative Human Cognition, 1983; Rogoff, 1982b; Rogoff, Gauvain, and Ellis, 1984). Many researchers interested in culture and development found in the writings of Vygotsky a theory that laid the groundwork for a necessary integration of individual development in social and cultural context.

Crucial to the sociohistorical approach is the integration of individual, social, and cultural/historical levels within the analytical unit of *activity* (Cole, 1985; Leont'ev, 1981; Vygotsky, 1987; Wertsch, 1985; Zinchenko, 1985). Activity involves individuals with others in shared efforts with societal organization and tools.

In contrast with most other theories of development – which focus on the individual and the social or the cultural context as separate entities, adding or multiplying one and the other – the sociohistorical approach assumes that individual development must be understood in (and cannot be separated from) the social context. Vygotsky stressed that cognitive development involves children internalizing skilled approaches from their participation in joint problem solving with more skilled partners, who bring the intellectual tools of society within the reach of children in the "zone of proximal development."

Cole (1985) suggested that in the zone of proximal development, culture and cognition create each other. Interactions in the zone of proximal development are the crucible of development *and* of culture, in that they allow children to participate in activities that would be impossible for them alone, using cultural tools that themselves must be adapted to the specific activity at hand and thus are both passed along to and transformed by new generations.

Such an approach views individual development as dependent on interaction with other people in activities involving societal values, intellectual tools, and cultural institutions. Although many researchers treat the zone of proximal development as interaction between children and their social partners, such analysis is incomplete unless it also considers the societal basis of the shared problem solving – the nature of the problem the partners seek to solve, the values involved in determining the appropriate goals and means, the intellectual tools available (e.g., language and number systems, literacy, and mnemonic devices), and the institutional structures of the interaction (e.g., schooling and political and economic systems).

Ironically, the sociohistorical school's formulation of the relation between individual, social, and cultural processes is not only its strength but its weakness. Despite the theory's emphasis on context and society, it nonetheless maintained assumptions regarding the contexts and societal approaches that are most valuable. Vygotsky focused on the sort of language and analysis that characterize academic learning, consistent with the agenda of his nation at the time he wrote (to establish a new Soviet nation with widespread literacy) and with Vygotsky's own upbringing and early career (as a Jewish intellectual and literary critic). In Vygotsky's collaboration with Luria (1976) on "cross-historical" studies in Central Asia, the bias of these views is apparent in the evaluation of the non-literate peasants' versus the literate subjects' ways of thinking,

This unidirectonal focus privileging academic, literate approaches – common to Vygotskian as well as to other major developmental theories – must be questioned if we are to understand the cultural context of development, as the goals of literacy and academic discourse are not universal. Understanding the development of children in the context of their own communities requires study of the local goals and means of approaching life.

From our perspective, each community's valued skills constitute the local goals of development. Societal practices that support children's development are tied to the values and skills considered important. It is not possible to determine if the goals or practices of one community are more adaptive than those of another, as judgments of adaptation cannot be separated from values. For middle-class US children, the skills and patterns of social interaction practiced in school may relate closely to those necessary for eventual participation in the economic and political institutions of their society. In other communities – within the United States and elsewhere – other goals and practices take prominence.

Guided participation and its similarities in two communities

The concept of *guided participation* (Rogoff, 1990) revises the idea of the zone of proximal development to include the developmental goals and means of communication of cultures other than those stressing literacy and academic analytical forms of discourse. The concept is also intended to address the everyday routine involvement of young middle-class children in the activities of their communities – involvement that is not captured in models of interaction based on didactic school lessons.

Guided participation stresses tacit forms of communication in the verbal and non-verbal exchanges of daily life and the distal arrangements involved in the regulation of children's activities, material goods, and companions. The notion of guided participation emphasizes the active role of children in both observing and participating in the organized societal activity of their care-givers and companions. In this more inclusive approach, the aim is to encompass more of the daily activities in which children participate and develop skill in and understanding of the valued approaches of their cultural community.

The emphasis on participation in the notion of guided participation has important implications for the question of how children gain from social interaction. With several theoretical approaches, the process is termed internalization, with the view that children bring external processes "inside." In contrast with such views, however, Rogoff (1990) suggested that the process is one of *appropriation*, emphasizing that children are already parti-cipants (either central or peripheral) in ongoing activity. As such, they already function *within* activities as they learn to manage them, rather than engaging in a two-stage process of, first, social lessons and then individual internalization in order to put the social lessons inside their heads. Chil-dren make later use of their changed understanding resulting from their contribution and involvement with joint problem-solving processes in new situations that resemble the ones in which they have participated. Rather than importing an external process to the internal plane, they appropriate a changed understanding from their own involvement and can carry to future occasions their earlier participation in and their gains in understanding of social activity. As Wertsch and Stone (1979, p. 21) put it, "the process *is* the product."

Although there are important cultural differences in valued activities and means of communication, dealt with in subsequent sections of this chapter, we believe that the processes of guided participation are widespread across differing cultural groups. In this section, we focus on processes of guided participation that we propose are similar across widely different cultural communities.

In almost all (44 of 47) of the episodes we observed involving the nesting doll, the dough, and the babydoll, the toddlers were closely involved with their parents, engaged with the same agenda (e.g., parent and child working the object together; or the parent attempting to assist the child with the object, and the child attempting to work the object with the parent's help). It is likely that if the event had not involved a focus on the toddler (due to the visitors' request to the mother to have the child work the objects), the extent of joint activity would have been much lower in both communities, a topic we will address in a subsequent report. Our point here is that in situations in which caregivers are focused on toddlers, caregivers and toddlers in both communities engaged in close communication.

Such communication between children and their caregivers involves two focal processes, discussed below, that we expect to be widespread across varying cultural communities: *creating bridges* to make connections to new ideas and skills, and *structuring the children's participation* in activities through opportunities available for their involvement and through social support and challenge in activities and roles valued in their community.

Bridging to make connections between known and new

Inherent to communication is a collaborative effort of partners to find a common ground of understanding on which to base their contributions in order to ensure mutual comprehension. Partners initially have somewhat (or greatly) discrepant views of a situation, but seek a common perspective or language through which to communicate their ideas. This effort to reach a common ground involves a stretch on the part of the participants. Middle-class adults often adapt their contribution to fit with what they think the children can understand, restructuring the problem definition to be within children's grasp (Wertsch, 1984). At the same time, children's efforts to participate in ongoing communication involve a stretch in the direction of a more mature definition of the situation and more skilled roles. From the collaboratively constructed common ground, which itself involves development, the participants may share in thinking as they extend their joint understanding together.

Bridging between two starting points involves emotional and non-verbal as well as verbal forms of communication. Children seek connections between old and new situations in their caregivers' emotional cues regarding the nature of a situation and how to handle it, in their interpretations of children's behavior, and in their labels for objects and events that inherently classify similarities across objects and events. All of the parents we observed indicated to the toddlers the nature of the activity with the object, orienting the children verbally in an average of 85 percent of the episodes and non-verbally in 91 percent of the episodes.

One kind of non-verbal bridging that provides young children with information about ambiguous situations is social referencing, in which infants as young as 10 months seek information from adults' expressions. They proceed to explore if the adult appears content but avoid the ambiguous situation if the adult appears fearful (Feinman, 1982; Gunnar and Stone, 1984; Sorce, Emde, Campos, and Klinnert, 1985).

An example is provided by a 20-month-old Mayan boy who attempted to gather information about an ambiguous situation: whether or not a playdough tortilla was edible. He had been skillfully patting the playdough that we had brought along into a "tortilla," with his mother's guidance:

The baby broke off a tiny corner of the little tortilla he had made and held it up expectantly to his mother. She absently nodded to the baby as she conversed with the adults present.

The baby brought the piece of play tortilla to his mouth and, looking at his mother fixedly, he stuck out his tongue and held the piece of tortilla toward it, with a questioning expression. His mother suddenly bolted out her hand and snatched his hand holding the piece of tortilla away from his mouth, blurting out "No! Not that!" The baby looked at her with a little surprise but was not disturbed by this clear message that the dough is not edible; he watched quietly as she laughingly put the little piece of dough back on the rest of the tortilla, put it back into the baby's hand and told him that it is not to eat. He resumed patting the dough contentedly.

The mutual adjustments in communication that provide the basis of bridging between adults and children reflect adherence to principles of communication (e.g., Clark and Haviland, 1977) that a speaker be sensitive to the perspective and knowledge of the listener and that conversation focus on what is deserving of comment from the joint perspective of speaker and listener. Although there are likely to be asymmetries in responsibility for adjustment according to the status of the participants, the situation, and societal standards of responsibility for adjustment (discussed later), the phenomenon of seeking shared meaning is in the nature of human communication. Indeed, some argue that intersubjectivity between infants and their caregivers is innate – that from the earliest interactions infants are involved in the sharing of meaning (Brazelton, 1983; Luria, 1987; Newson, 1977; Trevarthen, Hubley, and Sheeran, 1975).

Collaborative structuring of problem solving

Caregivers and children arrange the structure of situations in which children are involved through both distal arrangements and explicit interaction. Social activity is managed through assignment of and opportunity for participation in varying activities, such as the household chores in which 14 of the 16 toddlers were reported to engage, as well as through structuring children's responsibility for an activity through ongoing communication. Both adults and children are responsible for deciding children's activities and their role in them, often through tacit and pragmatic determination of children's skills and interests, as well as through more explicit arrangements for children's growing participation in the activities of their culture.

During caregiver–child communication, participants collaborate in structuring children's roles through division of responsibility for the activity. The more skilled partner may provide "metacognitive" support through handling higher-order goals as children handle the subgoals of which they are capable with assistance, allowing children to achieve more in collaboration than they can independently. With the nesting doll and playdough, most caregivers adjusted the object or its position to facilitate the toddlers' efforts, divided or simplified the task, and handled difficult moves for the child (in 94 percent, 75 percent, and 62 percent of the episodes, respectively). Such structuring was a little less frequent with the babydoll, perhaps owing to its familiarity to the children.

Children's roles in structuring an activity in social interaction may involve central responsibility for managing the situation – even when their partners have greater knowledge – and for adjusting their own level of participation. One-third of the toddlers clearly negotiated shifts in responsibility for handling the objects, seeking greater involvement or greater assistance, or resisting caregivers' suggestions. When there were tussles between caregivers and children regarding the agenda, the outcome was more likely to involve the toddlers' agenda, particularly in the Mayan community, which stresses respect for infants' autonomy. Children's interest and care-givers' constraints may ensure that young children's roles in routine activities adjust according to their interest and skills, within a dynamic zone of proximal development.

Cultural variation in the goals of development

Differences across cultures in guided participation involve variation in the skills and values that are promoted according to cultural goals of maturity. Cultural communities vary in their institutions and related tools and technologies. Cultural psychologists and sociocultural theorists have argued that underlying the cognitive differences across cultural (or historical) groups are intellectual tools such as literacy and arithmetic (Cole and Griffin, 1980; Rogoff, 1981b; Rogoff et al., 1984; Scribner and Cole, 1981; Vygotsky, 1978, 1987). Communities differ in the skills considered important (e.g., reading, weaving, sorcery, healing, managing people) and approaches valued (e.g., individual achievement, speed in performance, interpersonal harmony).

Skills for the use of cultural tools such as literacy begin to be practiced even before children have contact with the technology in its mature form. Middle-class US parents involve their children in "literate" forms of narrative in preschool discourse, as they embed their children in a way of life in which reading and writing are integral to communication, recreation, and livelihood (Cazden, 1988; Heath, 1982, 1983; Michaels and Cazden, 1986; Taylor, 1983).

Cultural differences in children's activities are apparent in the chores in which the mothers reported that their toddlers participated. Most of the toddlers helped with sweeping or food preparation, but most Salt Lake City toddlers also helped manage household machines such as vacuum cleaners and dishwashers; the Mayan children had less involvement with machines, but some had roles in economic activities of the adult world, such as running errands to a corner store and trying to weave.

Cultural variation in adult–child roles and communication

There appear to be striking cultural differences in the means available for children to observe and participate in culturally important activities as well as to receive instruction outside the context of skilled activity. These differences relate to variations in the explicitness and intensity of verbal and non-verbal communication and the interactional status of children and adults (Field, Sostek, Vietze, and Leiderman, 1981; Leiderman, Tulkin, and Rosenfeld, 1977; Whiting and Edwards, 1988). Rogoff (1990) suggested that these cultural differences fit together into patterns that vary in terms of the responsibility adults take for teaching children in cultures in which children do not participate in adult activities, and the responsibility children take for learning in cultures in which they have the opportunity to observe and participate in mature cultural activities.

Cultural variation in verbal and non-verbal communication

An emphasis on explicit, declarative statements – in contrast to tacit, procedural, and subtle forms of verbal and non-verbal instruction – appears to characterize cultures that promote Western schooling (John-Steiner, 1984; Jordan, 1977; Rogoff, 1981b, 1982a; Scribner, 1974; Scribner and Cole, 1973). The emphasis of Western researchers on talking as the appropriate means of adult–child interaction may reflect a cultural bias that overlooks the information provided by silence, gaze, postural changes, smells, and touch. Middle-class US infants have been characterized as "packaged" babies who do not have direct skin contact with their caregiver (Whiting, 1981) and often spend more than one-third of their time in a room separate from any other people. US infants are held approximately half the time, as are Gusii (Kenyan) infants (Richman, Miller, and Solomon, 1988).

The physical separation of US infants from other people may necessitate the use of distal forms of communication such as vocalizing. In contrast with US children's use of distal communication, children who are constantly in the company of their caregivers may rely more on non-verbal cues, such as direction of gaze or facial expression. Infants who are in almost constant skin-to-skin contact with their mothers may manage effective communication through tactile contact in squirming and postural changes.

In our observations, almost all of the toddlers received both explanations and demonstrations of what they were to do with the nesting doll, dough, and babydoll from their caregivers. However, the amount of parental talk to the Salt Lake City toddlers was much greater, as can be seen in Table 13.1. Most Salt Lake City caregivers used many sentences, whereas most Mayan caregivers spoke few sentences and some spoke none. The Salt Lake City

Table 13.1 Episodes with differing amounts of talk, by toddlers' age

	Salt Lake City		Mayan community	
	12–16 mo	20–23 mo	12–16 mo	20–23 mo
Total no. of episodes	12	12	12	11
Caregiver's talk				
Many sentences	8	8	2	4
A few sentences	4	2	6	5
Phrases at most	0	2	4	2
Toddlers' talk				
Many words; phrases	8	1	0	0
A few words	3	6	3	0
No words	1	5	9	11

caregivers averaged 2.0 episodes with extensive talk, whereas the Mayan caregivers averaged only 0.9 episodes with extensive talk, $F(1,14) = 4.8$, $p <0.05$.

The Mayan toddlers, in turn, were much less talkative: most of the older Salt Lake City toddlers' episodes involved speaking many words or phrases, whereas most of the Mayan episodes involved no talk at all by the toddler. (The community difference was significant, $F[1,14] = 24.9$, $p = 0.0003$, as was the age difference, $F[1,14] = 6.9, p = 0.02$.)

Caregivers' use of some forms of non-verbal communication was similar across the two communities. Most caregivers used action communication, guiding the toddlers' hands or the object or indicating with gestures.

There were differences between the caregivers from the two communities in other kinds of non-verbal communication as well. The Mayan caregivers' interactions relied more on information carried in gaze or postural or timing changes: the exchange of information by means of caregivers' gaze or by means of changes in caregivers' posture or pacing was essential for communication during an average of 1.9 and 2.2 Mayan episodes, respectively, and for only 0.5 and 0.2 Salt Lake City episodes, $F(1,14) = 6.3, p = 0.02$; $F(1,14) = 32.0, p = 0.0001$.

The Mayan babies, like the Mayan caregivers, relied more on non-verbal communication through action communication, gaze, and changes in posture or pacing. In an average of 1.6 and 1.9 Mayan episodes but only 0.5 and 0.8 Salt Lake City episodes, toddlers guided their partner's hands or the object, or gestured, $F(1,14) = 7.2, p <0.02$; $F(1,14) = 4.9, p = 0.04$. Toddlers' gaze and changes in posture or pacing were essential during an average of 1.8 and 2.1 of the Mayan episodes, respectively, but in only 0.4 and 0 of the Salt Lake City episodes, $F(1,14) = 6.9, p = 0.02$; $F(1,14) = 51.9, p = 0$.

The Mayan caregivers held their hands in readiness to assist the toddlers more frequently than the Salt Lake City caregivers (on 2.4 versus 1.1 episodes, $F[1,14] = 10.0$, $p < 0.007$), suggesting preparedness for the subtle communication of the Mayan children regarding a need for assistance.

Cultural variation in adult–child status and locus of responsibility for learning

Variations in the relative status of children and adults have been noted in observations of cultural differences regarding the likelihood of adults serving as play partners with children or carrying on conversations as if children were their peers. These status variations may relate to children's opportunities to participate in adult activities and thereby learn through involvement rather than needing separate child-focused teaching situations and interactions.

Adults in peer or asymmetrical roles with children

In some communities, young children are not expected to be conversational peers with adults, initiating interactions and interacting as equals in the conversation (Blount, 1972; Harkness and Super, 1977; Schieffelin and Eisenberg, 1984). Instead, they may speak when spoken to, replying to informational questions or simply carrying out directions. Children converse and play not with parents but with other children and kin such as older cousins, uncles, and grandparents (Farran and Mistry, personal communication; Ward, 1971).

Whiting and Edwards (1988) noted that of the 12 cultural groups they studied, the US middle-class mothers ranked highest in sociability with children – interacting in a friendly, playful, or conversational way, treating children at times as status equals – whereas in the other communities mothers stressed training or nurturant involvement with children, maintaining authority and dominance with respect to children.

In the Mayan community in which we carried out the research, when older children interact with adults it is in the context of adult work. Rogoff (1981a) observed that adults were as likely as or more likely than peers to be interacting with 9-year-olds when the children were doing household or agricultural work, but they were almost never involved with them when children were playing. Play is a domain for peer interaction, not adult companionship. During free time, children beyond age 3 or 4 move around town with a multi-age group of children, amusing themselves by observing ongoing events and imitating their elders in play, most of which involves emulation of adult activities.

Whereas US middle-class mothers consider it part of their role to play with their children – all eight of the Salt Lake City mothers reported that they and the children's fathers often play with the baby – seven of the eight Mayan mothers reported that neither parent played with the child. Several

Mayan mothers laughed with embarrassment at the idea of playing with their children, as being a playmate is the role of other children and occasionally grandparents. When a toddler is playing, reported the Mayan mothers, it is time for a mother to get her work done.

Ochs and Schieffelin (1984) contrasted two cultural patterns of speech between young children and their caregivers. In middle-class US families, caregivers simplify their talk, negotiate meaning with children, cooperate in building propositions, and respond to verbal and non-verbal initiations by the child. In Kaluli New Guinea and Samoan families, caregivers model unsimplified utterances for the child to repeat to a third party, direct the child to notice others, and build interaction around circumstances to which caregivers wish the child to respond. Ochs and Schieffelin pointed to the difference in adults adapting to children versus children adapting to adults. In both of these patterns, children participate in activities of the society, but the patterns vary in terms of children's versus caregivers' responsibilities to adapt in the process of learning or teaching mature forms of speech and action.

Opportunities for children to participate in and to observe adult activities

The adaptation of caregivers to children may be more necessary in societies that segregate children from adult activities, thereby requiring them to practice skills or learn information outside the mature context of use (Rogoff, 1981a, 1990). In the US middle class, children are segregated from the work and recreational world of adults, and they learn about skills they may eventually need in order to participate in their society as adults in a separate context specialized for the purpose (i.e., school).

Young US middle-class children seldom have much chance to participate in the economic functioning of the households and may be segregated from human company by the provision of separate bedrooms and a focus on attention to objects rather than people. Infants are often entirely alone for as much as 10 of 24 hours, managing as best they can to handle their hunger or thirst or comforting needs with objects (Morelli *et al.*, 1988; Ward, 1971; Whiting, 1981). All eight of the Salt Lake City toddlers had their own separate beds, and six of the eight had their own rooms; all eight of the Mayan toddlers slept in the same room as their parents, and seven slept in the same bed with their mothers (and usually with father or siblings as well).

In communities in which children are integrated in adult activities, children are ensured a role in the action, at least as close observers. Children are present at most events of interest in the community, from work to recreation to church. They are able to observe and eavesdrop on the ongoing processes of life and death, work and play, that are important in their community. As infants, they are often carried wherever their caregiver goes, and as young children they may do errands and roam the town in their free time, watching whatever is going on. As non-participants in ordinary adult conversation, they may eavesdrop on important adult activities from which non-participant adults may be excluded.

Gaskins and Lucy (1987) noted that children's lower status and freedom to observe in a Mayan community in Mexico means that children have access to information unavailable to adults, providing extra eyes and ears for their mothers who stay at home and extract information regarding village events from the children. Mothers' questions about events focus children's attention on the relevant features of ongoing activities, guiding the children as to what aspects of events are significant. Observation and eavesdropping serve as an active method of obtaining information.

Children's versus adults' responsibility for learning and teaching

Cultural variation in the symmetry of children's and adults' roles and in the opportunities for children to observe and participate in adult activities may relate to cultural expectations that children are responsible for learning or that adults are responsible for making children learn through teaching (Rogoff, 1990).

Eavesdropping versus peer-status conversation and language lessons

Ward (1971) offered an eavesdropping account of language learning in her description of a black community in Louisiana, in which "the silent absorption in community life, the participation in the daily commercial rituals, and the hours spent apparently overhearing adults' conversations should not be underestimated in their impact on a child's language growth" (p. 37). Small children are not conversational partners with adults, people with whom to "engage in dialogue." Children are not encouraged to learn skills in initiating and monopolizing conversation with adults on topics of their own choosing (skills useful in middle-class schooling). Questions between children and adults involve requests for information, not questions asked for the sake of conversation, or for parents to drill children on topics about which the parents already know the answers. However, mothers' speech to children, although not taking the form of a dialogue, is carefully regularized, providing workable models of the language used in the community.

Heath (1983) similarly reported that working-class black Carolina adults did not see young children as conversational partners. Rather, the toddlers were always surrounded by others and moved through phases of echoing and experimenting with variation on the speech around them – at first ignored but gradually participating by making themselves part of ongoing discourse. Adults encouraged verbal facility by instigating and appreciating preschoolers' involvement in assertive challenging and scolding exchanges with adults and other children. However, because children were not seen as information givers, they were not asked test questions for which adults already had an answer, such as questions of fact or detail.

An example of instructional discourse between an adult and a toddler, with peer interactional status and test questions, appears with a 21-month-old Salt Lake City child handling the babydoll with his mother:

> The mother handed the doll to the toddler, saying, "What is it? Is that a baby? Can you take care of the baby?" with babytalk intonation. The toddler explored the doll and pointed to the eye, commenting, "Eye." His mother confirmed, "eye," and he asked "What dat?" as he pointed at the doll's face. The mother clarified and answered his question: "What's that? Her mouth." After some further interaction, the mother chirped "Where's her belly button?" When he pointed to the doll's belly button, the mother evaluated his response, "All right!" in the classic question–response–evaluation sequence that Mehan (1979) has documented as teacher–student discourse in the classroom.

In an average of 2.2 Salt Lake City episodes, parents interacted with toddlers as conversational peers, asking their opinions, responding to their vocalizations as conversation, and providing openings for equal dialogic exchanges, whereas the Mayan toddlers were treated as conversational peers in only 1 of 23 episodes, $F(1,14) = 106$, $p = 0$. The Salt Lake City toddlers assumed a peer role in 1.9 of the episodes, offering comments and initiating optional conversation, but the Mayan toddlers never took a peer conversational role with their parents, $F(1,14) = 22.2$, $p = 0.0003$. Nonetheless, the toddlers in both communities interacted reciprocally with their parents in almost all episodes with joint action and action communication. It is the presence of verbal dialogue that most differentiates the interactions of the two communities.

Many of the episodes with the Salt Lake City toddlers involved talk that can be seen as lessons in language use; such language lessons almost never occurred in the Mayan episodes. The Salt Lake City caregivers used marked babytalk intonations and speech in an average of 2.5 episodes; the Mayan caregivers did in only 0.5 episodes, $F(1,14) = 18.7$, $p = 0.0007$. The Salt Lake City caregivers used test questions, asking for information they already knew, in an average of 1.4 episodes; the Mayan parents never did, $F(1,14) = 13.4$, $p = 0.002$. The Salt Lake City caregivers labeled events or object parts didactically, produced running commentaries describing and evaluating ongoing events, and they played word games in 2.1, 2.1, and 1.0 episodes, respectively; the corresponding amounts for the Mayan caregivers were 0.4, 0.1, and 0.1 episodes, $Fs = 19.6, 28.9, 8.8$, $ps < 0.01$.

This finding does not necessarily mean that the Salt Lake City parents were self-consciously producing such "lessons"; they may have been, or they may have interacted with their children in this manner in an intuitive fashion. Whatever their explicit purpose, the differences in types of adult–toddler talk in the two communities are striking.

In communities in which children are not conversational partners of adults, they may be poorly prepared for the pattern of discourse used in school, but they become proficient in the language and other skills of their community. They are able to learn from observing and eavesdropping as ever-present members of the community, their growing participation in daily activities from an early age, the questions and directives and demonstrations of adults, and their playful talk with other children.

Observation and attention management

With opportunities to observe ongoing activity and to help when necessary, children from many cultures begin to participate in chores and other activities from age 3 or 4, when they begin to see what to do; they assume responsibilities for child, animal, and house care by age 5 or 7 (Rogoff et al., 1975; Ward, 1971; Whiting and Edwards, 1988). Their role grows and their opportunities to practice are amplified by their interest in participation and by their parents' setting them tasks within their capabilities and providing suggestions and demonstrations *in the context of joint activity.* In observations in the Mayan community, native observers identified only 6 of 1,708 occasions in which 9-year-olds were explicitly being taught outside of school (Rogoff, 1981a).

An example of children's learning in the context of participation is Mayan mothers' reports of how their children learn to make tortillas. Although the Mayan mothers give pointers and structure their children's efforts, they do not regard the process as teaching; they claim that the children simply learn. They, along with researchers, seem to regard teaching as the sort of interaction that goes on in schools. According to Mayan mothers, 1- to 2-year-olds observe their mothers making tortillas and attempt to follow suit. The mothers give them a small piece of dough to use and facilitate their efforts by rolling the dough in a ball and starting the flattening process. The toddler's "tortilla" is cooked and eaten by family members. As the child gains skill in making tortillas, the mother adds pointers and demonstrations to facilitate holding the dough in a position that facilitates smooth flattening, and the children can witness the outcome of their own efforts and contribute to making meals. The child observes carefully and participates, and the mother simplifies the task to the child's level of skill and demonstrates and gives suggestions during the process of joint activity.

Questions by children to adults are rare in some communities (Heath, 1983). Learners' questions to a teacher may be regarded as impolite challenges in that they involve a subordinate obliging a superior to respond. This exchange implies that the subordinate has the right to hold the superior responsible for the information requested, as Goody (1978) observed in the apprenticeship of Gonja youths learning to weave.

Rather than relying on questions and explanations to organize their learning, observers may be skilled in picking up information through watching, on some occasions without hands-on participation. Nash (1967) reported that the method of learning to use the footloom in a weaving factory in Guatemala is for the learner (an adult) to sit beside a skilled weaver for a period of weeks, simply observing, asking no questions and receiving no explanation. The learner may fetch a spool of thread from time to time for the weaver but does not carry out the process, until after a period of weeks the learner feels competent to begin. At that point, the learner has become a skilled weaver simply by watching and by attending to whatever demonstrations the skilled weaver has provided.

In our observations, the Mayan toddlers appeared more likely to monitor peripheral social events outside their own activity or their activity with their caregiver (doing so during an average of 2.5 episodes) than were the Salt Lake City toddlers (who monitored during an average of 1.1 episodes). The Mayan toddlers appeared to be able to attend to several events simultaneously (e.g., working the object with the caregiver and monitoring other conversation, glancing at and being involved with the flow of events, on an average of 2.1 episodes), whereas the Salt Lake City toddlers seldom appeared to attend to several events simultaneously (averaging only 0.4 episodes, $F[1,14] = 25.4$, $p = 0.0002$). The Salt Lake City toddlers were more likely to attend to one event at a time: their own activity or a joint activity, either exclusively or alternating attention between their own activity and other events.

The Mayan caregivers, like the children, appeared able to engage attention with several events simultaneously. Their timesharing of attention may have been facilitated by their reserving verbal channels of communication for adult conversation and relying heavily on non-verbal channels – gaze, posture, timing, and action communication – with the toddlers. In an average of 2.2 episodes, they tracked several events simultaneously, compared with 0.5 Salt Lake City episodes, $F(1,14) = 22.9$, $p = 0.0003$. The Salt Lake caregivers usually alternated attention with other events if there were competing events that caught their attention.

In communities in which observation is possible, people may be especially active and skilled observers. Mainstream middle-class researchers, who may rely less on observation, tend to think of observation as passive. However, this research suggests that in some settings children and adults are skilled and active in attending to what they watch. In the guided participation of children in cultural communities that stress children's responsibility for learning, children may have the opportunity to observe and participate in the skills of the community and may develop impressive skills in observation, with less explicit child-centered interaction to integrate the child in the activities of society. Skilled observation may allow skilled participation by very young children, yielding impressive skill and responsibility in such activities as tending younger children (Weisner and Gallimore, 1977) or handling knives (Sorenson, 1979).

Efforts to aid children in learning may thus vary in terms of the children's responsibility to observe and analyze the task versus the caregivers' responsibility to decompose the task and motivate the child. Dixon, LeVine, Richman, and Brazelton (1984) noted that Gusii (Kenyan) mothers gave their 6- to 36-month-old infants the responsibility for learning. They used clear "advance organizers" in instruction, often modeling the expected performance in its entirety, and appeared to expect the task to be completed exactly as specified if the child attended to it. This method contrasted with the efforts of American mothers, who took the responsibility for teaching and making their babies learn. They concentrated on arousing the children's interest and shaping their behavior step by step, providing constant encouragement and refocusing.

In our observations, the Salt Lake City parents seemed to take greater responsibility for motivating their children and for managing their attention. The Salt Lake City parents attempted to manage their toddlers' attention in an average of 1.5 episodes, whereas only 0.4 Mayan episodes involved parental management of the child's attention, $F(1,14) = 7.2, p < 0.02$. Consistent with the observations of Dixon et al., the Salt Lake City caregivers often tried to arouse their children's interest, showing mock excitement about an activity in an average of 2.0 episodes, compared with only 0.4 episodes with Mayan caregivers, $F(1,14) = 12.5, p = 0.003$. Consistent with teachers' efforts to motivate, half of the Salt Lake City episodes involved praise for the child's performance, but such praise occurred only once in 23 Mayan episodes, $F(1,14) = 18.7, p = 0.0007$.

Two toddlers with their mothers and the nesting doll

A contrast in verbal versus non-verbal communication, status relations of partners, and teaching versus learning emphases is apparent if we compare a 20-month-old from each community. Both are first-born boys whose handling of the nesting doll was skilled and interested and included a counting routine with their mothers. For both communities, the interaction style was extreme in similar ways: counting routines were not usual with this toy in either community (these two boys are the only children of the 16 who counted or were encouraged to count the nesting doll pieces), and both mothers appeared more concerned with their children's performance than most other mothers from their communities. For the Salt Lake City mother, the concern took the form of greater directiveness and of putting herself at times into a more extreme peer role with the child, acting like a child herself, than the other

Salt Lake City mothers. The Mayan mother was somewhat more directive with the child than the other mothers from her community. So the style of both mothers is extreme for their communities, in the same direction.

The most important differences between these two dyads are in status roles – the Salt Lake City mother getting on the child's level and playing or teaching versus the Mayan mother assisting the child but maintaining a difference of status – and in responsiveness and subtlety of their verbal and non-verbal communication. The differences are consistent with the Salt Lake City child being treated as the object of teaching and the Mayan child being responsible for learning. This example is in line with differences in the sample as a whole, in which Salt Lake City caregivers acted as teachers in an average of 1.1 episodes and as playmates in 1.1 episodes, whereas Mayan caregivers never acted as teachers or playmates with the toddlers: $Fs = 10.3, 14.5, ps < 0.006$. Rather, the Mayan caregivers showed readiness to aid in their children's efforts to learn.

It is important to note that although the style of the two mothers differed, each mother used both verbal and non-verbal communication adjusted to her child, and each child was comfortably engaged with his mother in handling a problem that was challenging but supported in the interaction.

The Mayan mother monitored her son's actions with the object; and though she told him clearly what to do, her moves were generally responsive rather than initiatory, and she did not overrule his agenda. The Salt Lake City mother, in contrast, interrupted her child's pace and at many moves seemed to attempt to manage the agenda, even to the point of lack of coordination of the moves between mother and child. The communication between the Mayan mother and child was subtle, whereas that between the Salt Lake City mother and child involved loud and frequent talk and large movements. The Mayan mother managed to participate in adult conversation simultaneously with her support for the baby's efforts; the Salt Lake City mother focused exclusively on the child, though other adults were also present.

Salt Lake City mother and 20-month-old

The Salt Lake City mother began playing with the nesting doll as if she were herself a child, giggling and waving her hands in an animated fashion and bouncing up and down and squealing as she knelt on the floor with the child. She poked at the baby with the nesting doll and tickled him; she took pieces of the toy and made up new games with them, hiding them or putting them inside other objects. She sometimes turned the toy over to him by saying "Your turn," thereby emphasizing the equality of status.

When the baby handled the toy, she sometimes changed to an instructional tone: "*On*. Put the lid *on*" and cheered "Wonderful! Yay!" and applauded his moves, frequently gushing "Oh, you're so smaaart! You're so smaaart! I *love* you!" with a hug. The baby generally worked calmly with the object but sometimes giggled with his mother. The father sat nearby and watched placidly as if the mother's actions were not out of the ordinary.

Much later in the visit, the interviewer brought out a new version of the nesting doll, which the mother helped the baby take apart and put together, cheering "Yay! There you go, Buddy!" and jumping him up and down on her lap. When the littlest doll appeared, she gasped in exaggerated surprise and enthusiastically exclaimed, "There's three of them!" She proceeded to count them, with the child following her cues to count, but the counting efforts of the mother and child were uncoordinated, with the mother both instigating and echoing with a confusion of sequence that got more complicated during the next round of counting. When the mother said "two," the baby said "one," and when she finished with "three," the baby said "two." The mother then started counting again, saying "one" before the baby said "three."

Then the mother changed the routine, holding the bottom pieces out on her flat palm and encouraging him to put the nesting doll together, "Does the lady go in there?" She encouraged in a sweet babytalk intonation, "That's right! . . . Put her in. *In*," emphasizing the term. She used a sweet voice throughout, and when he did it differently than she suggested, she emphasized his independent choice, "OK, do you want to put her that way? . . . That's fine . . . Do you choose that way?" The mother went on with the lesson in putting the pieces together, directing the baby's actions with language instruction, cheering and providing commentary on his actions, and enthusiastically marking and praising his "individual" accomplishment.

Mayan mother and 20-month-old

The playmate and teacher roles taken by the Salt Lake City mother differed from the role taken and means used by the Mayan mother, although the Mayan mother appeared to be focused on encouraging her son's performance and is a member of a family that stresses schooling; she herself has a high level of education by community standards (ninth grade, the highest in the Mayan sample).

The mother demonstrated how the nesting doll comes apart and fits together, with a few words to encourage him to look. The baby insisted on handling the toy himself; after a moment the mother took the doll back and demonstrated again, leaning over with the two halves of the big doll, saying quietly, "I'll put it together." The baby held the small inside doll and complained to get access to the big outside doll. The mother looked into the baby's eyes and pointed out "Two . . . two . . ." and handed the big doll back to the baby, repeating "two" with a significant gaze. Then she demonstrated opening and closing the small inside doll, commenting only "Look" as the baby watched her pull the big outside doll apart, saying "Put it inside." She set down the two big halves carefully in front of the baby, and set the little doll inside to demonstrate the sequence to the baby, pausing a couple of times to look at the baby to be sure he was watching. He was.

The baby went on to handle the pieces himself for a while, as his mother conversed with adults at the same time as she occasionally demonstrated the actions to the baby, using gestures and timing to emphasize the essential aspects of the action to the baby while talking and looking at the adult with whom she spoke. She thus directed the baby in an unobtrusive fashion, and when he resisted her suggestions she did not insist.

When he had trouble, the mother instantly intervened and demonstrated, commenting, "Do this one first . . . and then cover it up with this one." The baby was attentive and attempted to work the nesting doll again, as the mother monitored his efforts and held her hands ready to help him, not interfering unless he had difficulty. This process continued until the doll was assembled, and the mother then subtly demonstrated again by carefully holding the pieces in position and making a few quiet comments. The baby watched patiently and acknowledged the demonstration with an "Okay" as if to say, "I see."

Now he could put the pieces in the right positions, and the mother merely monitored his actions as she chatted with the adults. The baby monitored the adult conversation as he worked the toy. Once the baby kissed the doll, and the mother and others encouraged him to do it again, responding with pleasure to his idea. He cheerfully continued. Then he turned and counted quietly as he put two pieces in her lap, "One . . . two . . ." The mother repeated "two" after him, and the baby put the third piece in her outstretched hand, "three," and the mother echoed, "three." There did not seem to be further acknowledgement of the baby's counting, though he had said little else during the session.

It is notable that the Mayan baby's counting, like his kissing of the doll, was at his instigation; it received a pleasant acknowledgment but did not become a public evaluation of his intelligence or a reason for expressions of love. The baby's actions, rather than being the exclusive, individual focus of the mother, fit into the flow of ongoing social events, with both the mother and child monitoring each other and the other social activities as they handled the object. Though the child received attention, it was not exclusive; rather, the child appeared to be smoothly integrated into the social fabric, not a recipient of baby-directed play or special registers of speech.

These two examples illustrate how middle-class US parents may assume didactic and dyadic roles as they rely on their own efforts to motivate children to learn, in contrast with caregivers in cultures in which children have the responsibility to learn and are involved with many other social partners in the process.

Conclusions

Children in a wide variety of cultural communities, including middle-class US communities, appear to have in common opportunities to learn through guided participation in culturally arranged activities, learning and developing in situations of joint involvement with more experienced people.

Variations across communities have to do with what is being learned, with differing values and practices regarding such skills as literacy and other school-related technologies or management of people as in child care. Goals of development have local variation (along with species' similarities, of course) according to local practices and values.

Related variation across communities involves contrasting means of teaching/learning, differing with children's opportunities to observe and participate in adult activities or in child-oriented instructional interactions. Differences in children's versus adults' responsibility for children's learning appear to be accompanied by variations in the interactional roles of children and adults and in reliance on explanation out of context or observation and participation in the context of important adult activities. Such differences may lead to variation in children's skill in managing their own attention and observation, and in managing verbal interactions with adults as conversational peers. These skills and interactional practices are differentially useful for participation in varying institutional contexts such as formal schooling and economic activities.

Underlying these varying circumstances, however, are similarities in guided participation: caregivers collaborate with children in determining the nature of children's activities and their responsibilities in participation. They work together, and in the process children learn to manage new situations under collaborative structuring of problem-solving attempts and regulation of their responsibilities. This guided participation includes tacit forms of communication and distal arrangements of children's learning environments, as well as explicit verbal interaction. The mutual roles played by caregivers and children in children's development rely on both the caregivers' interest in fostering mature skills and the children's own eagerness to participate in adult activities and push their own development. Guided participation involves children's participation in the activities of their community, with the challenge and support of a system of social partners including caregivers and peers of varying levels of skill and status.

Guided participation may be universal, although communities vary in the goals of development and the nature of involvement of children and adults. Observations of variations in guided participation across cultures draw attention to:

1   Goals of mature contribution to the community that organize the skills and values that children learn

2   Opportunities available to children for learning in the arrangements made for children's activities and companions
3   Responsibility that children take for learning from the activities in which they participate and from rich opportunities for observation and eavesdropping
4   Tacit but ubiquitous nature of children's guided participation
5   Unselfconscious nature of the roles of children as well as of their social partners in day-to-day arrangements and interaction.

Observations in cultures other than those of the researchers may make such aspects of guided participation more apparent. However, we suggest that these features of guided participation may also be more common for US middle-class children than the explicit, didactic, selfconscious instructional interaction that has been the focus of research. The interdependence of children and their social partners in valued and routine cultural activities may be a fact of children's lives that accounts for children's rapid development as participants in the skills and understanding of their community, whether it involves learning to weave or to read, to take care of livestock or young children or homework.

References

Blount, B. G. (1972). Parental speech and language acquisition: some Luo and Samoan examples. *Anthropological Linguistics*, *14*, 119–30.
Brazelton, T. B. (1983). Precursors for the development of emotions in early infancy. In R. Plutchik and H. Kellerman (eds). *Emotion: theory, research, and experience* (Vol. 2, pp. 35–55). Orlando, FL: Academic Press.
Cazden, C. B. (1988). *Classroom discourse.* Portsmouth, NH: Heinemann.
Clark, H. H. and Haviland, S. E. (1977). Comprehension and the given-new contract. In R. O. Freedle (ed.). *Discourse production and comprehension* (pp. 1–40). Norwood, NJ: Ablex.
Cole, M. (1985). The zone of proximal development: where culture and cognition create each other. In J. V. Wertsch (ed.). *Culture, communication, and cognition: Vygotskian perspectives* (pp. 146–61). Cambridge: Cambridge University Press.
Cole, M. and Griffin, P. (1980). Cultural amplifiers reconsidered. In D. R. Olson (ed.). *The social foundations of language and thought* (pp. 343–64). New York: Norton.
Dixon, S. D., LeVine, R. A., Richman, A., and Brazelton, T. B. (1984). Mother–child interaction around a teaching task: an African–American comparison. *Child Development*, *55*, 1252–64.
Feinman, S. (1982). Social referencing in infancy. *Merrill-Palmer Quarterly*, *28*, 445–70.
Field, T. M., Sostek, A. M., Vietze, P., and Liederman, P. H. (eds) (1981). *Culture and early interactions.* Hillsdale, NJ: Lawrence Erlbaum Associates.
Gaskins, S. and Lucy, J. A. (1987, May). The role of children in the production of adult culture: a Yucatec case. Presented at the meeting of the American Ethnological Society, San Antonio.

Goody, E. N. (1978). Towards a theory of questions. In E. N. Goody (ed.). *Questions and politeness* (pp. 17–43). Cambridge: Cambridge University Press.

Gunnar, M. R. and Stone, C. (1984). The effects of positive maternal affect on infant responses to pleasant, ambiguous, and fear-provoking toys. *Child Development*, 55, 1231–36.

Harkness, S. and Super, C. M. (1977). Why African children are so hard to test. *Annals of the New York Academy of Sciences*, 285, 326–31.

Heath, S. B. (1982). What no bedtime story means: narrative skills at home and school. *Language in Society*, 11, 49–76.

Heath, S. B. (1983). *Ways with words: language, life, and work in communities and classrooms.* Cambridge: Cambridge University Press.

John-Steiner, V. (1984). Learning styles among Pueblo children. *Quarterly Newsletter of the Laboratory of Comparative Human Cognition*, 6, 57–62.

Jordan, C. (1977, February). Maternal teaching, peer teaching, and school adaptation in an urban Hawaiian population. Presented at the meeting of the Society for Cross-Cultural Research, East Lansing.

Laboratory of Comparative Human Cognition (1983). Culture and cognitive development. In W. Kessen (ed.). *History, theory, and methods.* In P. H. Mussen (ed.). *Handbook of child psychology* (Vol. 1, pp. 294–356). New York: Wiley.

Leiderman, P. H., Tulkin, S. R., and Rosenfeld, A. (eds.) (1977). *Culture and infancy: variations in the human experience.* Orlando, FL: Academic Press.

Leont'ev, A. N. (1981). The problem of activity in psychology. In J. V. Wertsch (ed.). *The concept of activity in Soviet psychology.* Armonk, NY: M. E. Sharpe.

Luria, A. R. (1976). *Cognitive development: its cultural and social foundations.* Cambridge, MA: Harvard University Press.

Luria, A. R. (1987). Afterword to the Russian edition. In R. W. Rieber and A. S. Carton (eds.). *The collected works of L. S. Vygotsky. Vol. 1. Problems of general psychology.* New York: Plenum.

Mehan, H. (1979). *Learning lessons.* Cambridge, MA: Harvard University Press.

Michaels, S. and Cazden, C. B. (1986). Teacher/child collaboration as oral preparation for literacy. In B. B. Schieffelin and P. Gilmore (eds). *The acquisition of literacy: ethnographic perspectives* (pp. 132–54). Norwood, NJ: Ablex.

Morelli, O. A., Fitz, D., Oppenheim, D., Nash, A., Nakagawa, M., and Rogoff, B. (1988, November). Social relations in infants' sleeping arrangements. Presented at the meeting of the American Anthropological Association, Phoenix.

Nash, M. (1967). *Machine age Maya.* Chicago: University of Chicago Press.

Newson, J. (1977). An intersubjective approach to the systematic description of mother–infant interaction. In H. R. Schaffer (ed.). *Studies in mother–infant interaction* (pp. 47–61). Orlando, FL: Academic Press.

Ochs, E. and Schieffelin, B. B. (1984). Language acquisition and socialization: three developmental stories and their implications. In R. Schweder and R. LeVine (eds). *Culture and its acquisition.* Chicago: University of Chicago Press.

Richman, A. L., Miller, P. M., and Solomon, M. J. (1988). The socialization of infants in suburban Boston. In R. A. LeVine, P. M. Miller, and M. M. West (eds). *Parental behavior in diverse societies* (pp. 65–74). San Francisco: Jossey-Bass.

Rogoff, B. (1981a). Adults and peers as agents of socialization: a highland Guatemalan profile. *Ethos*, 9, 18–36.

Rogoff, B. (1981b). Schooling and the development of cognitive skills. In H. C.

Triandis and A. Heron (eds). *Handbook of cross-cultural psychology* (Vol. 4, pp. 233–94). Rockleigh, NJ: Allyn & Bacon.

Rogoff, B. (1982a). Mode of instruction and memory test performance. *International Journal of Behavioral Development, 5,* 33–48.

Rogoff, B. (1982b). Integrating context and cognitive development. In M. E. Lamb and A. L. Brown (eds). *Advances in developmental psychology* (Vol. 2). Hillsdale, NJ: Lawrence Erlbaum Associates.

Rogoff, B. (1990). *Apprenticeship in thinking: cognitive development in social context.* New York: Oxford University Press.

Rogoff, B. and Gauvain, M. (1986). A method for the analysis of patterns, illustrated with data on mother–child instructional interaction. In J. Valsiner (ed.). *The individual subject and scientific psychology* (pp. 261–90). New York: Plenum.

Rogoff, B., Gauvain, M., and Ellis, S. (1984). Development viewed in its cultural context. In M. H. Bornstein and M. E. Lamb (eds). *Developmental psychology.* Hillsdale, NJ: Lawrence Erlbaum Associates.

Rogoff, B., Mistry, J., Göncü, A., and Mosier, C. (1993) Guided participation in cultural activity by toddlers and their caregivers. *Monograph of the Society for Research in Child Development, 236,* Vol. 58, No. 8.

Rogoff, B., Sellers, M. J., Pirotta, S., Fox, N., and White, S. H. (1975). Age of assignment of roles and responsibilities to children: a cross-cultural survey. *Human Development, 18,* 353–69.

Schieffelin, B. B. and Eisenberg, A. R. (1984). Cultural variation in children's conversations. In R. Schiefelbusch and J. Pickar (eds). *The acquisition of communicative competence* (pp. 377–420). Baltimore: University Park Press.

Scribner, S. (1974). Developmental aspects of categorized recall in a West African society. *Cognitive Psychology, 6,* 475–94.

Scribner, S. and Cole, M. (1973). Cognitive consequences of formal and informal education. *Science, 182,* 553–9.

Scribner, S. and Cole, M. (1981). *The psychology of literacy.* Cambridge, MA: Harvard University Press.

Sorce, J. F., Emde, R. N., Campos, J., and Klinnert, M. D. (1985). Maternal emotional signaling: its effect on the visual cliff behavior of 1-year-olds. *Developmental Psychology, 21,* 195–200.

Sorenson, E. R. (1979). Early tactile communication and the patterning of human organization: a New Guinea case study. In M. Bullowa (ed.). *Before speech: the beginning of interpersonal communication* (pp. 289–305). Cambridge: Cambridge University Press.

Taylor, D. (1983). *Family literacy.* Exeter, NH: Heinemann.

Trevarthen, C., Hubley, P., and Sheeran, L. (1975). Les activités innées du nourrisson. *La Recherche, 6,* 447–58.

Vygotsky, L. S. (1978). *Mind in society: the development of higher psychological processes.* Cambridge MA: Harvard University Press.

Vygotsky, L. S. (1987). *Thinking and speech.* In R. W. Rieber and A. S. Carton (eds). *The collected works of L. S. Vygotsky* (N. Minick, trans; pp. 37–285). New York: Plenum.

Ward, M. C. (1971). *Them children: a study in language learning.* New York: Holt, Rhinehart & Winston.

Weisner, T. S. and Gallimore, R. (1977). My brother's keeper: child and sibling caretaking. *Current Anthropology*, *18*, 169–90.

Wertsch, J. V. (1984). The zone of proximal development some conceptual issues. In B. Rogoff and J. V. Wertsch (eds). *Children's learning in the "zone of proximal development"* (pp. 7–18). San Francisco: Jossey-Bass.

Wertsch, J. V. (1985). *Vygotsky and the social formation of mind.* Cambridge, MA: Harvard University Press.

Wertsch, J. V. and Stone, C. A. (1979, February). A social interactional analysis of learning disabilities remediation. Paper presented at the International Conference of the Association for Children with Learning Disabilities, San Francisco.

Whiting, B. B. and Edwards, C. P. (1988). *Children of different worlds: the formation of social behavior.* Cambridge, MA: Harvard University Press.

Whiting, J. W. M. (1981). Environmental constraints on infant care practices. In R. H. Munroe, R. L. Munroe, and B. B. Whiting (eds). *Handbook of cross-cultural human development* (pp. 155–79). New York: Garland.

Zinchenko, V. P. (1985). Vygotsky's ideas about units for the analysis of mind. In J. V. Wertsch (ed.). *Culture, communication and cognition: Vygotskian perspectives* (pp. 94–118). Cambridge MA: Cambridge University Press.

Chapter 14

Socialization of Nso children in the Bamenda Grassfields of Northwest Cameroon*

A. Bame Nsamenang and Michael E. Lamb

In this chapter, we explore the ideas and values that give directive focus to the socialization of children – especially Nso children – in the Bamenda Grassfields of Cameroon, shaping their affective, social, and cognitive development. We highlight the continuity across generations in the face of discontinuities introduced by such factors as formal schooling, urbanization, and the economic necessity for parents, especially mothers, to relinquish their traditional roles and participate instead in the labor force. Familial values foreshadow the content and mode of cultural transmission and, eventually, the pattern of intelligence children acquire and cherish.

Today, the Bamenda Grassfields roughly comprise the Northwest Province, one of Cameroon's 10 Provinces. It is composed of several centralized fondoms (ethnic kingdoms) whose demographic history reveals population movements, the adjustment of cultural patterns, and the adaptation of customary traditions to accommodate the savanna (grassland) ecology (Nkwi, 1983). Nso is the largest of the Bamenda Grassfields fondoms.

We begin the chapter by providing a conceptual framework for the understanding of Nso enculturation. Next, we describe the values and beliefs of parents from the Bamenda Grassfields, emphasizing the high value placed on community spirit, social intelligence, and the demarcation of life stages by social criteria. Third, we describe the processes of socialization, showing how parents and other members of society directly and indirectly influence the acquisition of socioaffective and cognitive skills by young children. The findings are placed in context in the final section.

Conceptual framework

Human development always occurs in a specific ecoculture, defined by geography, history, climate, and the sociocultural system. Physical and social

---

* This is an edited version of a chapter that appeared in *Cross-Cultural Roots of Minority Child Development*, Hillsdale, New Jersey: Lawrence Erlbaum Associates, 1994.

environments provide culturally meaningful experiences for their occupants. In addition, the sociocultural system offers the agents, institutions, and scripts that permit and facilitate the humanization of offspring and their social integration and enculturation (Nsamenang, 1992a). Whereas some – especially Western – cultures emphasize academic, technological, or cognitive modes of social integration, other – especially African – cultures place primacy on socioaffective socialization (cf. Mundy-Castle, 1968, 1974). Both social and technological intelligence are embedded in the ecocultural imperatives that focus and channel individuals to acquire the right moral posture, the appropriate social graces, and the technical skills required for acceptable, functional membership in the culture. The school system is a cultural artifact of external colonial origin that, like other societal institutions, "provides practice in the use of specific tools and technologies for solving particular problems" (Rogoff, 1990, p.191).

In virtually every culture, there are three major sources of parenting values: folk knowledge, ontogenetic experience, and literature or expert advice (Harkness, Super, and Keefer, 1992). The directive force of each of these sources of knowledge varies across individuals and societies, depending on an array of such background factors as world view, social history, education, religion, place of residence, and so on.

Values and norms

Collectivism

A frame of reference that focuses on the individual does not come to the West African readily. To use the terminology of Triandis (1985, 1989), West Africans differ from Europeans and North Americans in their perspective, which is collectivistic rather than individualistic. In the West-African world view, "man is not man on his own; the individual gains significance from and through his relationships with others" (Ellis, 1978, p. 6). The nature of the self is interdependent more than independent (Kitayama and Markus, 1992; Markus and Kitayama, 1991).

Traditional life fosters a sense of community that supports individuals and families; it accords them a deep and comforting sense of tradition and community, thus promoting collective responsibility and rendering individual and collective miseries more bearable (Nsamenang, 1992a). This kind of social ecology certainly enriches some but undoubtedly stifles other aspects of development. For instance, losses in individuality and personal freedom are as inevitable as gains in the security that may accrue from active membership in an extensive supportive social network (Nsamenang, 1989b).
[. . .]

Social intelligence and social stages

West Africans clearly distinguish between illiterate intelligence and print (literate) intelligence, as well as between social and technological intelligence. For example, the Baoulé of the Ivory Coast, like other West Africans, hold that "One may know how to read and write but be quite dumb" because one "may know much of Baoulé intelligence without knowing much on paper" (Dasen, 1984, p.427). Thus, the common feeling is that academic or technological intelligence must be integrated with social intelligence because a person's abilities are useless unless they are applied for the good and well-being of the social group (Dasen, 1984).

For West Africans, the infant is a "project-in-progress" (Nsamenang, 1992a), and stages of social integration are demarcated using social rather than biological signposts. In other words, children are progressively assigned different roles at different life stages, depending on their perceived level of social competence rather than on their biological maturation. This emphasis reflects the fear that some persons who are mature in chronological terms may behave irresponsibly. Thus, the notion of social intelligence changes according to ontogenetic status, as children are systematically incorporated into different roles at different stages of life. Without functional integration into "this" or "that" social stratum, individuals are considered mere "danglers" to whom the designation of *person* does not appropriately and fully apply. Therefore, human offspring need other humans to attain full selfhood: a sense of self cannot be attained without reference to the broader community.

However alien it may appear to those whose world view promotes individualism and freedom of choice, students of West Africa must understand the significance of deference and obedience to elders and superiors, including older siblings. Such orientations are the product of a socialization pattern in which emphasis is placed on notions of authority, with a fear that children will be "spoiled" if they do not serve or perform some duties.

In summary, Nso parents have a particular ethnotheory of development (Kagitçibasi and Berry, 1989; Super and Harkness, 1986). Socialization in the Bamenda Grassfields exposes children to a social reality and a set of experiences that channel their development with different purposes and in different directions than children in Western cultures. Socialization is not organized to train children for academic pursuits or to become individuals outside the ancestral culture. Rather, it is organized to teach social competence and shared responsibility within the family system and ethnic community. As Kagitçibasi (1982, 1985, 1988) noted, this pattern of socialization is typical of traditional, rural agricultural groups with large, close-knit family systems.

Contemporary forces and changes

Currently, however, the social system is in total flux. For instance, children are frequently more knowledgeable in matters of contemporary life than their (illiterate) parents. This reverses traditional roles and makes it difficult for parents to be role models or to teach their children "the correct ways of the world." Unfortunately, little is known of the extent to which traditional values are being renounced in the process. To address the question, we have attempted to explore ideas and attitudes of parents of diverse ages, backgrounds, and economic stations. In this research, we are comparing the ideas and values of parents and grandparents, from rural and urban areas, both to give life and voice to the Nso people, as well as to quantify the extent to which there is a generational change in belief systems. Interestingly, although we sought largely to describe popular beliefs, many respondents claimed that our interview was the first time they had ever verbalized their parenting attitudes and practices.

An empirical study

Our study involved 211 men and 178 women who were either parents (persons who had at least one child 10 years of age or younger) or grandparents (persons with at least one grandchild). Nearly 25% (95) claimed adherence to African theodicy, 58% (226) were Christian, and 18% (68) were Moslem. Two thirds (263) lived in Nso villages, whereas the remainder (126) lived in Bamenda town.

[. . .]

One parent in each of the 389 families volunteered to participate in the study. Data were collected using the Lamnso (Nso language) version of the open-ended Parent Interview Guide (PIG), developed by Nsamenang and Lamb (1988).

[. . .]

When asked why Nso people might want children, respondents tended to give answers that conveyed a very traditional view of the value of children. Thus, 56% mentioned the performance of domestic chores, another 30% mentioned running errands, and 36% mentioned respect for and obedience to parents. However, when asked about their expectations of children, only 27% mentioned filial service. Instead, half mentioned good progress in school, and 45% "success in life," although less than a fifth of them mentioned either vocational or social competence specifically. Of the mothers and fathers, 40% felt that boys and girls should be raised differently, although they were not very articulate about the specific ways in which they should be treated differently.

There was considerable agreement between parents and grandparents in the perceptions of desirable and undesirable characteristics. "Good children" were expected to display (a) obedience and respect (90%), (b) filial service (89%), (c) hard work (91%), (d) helpfulness (90.5%), (e) honesty (100%), and (f) intelligence (100%). In contrast, the following characteristics were deemed undesirable: (a) disobedience and disrespect (92.5%), (b) laziness (96.7%), (c) fighting (95.4%), (d) greed (99%), (e) playfulness (99%), (f) fearfulness (100%), and (g) inquisitiveness (100%). These preferences were especially prominent in the responses of the rural parents, who endorsed slightly more traditional views than did the urban respondents.

[. . .]

Ellis (1978) noted that all African cultures have been exposed to extremely powerful external cultural influences. This fact notwithstanding, Nso socialization values seem to be of indigenous origin, reflecting "the influence of a well-defined cultural background that has strong roots" (Palacios, 1990, p. 150), rather than of alien world views and cultural values. For example, parental concern with school progress, although not strictly an indigenous motive, derives from a cultural belief in social competence. It also derives from the realization that, because education and farming are incompatible (Ohuche and Otaala, 1982), contemporary realities demand that raising children be guided by what provides the basic requirements for functional and meaningful citizenship. A plausible explanation for the tenacity of Nso socialization values in face of potent modifying forces is Uka's (1966) claim that childrearing beliefs "are never amenable to easy changes because beliefs about the origin of life are not held on a rational basis" (p. 29).

[. . .]

Socialization and social interaction

As explained earlier, the socialization values of the Nso primarily stress social competence and social intelligence. However, "children's cognitive development is inseparable from the social milieu in that what children learn is a cultural curriculum: from the earliest days, they build on the skills and perspectives of their society with the aid of other people" (Rogoff, 1990, p. 190). Parents in the Bamenda Grassfields are oriented toward this pattern of cognitive socialization. The ecoculture is represented to children by the people who instruct, explain, or act as models; "but even more pervasively by those with whom the child cooperates in shared functioning" (Tharp et al., 1984, p. 93) – hence the significance of the ubiquitous peer group in West-African communities.

How then do children learn from adults? Adults construct the social context, shaping the behavioral settings that provide opportunities for children to learn and develop. In general, "much knowledge filters from adults through older children" (Tharp et al., 1984, p. 100) who are co-participants, alongside adults, in the routine tasks and activities of teaching younger ones. For example, among the Wolof of Senegal, some of the basic social norms of the culture begin to be systematically and, in the main, painlessly instilled into the children almost immediately after weaning through the powerful agency of the sibling group in this process (Rabain, 1979; Zempleni-Rabain, 1973).

In the Bamenda Grassfields, as elsewhere in West Africa, social and cognitive stimulation literally begin at birth. Although Ellis (1978) suggested that West Africans do not talk to babies because they believe that babies do not "hear" baby talk, West Africans freely tell babies whom they resemble, what their names should be, what they signify, and what sort of adults they are expected to become.

Nso children learn culturally appropriate forms of behavior and thought systems primarily through "hands-on" socialization (Harkness et al., 1992; Whiting and Whiting, 1975), more under the mentorship of older siblings and peers than of parents or other adults. Regularities or continuities in the ecoculture and the expectable social roles and culturally defined life stations "provide material from which the child abstracts the social, affective, and cognitive rules of the culture, much as the regularities of grammar are abstracted from the speech environment" (Super and Harkness, 1986, p. 552).

The reported parental values encourage "an active apprenticeship experience for children" (Weisner, 1987, p. 238). Typically completed by adolescence, this apprenticeship usually proceeds while the individual learns to perform the domestic tasks essential for family and community survival. By encouraging children to take part in different tasks of social life, to observe seniors, and to listen to and later join in discussions, the Grassfields' adolescent acquires a sense of solidarity and responsibility as he or she completes his or her physical, intellectual, and practical education (*Encyclopedie de la Republique unie du Cameroun*, 1981).

The fact that parents endorse the assignment of responsibilities to children underscores their assumption that children are capable and socially responsible (Nsamenang, 1989a). It also connotes an awareness of developmental milestones. The pattern of socialization is such that children are systematically "graduated" from one role position to another until they assume adult roles. By permitting children to learn to speak and act within "pivot roles," the Grassfields' caregiving milieu facilitates this kind of socialization.

Children in the Bamenda Grassfields acquire cultural competence primarily by way of (a) observation and imitation, (b) attention to the themes of prototypic stories, and (c) co-participation in major activities, especially within the peer culture (peer mentoring). Socialization practices depend on watching and learning from adults, siblings, and peers in role rehearsal or reenactment when error occurs.

Children are expected to observe the performance of tasks and to imitate or rehearse them, especially while playing with peers, with little if any instruction. Consequently, it is common to find toddlers playing mother or father, typically under the corrective surveillance and mentorship of elder siblings or peers, rather than that of parents and other adults. Strangers are often surprised at the extent to which children spontaneously respond to sign or symbolic (hidden) language.

As in Hawaii, learning occurs in a mode of "enterprise engagements," whereby the child actually performs or attempts to practice the skill or task that he or she is learning. The emphasis is not on "I'll tell you how to do it," but on "watch," "listen," participate," and "try" (Tharp *et al.*, 1984, p. 101).

Shared functioning of this sort eases the passage from play to productive activities (Bekombo, 1981). For example, because it is not a West-African tradition to provide children with commercial toys, they are usually encouraged to create their own playthings or to make miniature replicas of common objects. The immediate recognition of such "creations" as "products" certainly enhances the creator's self-image. "The process of making these toys teaches the children how to plan work, organize tools and materials, to make measurements, and to conceive of objects in three-dimensional space . . . " (Segall *et al.*, 1990, p. 123). The genesis of the rich tradition of African sculpture, embroidery, leather works, and pottery is rooted in this pattern of socialization.

Traditionally, an adult is responsible for a particular task or service and is usually assisted by children and younger persons of the same gender (Oppong, 1983) who are expected to observe and rehearse the roles, especially during play. At moments in a typical scenario, the child must defer to older persons, especially parents, older siblings, and peer mentors. Later, the child becomes the primary enactor of the same role, "assuming responsibility and utilizing decision-making skills" (Weisner, 1987, p. 248), particularly in sibling care and collective performance of chores.

This implies that the child's behavior varies depending on whether older, more senior members of the social niche are present. When older persons are available, the child's direct responsibility and activities are limited and stereotyped because of "the child's low status rank in that setting at that point in time. A later point in the day may find the child to be relatively senior in rank and in charge, directing other children and displaying" more responsible behaviors (Weisner, 1987, p. 248).

Nso children experience the intimacies and conflicts engendered in social interactions within extended families and peer groups from an early age. The "free" climate and absence of overt adult control within the peer culture breed conflicts as well as compromises. They permit and facilitate peer mentoring and perspective-taking (Dunn and Kendrick, 1982), encouraging children to notice and even anticipate the feelings and needs of younger children. This mode of informal education offers opportunities to learn performance skills, particularly during play, as well as social skills such as learning to (a) collaborate or disagree, (b) lead and follow others, (c) cooperate in collective responsibility, and (d) disagree about diverse tasks and issues (Nsamenang, 1989b). It also provides opportunities for children to discover their abilities and limitations and to learn adult roles. "Children learn skills for household, child-care, and self-care tasks by participating in those tasks with and, initially, under the supervision of, older children" (Tharp *et al.*, 1984, p. 100). "When these children are not involved in tasks and chores, they are usually engaged in friendly sociability" (Weisner, 1987, p. 253). Thus, it is clear that the extent of child-to-child socialization of skills, affect, and cognition is substantial – perhaps far more extensive and developmentally more critical than direct parental socialization (Nsamenang, 1992b).

Many lessons are also taught with proverbs and folktales that contain moral themes and describe virtuous acts for children to emulate. Other tales are suffused with myth to give a sense of the strange and fearful, and thus deter children from wrongdoing (Nsamenang, 1992c). Failure to learn to behave appropriately is admonished, usually with a terse proverb or verbal abuse, and sometimes punished by the withdrawal of privileges. In general, children accept punishment without rancor and accept that parents have the "right to deal with them" as they think fit (Jahoda, 1982, p. 110). Parents rationalize the strictness of their behavior by referring to such folk maxims as: "If a person is trained strictly then that person becomes a good person" (Ellis, 1978, p. 156); "to beat a child is not to hate it" (Jahoda, 1982, p. 111). Children accept parental punishment because "my father punishes me to correct my behavior; my mother rebukes me because I am wrong" (Ellis, 1968, p. 156).

The authority of elder siblings over youngsters is derived from parental authority over children. With such authority, older siblings are usually charged with the care and supervision of younger brothers and sisters whom they can reprimand and correct. A distinctive feature of socialization in much of West Africa is that parents do not retain the sole responsibility for fostering socioaffective and cognitive development in children; children themselves are co-participants in other children's socialization. Thus, socialization is a shared responsibility among members of the social network. In fact, a daily routine that keeps both parents away from the home at work, the market-place, or other activities, and a heavy work load for adult women in particular, encourages sibling care (Weisner, 1987).

Child caregiving generally involves multiage, multigender groups with charges ranging in age from 20 months to 6 or 7 years under the supervision and guidance of one or two children (usually girls) aged 8 to 10 years (Nsamenang, 1992b). After they have been weaned, infants spend most of their time in such peer and sibling groups, and most socialization takes place in this context (Nsamenang, 1992b). Although children spend a considerable amount of time in child-to-child interactions and engage in creative activities by themselves, they are still constrained by adult norms because "a mechanism of self-regulation exists in the fraternal group, due to the power inherent in the word of the adult, whose direct intervention is no longer needed" (Zempleni-Rabain, 1973, p. 233).

Because Bamenda Grassfields children spend far more time in direct interaction with one another than with adults, they, like their Kokwet counterparts, learn to talk more from each other than from their parents (Super and Harkness, 1986). Children also consolidate the social graces, moral imperatives, and skilled activities of their culture through shared functioning within the peer culture.

Child caregiving is but one form of children's roles. Child "work" is an indigenous mechanism for social integration – a strategy that keeps children in contact with existential realities and the activities of daily life. It represents the participatory component of social integration, an essential preparation for economic and civic participation in societies where the school system has distanced itself from the realities and basic skills needed for agrarian economies (Serpell, 1992). In summary, children in the Bamenda Grassfields are integrated into a dense social network characterized by norms of sharing and exchange. Unfortunately, many aspects of this traditional system of education and socialization are under siege, disrupted by the competing demands of the "modern" nation-state.

Summary and conclusion

The central idea in this chapter is that children's affective and cognitive development is dependent on and shaped by their sociocultural milieu. Social, affective, and cognitive skills are closely linked to the familiar tasks and interpersonal encounters in which children and adults engage. They are embedded in the social contexts and cultural institutions in which the skills are demanded and enacted. Communication, both verbal and non-verbal, is central to the acquisition of cultural forms of behavior and thought. Cultural differences in social orientation, affective posture, and cognition emerge primarily from varying ecocultural imperatives, the socialization values that direct how children progress toward adult cultural forms, and the extent to which cultural repertoires of skills and competencies are encoded in the language. Within shared-function social niches characterized by deference and hierarchy, Nso children, in collaboration with their families, are active participants in their own socialization. The emphasis in socialization is on obedience and social responsibility, rather than on proficiency in verbal expression and individuality. Despite obvious Westernization, Nso socialization values are still deeply rooted in their ancestral traditions. Nevertheless, compared with the parents of previous generations, contemporary parents may be less certain about their socialization values and the changing world for which their children are being prepared.

References

Bekombo. M. (1981). The child in Africa: Socialization, education and work. In G. Rodgers and G. Standing (Eds), *Child work, poverty, and underdevelopment*. Geneva: World Health Organization.

Dasen, P. R. (1984). The cross-cultural study of intelligence: Piaget and the Baoule. *International Journal of Psychology*, *19*, 407–434.

Dunn, J. and Kendrick, C. (1982). The speech of two- and three-year-olds to infant siblings. *Journal of Child Language*, *9*, 579–595.

Encyclopedie de la Republique unie du Cameroun [Encyclopedia of the United Republic of Cameroon]. (1981). Douala, Cameroon: Eddy Ness.

Ellis, J. (1968). Child-rearing in Ghana, with particular reference to the Ga tribe. Unpublished master's thesis, University of Ghana, West Africa.

Ellis, J. (1978). The child in West African society. In J. Ellis (Ed.), *West African families in Britain*. London: Routledge & Kegan Paul.

Harkness, S., Super, C. M., and Keefer, C. H. (1992). Learning to be an American parent: How cultural models gain directive force. In R. G. D'Andrade and C. Strauss (Eds), *Cultural models and motivation*. New York: Cambridge University Press.

Jahoda, G. (1982). *Psychology and anthropology*. London: Academic Press.

Kagitçibasi, Ç. (1982). *The changing value of children in Turkey*, Honolulu, HI: East–West Population Institute.

Kagitçibasi, Ç. (1985). Culture of separateness – culture of relatedness. In *1984: Vision and reality*. Columbus: Ohio State University Press.

Kagitçibasi, Ç. (1988). Diversity of socialization and social change. In P. R. Dasen, J. W. Berry, and N. Sartorius (Eds), *Health and cross-cultural psychology: Toward applications* (pp. 25–47). Newbury Park, CA: Sage.

Kagitçibasi, Ç. and Berry, J. W. (1989). Cross-cultural psychology: Current research and trends. *Annual Review of Psychology*, *40*, 493–531.

Kitayama, S. and Markus, H. R. (1992, May). Construal of the self as cultural frame: Implications for internationalizing psychology. Paper prepared for symposium on Internationalization and Higher Education, University of Michigan, Ann Arbor.

Markus, H. and Kitayama, S. (1991). Culture and the self: Implications for cognition, emotion, and motivation. *Psychological Review*, *98*, 224–253.

Mundy-Castle, A. C. (1968, December) Paper presented at a workshop in social psychology organized by the Makerere Institute of Social Research and Syracuse University, New York.

Mundy-Castle, A. C. (1974). Social and technological intelligence in Western and non-Western cultures. *Universitas*, *4*, 46–52.

Nkwi, P. N. (1983). Traditional diplomacy, trade and warfare in the nineteenth century Western Grassfields. *Science and Technology Review*, *1*, 3–4.

Nsamenang, A. B. (1989a, May). Another style of socialization: The caregiving child. Poster presented to the Conference of the Iowa International Network on Personal Relationships, Iowa City, IA.

Nsamenang, A. B. (1989b, July). The social ecology of Cameroonian childhood. Poster presented to the International Society for the Study of Behavioral Development, Jyvaskyla, Finland.

Nsamenang, A. B. (1992a). *Human development in cultural context: A third-world perspective*. Beverly Hills, CA: Sage.

Nsamenang, A. B. (1992b). Early childhood care and education in Cameroon. In M. E. Lamb, K. J. Sternberg, C. P. Hwang, and A. G. Broberg (Eds), *Child care in context: Cross-cultural perspectives* (pp. 419–439). Hillsdale, NJ: Lawrence Erlbaum Associates.

Nsamenang, A. B. (1992c). Perceptions of parenting among the Nso of Cameroon. In B. S. Hewlett (Ed.), *Father–child relationship: Anthropological perspectives* (pp. 321–343). Hawthorne, NY: Aldine.

Nsamenang. A. B. and Lamb, M. E. (1988). Parent interview guide (Unpublished interview schedule). Bethesda, MD: National Institute of Child Health and Human Development.

Ohuche, R. O. and Otaala, B. (1982). *The African child in his environment* Oxford, England: Pergamon.

Oppong, C. (Ed.). (1983). *Female and male in West Africa*. London: Allen & Unwin.

Palacios, J. (1990). Parents' ideas about the development and education of their children: Answers to some questions. *International Journal of Behavioral Development*, *13*, 137–155.

Rabain, J. (1979). *L'Enfant du lignage: Du sevrage a la classe d'age* [Child of the lineage: From weaning to age-graded peer group]. Paris: Payot.

Rogoff, B. (1990). *Apprenticeship in thinking: Cognitive development in social context*. New York: Oxford University Press.

Schwartz, T. (1981). The acquisition of culture. *Ethos*, *9*, 4–17.

Segall, M. H., Dasen, P. R., Berry, J. W., and Poortinga, Y. H. (1990). *Human behavior in global perspectives*. New York: Pergamon.

Serpell, R. (1992). African dimensions of child care and nurturance. In M. E. Lamb, K. J. Sternberg, C. P. Hwang, and C. P. Broberg (Eds), *Child care in context: Cross-cultural perspectives* (pp. 463–476). Hillsdale, NJ: Lawrence Erlbaum Associates.

Super, C. M. and Harkness, S. (1986). The developmental niche: A conceptualization at the interface of child and culture. *International Journal of Behavioral Development*, *9*, 545–569.

Tharp, R. G., Jordan, C., Speidel, G. E., Au, K. H.-P., Klein, T. W., Calkins, R. P., Sloat, K. C. M., and Gallimore, R. (1984). Product and process in applied developmental research: Education and the children of a minority. In M. E. Lamb, A. L. Brown, and B. Rogoff (Eds), *Advances in developmental psychology* (Vol. 3, pp. 91–141). Hillsdale, NJ: Lawrence Erlbaum Associates.

Triandis, H. C. (1985). Collectivism vs individualism: A conceptualization of a basic concept in cross-cultural social psychology. In C. Bagley and G. K. Verma (Eds), *Personality, cognition and values*. London: MacMillan.

Triandis, H. C. (1989). Cross-cultural studies of individualism and collectivism. In *Nebraska Symposium on Motivation*. Lincoln: University of Nebraska Press.

Uka, N. (1966). *Growing up in Nigerian culture*. Ibadan, Nigeria: Ibadan University Press.

Weisner, T. S. (1987). Socialization for parenthood in sibling caretaking societies. In J. B. Lancaster, J. Altman, A. S. Rossi, and L. R. Sherrod (Eds), *Parenting across the lifespan: Biosocial dimensions* (pp. 237–270). Hawthorne, NY: Aldine de Gruyter.

Whiting, B. B. and Whiting, J. W. M. (1975). *Children of six cultures: A psycho-cultural analysis*. Cambridge, MA: Harvard University Press.

Zempleni-Rabain, J. (1973). Food and the strategy involved in learning fraternal exchange among Wolof children. In P. Alexandre (Ed.), *French perspectives in African studies* (pp. 221–233). Oxford, England: Oxford University Press.

Chapter 15

Komatsudani: a Japanese preschool*

Joseph J. Tobin, David Y. H. Wu and Dana H. Davidson

Komatsudani Hoikuen, a Buddhist preschool located on the grounds of a three-hundred-year-old temple on a hill on the east side of Kyoto, has one hundred and twenty students. Twelve of these children are infants, under eighteen months, who are cared for in a nursery by four teachers. Another twenty Komatsudani children are toddlers, under three years of age, who are cared for in two groups of ten by three teachers and an aide. The rest of the children are divided into three-year-old, four-year-old, and five-year-old, classes each with twenty-five to thirty students and one teacher. Each class has its own homeroom within the rambling old temple. In this chapter, a description of the children's day is the starting-point for discussion about Japanese approaches to child development, as expressed in the comments of a teacher at the school (Fukui-sensei) and her supervisor (Higashino-sensei), as well as preschool educators from China and the USA.

A day at Komatsudani

The school opens each morning at 7:00 a.m., and soon after, children begin to arrive, brought to school by a parent or grandparent on foot, by bicycle, or, less commonly, by car. By 9:00 most of the children have arrived, put their lunch boxes and knapsacks away in the cubbyholes in their homerooms, and begun playing with their friends in the classrooms, corridors, or playground. Some of the older children stop by the nursery to play with the babies or to take toddlers for a walk on the playground. At 9:30 the "clean-up" song is played over loudspeakers audible throughout the entire school area. As the children put away toys, balls, and tricycles, the music changes from the clean-up song to the equally lively exercise song, and, with their teachers' encouragement, the children form a large circle on the playground and go through ten minutes of stretching, jumping, hopping, and running together in a group.

*   This is an edited version of a chapter that appeared in *Preschool in Three Cultures*, New Haven, Connecticut: Yale University Press, 1989.

Taisō (morning exercise) complete, the "end-of-exercise-go-to-your-room" song comes over the loudspeakers, and the children, led by their teachers, run in a line into the school building, class by class, each child removing his or her shoes in the entranceway. Inside, the twenty-eight four-year-olds of Momogumi (Peach Class) enter their homeroom, which is identified by pictures of peaches on the door and the word *momogumi* written in *hiragana* (the phonetic alphabet). The Momogumi room has four child-sized tables, each with eight chairs that are covered with gaily embroidered seat covers the children have brought from home.

The *Momogumi-san-tachi* (Peach Class children) come in and stand behind their chairs while their teacher, Fukui-sensei, a twenty-three-year-old university graduate, plays the morning song on a small organ and the two *toban* (daily monitors) lead the class in singing:

> *Sensei. Ohayō* (Teacher, good morning)
> *Minna-san. Ohayō* (Everyone, good morning)
> *Genki ni asobimashō* (Let's play happily)
> *Ohayō, Ohayō* (Good morning, good morning)

After attendance is taken by roll call, a counting song is sung to the tune of "Ten Little Indians" to determine how many children are in school that day. Fukui-sensei then leads the children in recitation, each of her words echoed by the children's choral response:

> Today . . . *today* . . . is May . . . *is May* . . . twenty-sixth . . . *twenty-sixth* . . . today . . . *today* . . . twenty-eight children . . . *twenty-eight children* . . . have come to school . . . *have come to school* . . . today . . . *today* . . . is a fine spring day . . . *is a fine spring day.*

These housekeeping chores and morning ceremonies completed, the children begin a workbook project that lasts about thirty minutes. Under Fukui-sensei's direction, they color in boxes indicating how many pigs are riding bicycles in a picture, how many foxes are riding motor-cycles, and how many rabbits are riding in cars.

Throughout this workbook session there is much laughing, talking, and even a bit of playful fighting among tablemates. As the workbook pages are completed, the children grow increasingly restive; some leave their seats to talk and joke with friends or visit the bathroom. Fukui-sensei makes no attempt to stop them, but forges ahead with the task at hand, "How many rabbits are there? Color in one of these boxes for each rabbit you see in the car."

Workbooks completed, Fukui-sensei puts a sticker on each child's finished pages as the books are brought to her. After they turn in their workbooks, the children begin to play loud chasing games, *janken* (paper–rock–scissors), and to engage in mock karate and sword fights. After twenty minutes or so of this free and raucous play and trips to the bathroom, the children, heeding their teacher, grab their *bentō* (lunch box) from their cubbies and take their place at the table, arranging their lunch and cups and placemats in front of them. The food from home is supplemented by one warm course provided by the school and by a small bottle of milk. All the children sing in unison, under the direction of the daily *toban* and to the accompaniment of the organ:

> *Obentō o tabete iru toki* (As I sit here with my lunch)
> *Okāsan no koto kangaeru* (I think of mom)
> *Oishii na* (I bet it's delicious)
> *Nan daro ka* (I wonder what she's made?)

After the song the children stand, bow their heads, put their hands together, and recite:

> *Hotokesama* (Buddha)
> *Arigatō* (Thank you)
> *Otōsama* (Honorable Father)
> *Okāsama* (Honorable Mother)
> *Arigatō Gozaimashita* (We humbly thank you)

Lunch itself is loud and lively, each child eating at his or her own pace, which varies from less than ten minutes for some to forty-five minutes or more for others. Fukui-sensei sits with the children at one of the four tables each day (the children keep careful track of whose turn it is), talking quietly to the children near her and occasionally using her chopsticks to help a child snare a hard-to-pick-up morsel from his *bentō*.

When children finish eating, they wrap up their chopsticks, placemats, and lunch boxes. Some girls ask Fukui-sensei for help in properly tieing up their lunch things in the large cloth *furoshiki* they have brought from home.

By this time children who have finished with their lunch have gathered on the narrow covered porch adjoining their classroom. Four girls stand in a cluster, talking and laughing. Several boys are singing songs from television cartoon shows, engaging in more mock-fighting, and playing a game with flash cards meant to teach the *hiragana* syllabary. One especially energetic boy, Hiroki, who has been much the noisiest and most unruly child in the class throughout the day (though it must be said that no one has tried very hard to control or quiet him), becomes increasingly raucous in his play, his mock karate blows becoming by the moment more like actual punches. While Fukui-sensei is quietly exhorting children still in the classroom to finish their lunches and clear and wipe off the tables, Hiroki has been throwing flash cards off the porch balcony. Midori runs inside to tell the teacher of

Hiroki's misconduct and is encouraged by Fukui-sensei with a "go get 'em" sort of pat on the back to return to the balcony and deal with the problem herself. After sweeping up rice and other detritus from underneath the tables in the classroom, Fukui-sensei comes out to the porch, announcing to the children that it is clean-up time. Catching sight of Hiroki pounding on the back of another boy, Fukui-sensei chooses to ignore the ruckus and returns to the classroom to help stragglers wrap up their lunches. Out on the porch, Hiroki and the other children continue to throw cards, sing, and fight. When Fukui-sensei returns, to the balcony ten minutes later to urge the children to finish cleaning up the flash cards they've been playing with, she again finds Hiroki involved in a fight and again does little to break it up.

Eventually the fighting ceases, the cards are cleaned up (with Fukui-sensei's help), and the children settle in at their desks, where they sing the after-lunch song ("Thank you: It was delicious . . .") and then rest with their heads on the table for five minutes or so while Fukui-sensei plays a soothing tune on the organ.

Rest time over, a major origami project begins, the children led by their teacher through a twenty-step process resulting in the production by each child of an inflatable ball. ("Can you make a triangle? Good, now take these two ends of the triangle and make a smaller triangle, as I'm doing. . .") The project takes about thirty minutes, with another ten minutes spent by Fukui-sensei on repairs to improperly folded balls that refuse to inflate. Soon the children, paper balls in hand, run laughing and screaming from the classroom to the playground for an extended period of outdoor play.

Back inside later in the afternoon, Fukui-sensei reads a story to the class, using not a book but a *kami shibai* (literally, a paper show), a series of a dozen or so large cards, each with a picture on one side and the narrative to be read by the teacher on the back. A song and a snack round out the schedule. After singing the good-bye song ("Teacher, good-bye, everyone, good-bye . . ."), the children go outside to the playground once more to play until their parents come for them between 4:30 and 6:00 p.m.

Dealing with a difficult child

On the day we videotaped at Komatsudani, Hiroki started things off with a flourish by pulling his penis out from under the leg of his shorts and waving it at the class during the morning welcome song. During the workbook session that followed, Hiroki called out answers to every question the teacher asked and to many she did not ask. When not volunteering answers, Hiroki gave a loud running commentary on his workbook progress ("now I'm coloring the badger, now the pig . . .") as he worked rapidly and deftly on his assignment. He alternated his play-by-play announcing with occasional songs, entertaining the class with loud, accurate renditions of their favorite cartoon themes, complete with accompanying dancing, gestures, and occasional instrumental flourishes. Despite the demands of his singing and announcing schedule, Hiroki managed to complete his workbook pages before most of the other children (of course, those sitting near him might have finished their work faster, had they a less distracting tablemate).

Work completed, Hiroki threw his energies wholeheartedly into his comedy routine, holding various colored crayons up to the front of his shorts and announcing that he had a blue, then a green, and finally a black penis. We should perhaps mention at this point that penis and butt jokes were immensely popular with four-year-old children in nearly every school we visited in all three countries (China, Japan and USA). The only noticeable difference was that such humor was most openly exhibited in Japan, where the teachers generally said nothing and sometimes even smiled, whereas American teachers tended to say something like "We'd rather not hear that kind of talk during group time," and in China such joking appeared to have been driven largely underground, out of adult view.

As the children lined up to have Fukui-sensei check their completed work, Hiroki fired a barrage of pokes, pushes, and little punches at the back of the boy in front of him, who took it all rather well. In general, as Hiroki punched and wrestled his way through the day with various of his male classmates, they reacted by seeming to enjoy his attentions, by becoming irritated but not actually angry, or, most commonly, by shrugging them off with a "That's Hiroki for you" sort of expression. The reaction of Satoshi, who cried when Hiroki hit him and stepped on his hand, was the exception to this rule.

During the singing of the prelunch song, Hiroki, who was one of the four daily lunch monitors, abandoned his post in front of the organ to wrestle with a boy seated nearby. While eating, Hiroki regaled his classmates with more songs and jokes. Finishing his lunch as quickly as he had his workbook, Hiroki joined other fast diners on the balcony, where he roughhoused with some other boys and then disrupted a game by throwing flash cards over the railing to the ground below. The other children seemed more amused than annoyed by these antics, although one girl, Midori, ran inside to tattle to the teacher, who was by now sweeping up under the tables. Fukui-sensei sent Midori back to the balcony with some instructions. A few minutes later, Fukui-sensei walked out to the balcony, looked over the railing, and said, "So that's where the cards are going." Soon several of the children, with the conspicuous exception of Hiroki, ran down the steps to retrieve the fallen cards. This proved to be a losing battle as Hiroki continued to rain cards down upon them. It was now that Hiroki (purposely) stepped on Satoshi's hand, which made him cry. Satoshi was quickly ushered away from the scene by Midori, the girl who had earlier reported the card throwing. Midori, arm around Satoshi's neck, listened very empathetically to his tale of woe and then repeated it several times with gestures to other girls who came by: "Hiroki threw cards over the balcony and then he stepped on Satoshi's hand, and then he punched Satoshi like this." The girls then patted Satoshi on the back, suggesting that in the future he find someone other than Hiroki to play with.

Lunch over and the room cleaned up, Fukui-sensei returned to the balcony where, faced with the sight of Hiroki and another boy involved in a fight (which consisted mostly of the other boy's being pushed down and climbed on by Hiroki), she said neutrally, "Are you still fighting?" Then she added, a minute later, in the same neutral tone. "Why are you fighting anyway?" and told everyone still on the balcony, "Hurry up and clean up [the flash cards]. Lunchtime is over. Hurry, hurry." Hiroki was by now disrupting the card clean-up by rolling on the cards and putting them in his mouth, but when he tried to enter the classroom Fukui-sensei put her hand firmly on his back and ushered him outside again. Fukui-sensei, who by now was doing the greatest share of the card picking-up, several times blocked Hiroki from leaving the scene of his crime, and she playfully spanked him on the behind when he continued to roll on the cards.

The rest of the day wound down for Hiroki in similar fashion. At one point in the afternoon Komatsudani's assistant principal, Higashino-sensei, came over to Hiroki and talked softly but seriously to him for three or four minutes, presumably about his behavior. During the free playground period that ends the day, Hiroki played gently with a toddler and more roughly with some of the older boys. He was finally picked up shortly before 6:00 by his father, making him one of the last children to go home.

Interpreting Komatsudani

In these first pages we have provided a description of a day at Komatsudani as recorded in our videotape. Now we turn to Komatsudani's teachers and administrators' explanations of our videotape.

The perspective of Hiroki's teachers

When we showed Fukui-sensei and her supervisors the film we made in her classroom, we were most curious to see if Fukui-sensei would be at all defensive about the way the film depicted her dealing with – and seeming not to deal with – Hiroki's misbehavior. Both Fukui-sensei and her supervisors told us they were very satisfied with the film and felt that it adequately captured what they are about. Indeed, they said, the way Fukui-sensei dealt with Hiroki in the film, including ignoring his most provocatively aggressive and exhibitionistic actions, reflected not negligence but just the opposite, a strategy worked out over the course of countless meetings and much trial and error.

Japanese preschool teachers and, to a lesser extent, preschool administrators generally are pragmatists rather than ideologues, and thus their discipline and classroom-management techniques tend to be eclectic, focusing on what works. And for most Japanese teachers, for most situations, what seems to work best is a non-confrontational, energetic, friendly, yet affectively neutral approach.

[. . .]

Komatsudani's teachers are careful not to isolate a disruptive child from the group by singling him out for punishment or censure or excluding him from a group activity. Similarly, whenever possible they avoid direct confrontations with children. As Higashino-sensei told us, "The moment a teacher raises her voice or begins to argue or plead with a child, the battle is already lost." Catherine Lewis (1984) suggests that Japanese teachers think their most powerful source of influence over children is their being viewed unambivalently as benevolent figures; teachers are therefore careful to avoid interacting with children in unpleasant, stressful, emotionally complex ways. (Of course this is an ideal: teachers in Japan, as in other countries, occasionally lose their tempers and say and do things they later regret.) Lewis also suggests that teachers maintain order without intervening directly in children's disputes and misbehavior by encouraging in various ways other children to deal with their classmates' troubles and misdeeds.

Fukui-sensei's approach to dealing with Hiroki illustrates each of these Japanese strategies of discipline and classroom management. She scrupulously avoided confronting or censuring Hiroki even when he was most provocative. (Indeed, she remained composed even during those moments when it was all we could do not to drop our camera and our posture of scholarly neutrality and tell Hiroki to cut it out.)

Fukui-sensei encouraged the other children in the class to take responsibility for helping Hiroki correct his behavior – for instance, when she told Midori to go do something herself about Hiroki's throwing cards. And Fukui-sensei diligently avoided excluding Hiroki from the group in any way. In fact, she insisted he participate in the balcony clean-up to the bitter end, though his presence clearly made the others' task much more difficult.

[. . .]

Intelligence and behavior

Why does Hiroki misbehave? Dana Davidson, who has a background working in assessment and in gifted and talented programs in the USA, speculated that Hiroki's behavior problems might be related to his being intellectually gifted and easily bored. When we returned to Komatsudani to talk with the staff about our tape, Davidson suggested to Fukui-sensei and Higashino-sensei that Hiroki might be quicker and smarter than the other children and that this "giftedness" (which proved to be a very difficult concept for us to express in Japanese) might provide at least a partial explanation for Hiroki's behavior in the classroom. Fukui and Higashino looked a bit confused and even taken aback by this suggestion:

Higashino: Hiroki's intelligence is about average, about the same as most other children, I would say.

Davidson: But he finishes his work so quickly. And he looks like he knows the words to so many songs. He just seems so bright, gifted.

Higashino: What do you mean by "gifted"?

Davidson: Well, by "gifted" in the United States we mean someone who is exceptionally talented in some area, like intelligence. Like Hiroki who seems to be so smart, so quick. He has such a bright look in his eyes. We would say that a boy like this has a lot of energy and is so bright that he is quickly bored by school. To me, it seems that his incidents of misbehavior occur when he has finished his work before the other children. He provokes his teacher and the other children in an attempt to make things more exciting, better matched to the pace and level of stimulation he needs.

Higashino: It seems to me that Hiroki doesn't necessarily finish his work first because he is smarter than the other children. Speed isn't the same thing as intelligence. And his entertaining the other children by singing all those songs is a reflection not so much of intelligence as it is of his great need for attention.

The different perspectives that are apparent in this discussion suggest important cultural differences between Americans and Japanese, not only in definitions of and attitudes toward intelligence, but also in views of character, behavior, and inborn dispositions and abilities.

One possible explanation for Higashino's insistence that Hiroki is of only average intelligence might lie in the great value Japanese teachers and contemporary Japanese society place on equality and on the notion that children's success and failure and their potential to become successful versus failed adults has more to do with effort and character, and thus with what can be learned and taught in school, than with raw inborn ability. Thus, even if we were to assume, for the moment, that Hiroki is in fact of exceptional intelligence, his Japanese teachers would be hesitant to acknowledge this special gift because of their reluctance to explain or excuse behavior in terms of differences in abilities. We suspect that many Japanese preschool teachers and administrators we talked with found our questions about giftedness hard to understand, in part because of their distaste for the notion of inborn abilities and their suspicion that the identification of children as having unequal abilities would inevitably lead to an unequal allocation of educational effort, resources, and opportunity.

The Japanese do, of course, recognize that children are born with unequal abilities and that some children have special gifts, but Japanese society in general and teachers in particular view the role of education and perhaps especially of primary and preschool education as to even out rather than sort out or further accentuate these ability differences. Thus one Japanese pre-school teacher responded to our description of programs for gifted children in American preschools by saying, "How sad that by age three or four a child might already be labeled as having less chance for success than some of his classmates."

[. . .]

Since Japanese pedagogy, from primary school on, stresses the need for children to be able to work productively and harmoniously in large mixed-ability classrooms and in smaller mixed-ability work groups (*han*: see M. White, 1987, pp. 114–115), preschool teachers see as one of their chief tasks encouraging children to see themselves as like others in fundamental ways. This includes an effort by teachers to speed up and encourage slower learners and at times to slow down more talented members of the class. Teachers do not view as a disservice this holding back and slowing down of the more capable students, because they believe that students benefit in the long run by developing an increased sensitivity to the needs of others and a sense of security that comes from being a member of a seemingly homogeneous group.

When Japanese preschool teachers do talk about inborn differences in ability, it is usually in the context of praising a child of less than average ability for struggling to keep up with his classmates. For instance, on school sports days it is not unusual to hear a teacher say: "Look at him go! His legs are shorter than everyone else's, but he sure is trying hard." When Fukui-sensei watched the section of our film that shows Kuniko, a pudgy, slowish sort of girl, struggling to make an origami ball with her fat, uncooperative fingers, the teacher said, "Things never come easily to Kuniko, but she really gives it her best."

The Japanese, in contrast to Americans, seldom view intelligence in a young child as a value-free trait that can be used to good or bad result (LeVine and White, 1986). Rather, Japanese tend to view intelligence as closely linked to moral action and to associate the terms *oriko* (smart) and *atama ga ii* (intelligent), when applied to young children, with traits such as *kashikoi* (obedient, well behaved), *erai* (praiseworthy), *ki ga tsuku* (sensitive to others), and *wakareru* (understanding). Intelligence or smartness in a child in America is just as likely to be associated with asocial (naughty) as with desirable behaviors, as can be seen in such expressions as "smart-alec," "too smart for her own good," and "don't get smart with me, young man." But in Japan misbehavior is more likely to be associated with being not smart enough (lacking understanding). Lewis gives the example of the teacher who explains her young charges' misbehavior on an outing (throwing rocks at carp) by saying, "If they *understood* it was wrong, they wouldn't do it" (1984, p. 77).

One often hears Japanese preschool teachers and Japanese adults in general use the word *smart* to compliment preschool-aged children for a variety of socially approved actions, including behaviors Americans might consider indicative of intelligence but also behaviors that to Americans have little or nothing to do with intelligence, such as helping to clean up. In these situations the words *smart* and *intelligent* are used more or less synonymously with the words *well behaved* and *praiseworthy*.

These linguistic and cultural factors make it difficult for Hiroki's teachers to think of him as especially intelligent. Their reasoning would go, "If he is so smart, why doesn't he understand better? If he understood better, he would behave better."

Misbehavior as a dependency disorder

Many of the Chinese and American parents, teachers, and administrators who watched "A Day at Komatsudani" were bothered by Hiroki's misbehavior and Fukui-sensei's failure, in their minds, to respond adequately to his provocations. Our respondents offered various explanations of Hiroki's problem. Many of the Chinese respondents called him spoiled. For example, one teacher asked: "Why are the teachers so easy on a boy who is so spoiled, a boy so used to having his own way and monopolizing so much of his class's energy and attention?" Higashino-sensei responded:

> I suppose you could say in a sense that Hiroki is spoiled, but we believe that his problem is really just the opposite. To me spoiling implies getting too much care and attention, and Hiroki's problem is that he hasn't really received enough of the right kind of care and attention and doesn't know how to receive care and attention. Hiroki, you know, is a boy without a mother. He has been cared for since his birth by his father, who had him while still really just a boy himself, and by his father's mother. Without a mother things have of course been hard for Hiroki. He wants attention and to be cared for [*amae*], but he asks for it in the wrong way. We would only make this problem worse by yelling at him.

Higashino-sensei's description of Hiroki's problem as an inability to know how appropriately to solicit, receive, and respond to care and attention is consistent with Doi Takeo's work on *amaeru* (a Japanese word meaning to presume on the benevolence of others, to be dependent) and specifically with Doi's discussion of common disorders of *amae*: "*Tereru* describes the behavior of a child or an adult who is ashamed of showing his intimate wish to *amaeru*. . . . *Hinekureru* describes the behavior of a child or an adult who takes devious ways in his efforts to deny the wish to *amaeru*" (1974, p. 148). It is believed in Japan, as Doi explains, that *amae*, dependence, is not something an infant is born with, but something that must be learned and developed, and thus something that must be taught. Following this logic, we can see that a child like Hiroki, who is diagnosed as being awkward in the ways of *amae*, must be given help to overcome this problem.

From a Japanese perspective, Hiroki's problems have both an emotional and a cognitive component, as he suffers from an inability to *amaeru* (to be dependent) and an inability to *wakareru* (to understand; White and LeVine, 1986). But this inability to understand and thus to know how to be more obedient and more sensitive to others is attributed by his teachers to his lack of a mother and thus to his emotional problem, his inability to be dependent.

Some Japanese (including Doi) would reason that even if Higashino is wrong and Hiroki's outbursts do not stem from a disorder of *amae*, nothing would be lost and much might be gained by approaching Hiroki as if frustrated, misguided dependency urges were the core of his problem. Fukui-sensei and the other teachers at Komatsudani often diffuse children's anger and overcome their stubbornness by assuming that behavior problems such as these are at heart problems of *amae* and responding with concern and sympathy rather than anger or criticism.

[. . .]

Developing self-control

The staff of Komatsudani believes that children best learn to control their behavior when the impetus to change comes spontaneously through interactions with their peers rather than from above (Lewis, 1984). Thus Hiroki's best chance to learn self-control lies not in encounters with his teachers but in play with his classmates.

Fukui: I told Midori and the other children that if they felt it was a problem, then they should deal with Hiroki's throwing the cards. If I tell Hiroki to stop, it doesn't mean much to him, but if his classmates tell him, it affects him.

Tobin: But he kept throwing the cards even after Midori told him to stop.

Fukui: Because he's so proud. He won't ever change his behavior if someone orders him to. He'll always do the opposite in the short run. But in the long run, his classmates' disapproval has a great effect on him.

We saw an example of the effect of social opprobrium on Hiroki when we visited Komatsudani nine months after making the original videotape. On this day we were surprised to find Hiroki, now five years old, sitting alone at the front of the classroom, eating his lunch, while the other children ate at tables of six and seven.

Tobin:	(to a group of children eating lunch): Why is Hiroki eating alone up there?
Several children:	[We] don't know.
Tobin:	(to Hiroki) Why are you eating up here in front of the room alone.
Hiroki:	Because I'm the leader of the class!
Tobin:	(to some other children) Is that why? Is Hiroki the leader of the class?
Yasuko:	(laughing) He thinks he's the leader, anyway.
Kenichi:	(on his knees, bowing toward Hiroki) O Honorable Leader.
Tobin:	(quietly, to Fukui) Is Hiroki really up there because he's the leader? Did you put him up there?
Fukui:	No, no one told him to sit there. It just kind of evolved. I guess the other children gradually got tired of sitting next to him during lunch because he is so irritating. Everyone eventually decided they didn't like sitting next to him, and he's very proud, so he came up with this idea on his own of eating in the front of the room as the leader. It seems to be working out, so I'm letting him sit there.

We asked Fukui, Higashino, and Yoshizawa, Komatsudani's director, if it was not a problem for the other children that Hiroki causes so much chaos in the classroom and uses up a disproportionate amount of staff time and energy.

Yoshizawa:	No, I'd say it was just the opposite. The children in that class are lucky to have Hiroki there. [Laughing] He makes things interesting.
Higashino:	It's hard on Fukui-sensei, but I wouldn't say it's hard on the other children. By having to learn how to deal with a child like Hiroki, they learn to be more complete human beings.

When we returned to Komatsudani and showed the children in the peach class a twenty-minute version of the tape we made in their class, Hiroki at first was proud and excited, dancing in front of the monitor, making peace signs and pointing to himself on the screen. But halfway through the screening, as Hiroki could be seen on the monitor stepping on Satoshi's hand, and as the children in the class shouted out, "Look at what Hiroki is doing to Satoshi!" Hiroki grew agitated, then visibly embarrassed, and he covered first his ears, then his eyes, with his hands. Hiroki stood for a moment in front of the monitor and tried to distract his classmates with a silly song, but children shouted at him to get out of the way so they could see. Hiroki then pulled Kazumi to his feet, and led him off to play outside while the video continued inside.

Childlike children

The answer given most frequently at Komatsudani to our question, "What kind of child are you trying to produce in your preschool?" was a "*kodomo-rashii kodomo*" (a childlike child). What, then, is a childlike child? Irene Shigaki (1983) polled Japanese teachers on this question and found the traits most highly valued by preschool teachers to be *omoiyari* (empathy), *yasashii* (gentleness), *shakaisei* (social consciousness), *shinsetsu* (kindness), and *kyōchōsei* (cooperativeness). White and LeVine (1986) add to this list of traits *sunao* (obedience), *akarui* (enthusiasm), *genki/hakihaki* (energy, liveliness), *gambaru/ nintai* (perseverance), and *yutaka* (openness, receptivity).

Our interviews with Japanese preschool teachers generally corroborated Shigaki's and White and LeVine's descriptions of the Japanese concept of the ideal preschooler. We should point out, however, that in addition to these highly valued, traditionally Japanese traits, teachers and administrators also voiced appreciation for some values associated with the West, such as *dokoritsu* (independence), *kosei* (individuality), and *sōzō* (creativity).

Of the people we interviewed, we found preschool administrators who are Christian, Western-trained, or advocates of a particular philosophy of preschool education (Montessori, Waldorf, and so on) most likely to emphasize the importance of these individualistic Western values and to criticize traditional Japanese values as old-fashioned, incompatible with creativity, and conducive to a revival of militarism or fascism. In contrast, conservative or traditional preschool administrators we talked with often disparaged creativity, self-actualization, and individuality as false values transplanted from the West that threaten to undermine Japanese character and culture. Most administrators, however, attempt to steer a path between traditionalism and Westernism and to stress the need to offer a curriculum and a teaching style that balance the values of group harmony, interpersonal sensitivity, and obedience with creativity, independence, and self-confidence. And nearly all preschool teachers, who tend to be more pragmatic and less concerned with issues of pedagogy and ideology than their bosses, espouse a balanced approach mixing traditionally Japanese and Western values.
[. . .]

Group life

Virtually all the Japanese preschool teachers who viewed our tape of an American preschool contrasted the individualism (*kojin-shugi*) they perceive as characterizing preschool in America with the groupism (*shuudan-shugi*) they believe characterizes their own society and schools. The more Westernized Japanese teachers and administrators thought the individualized educational style they associated with America a good thing; others thought a group approach better; and some said that a mixture of the two would be ideal. But virtually all agreed that groupism is the key distinguishing factor between Japanese and American preschools and, indeed, between the two societies.

By groupism, these Japanese teachers and administrators did not mean, evidently, what they saw on our film of a Chinese preschool. Dong-feng, the Chinese preschool in our study, was rated as very group-oriented by Americans and Chinese – "too much" so by sixty-five percent of the American and eighty-five percent of the Chinese parents, teachers, and administrators who viewed "A Day at Dong-feng." Thus we were surprised to find that sixty percent of our Japanese respondents rated Dong-feng as having "too few group activities," especially since it looked to us as though the children in the Chinese school do everything in groups. Principal Kumagai of Senzan Yōchien explained, "Well, of course, I can't say for sure why you got the results you did, but I wonder if perhaps to Japanese viewers the Chinese school didn't lack a real group feeling. Everyone doing the same thing at the same time isn't the same as real group life, is it?"

Several other Japanese informants explained that the real problem they saw in the Chinese preschool film was not groupism but the manner in which group-oriented behaviors are taught to children. They felt that the best alternative to Chinese authoritarianism was not American individualism but a gentler, more joyful, more understanding, flexible, Japanese sort of groupism. Yano-sensei said: "What bothers me isn't so much that the Chinese teachers expect the children in their schools to do things in groups so much as that their group activities seem so joyless and unspontaneous, so lacking in human feeling." The key point here, we believe, lies in the Japanese teacher's assumption that groupism can and should be compatible with human feeling. This runs contrary to the assumption many of our American informants made that groups are necessarily unspontaneous, repressive, and antithetical to human feeling.

To teachers at Komatsudani, groupism does not inhibit the expression of natural feelings and joyful behavior. Rather, it makes possible the fullest realization of something truly human, the experience of camaraderie, of fusion, of unity with something larger than the self. A child's humanity is realized most fully not so much in his ability to be independent from the group as in his ability to cooperate with and feel part of the group (M. White, 1987, pp. 184–185). Assistant Principal Kumagai of Senzan Yōchien, commenting on the Chinese preschool tape, said:

> The feeling I get from this tape is that, to the Chinese, groupism means subjugating yourself to the group. But to us, in our preschools, we don't tell children they must be in groups, or they must participate in group activities, or that doing things alone is selfish or bad. Instead, we just try to show them, to teach them the fun and the sense of belonging one can get only by being part of a group.

Most Japanese preschools attempt to steer a course between the loneliness and anomie they associate with individualism in the West and the tyranny and authoritarianism they associate with Chinese and, for some, with traditional Japanese forms of group organization. One teacher commented: "This film of the Chinese preschool reminds me of what Japanese education must have been like in the prewar period, when duty and sacrifice were stressed and teachers were expected to be very severe with children."

How is this supposedly gentler, more humane, more joyful sort of group feeling achieved in the Japanese *yōchien* and *hoikuen*? The first and most obvious signs of groupism are the uniforms worn by most *yōchien* students. Typically, a *yōchien* child goes to school wearing navy-blue knee-length overalls or skirt, a white shirt with a round collar, a lightweight navy-blue coat, a felt or straw hat with a ribbon or tassel, and a blue or red knapsack. Each *yōchien*'s uniform is distinctive, differing from the uniforms of neighboring *yōchien* most dramatically in the shape and color of the hat. Some *yōchien* uniforms are nautical in flavor. Some use capes instead of jackets, or they are maroon instead of navy blue. Uniforms in Tokyo and in wealthy areas of any city are likely to be fancier, those in rural and poor districts somewhat plainer and more functional (lightweight blue smocks instead of jackets and shorts). But nearly always the *yōchien* child goes to school dressed in clothes that clearly identify him to the outside world, to his classmates, and to himself as a preschooler and, more important, as a member of a particular preschool, a special group.

Children in *hoikuen*, where uniforms are usually not worn, wear badges on their shirts bearing their family and given names, their school's name, and the name of their class. Children at many *hoikuen* are picked up by distinctive, brightly painted buses; others walk to school behind teachers carrying school flags. Some schools also issue children a pin or emblem in the shape of the flower or animal that has provided the name for their class. On school sports days children wear special sports uniforms and brightly colored caps, color-coded to identify them by their class. On field trip days *hoikuen* children wear special white, yellow, or red caps, which, besides making it easier for the teachers to round up runaways and strays, give the children a feeling of shared group membership while in the outside world.

Uniforms and other symbols such as pins, name tags, and signs over shoe lockers, cubbies, and classroom doorways emphasize the child's membership in a school and, within a school, in a class. Upon enrolling in preschool, a Japanese child receives not just a uniform but a group identity. She becomes instantly *Komatsudani Hoikuen no Midori-gumi no Yoko* (Yoko of the Green Class of Komatsudani Day-care Center) or *Senzan Yōchien no Tampopo-gumi no Chiseko* (Chiseko of the Dandelion Class of Senzan Nursery School). Japanese children are referred to throughout their preschool careers not only by the name of their class but also by their school-year cohort, as, for instance, in such announcements heard at school during the day as "*Nencho-gumi-san-tachi*

[Children in the oldest classes], please line up by the swings for morning exercise," or "*Onenshō-san-tachi* [the first-year students] will now entertain you with their version of 'Snow White and the Seven Dwarfs.'"

Competition among classes in a school is often used to encourage group effort and to promote a sense of group identification and pride. During morning clean-up time at Senzan Yōchien, for example, the assistant principal's voice can be heard over the loudspeaker in each room intoning, "Let's see which class can be first to clean up their room today." During school sports days (*undōkai*), vigorous competition between classes of children and even between the mothers or fathers of a class is enthusiastically encouraged by the teachers, principals, and spectators watching the races. In these events the feeling of group solidarity experienced by the losers, who commiserate with each other, "*Zannendakedo, gambarimashita* [It's too bad, but we did our best]", is perhaps even more keenly felt than is the collective sense of group accomplishment of the victors.

Japanese preschools achieve nearly one hundred percent participation levels in group activities by making it extremely easy as well as attractive to be included. Indeed, the harder trick in a Japanese preschool would be to figure out a way not to be included in group activities. For example, during the schoolwide daily morning exercise period, though teachers hope that all the children will participate actively, no child is ordered or threatened or even very aggressively cajoled into running, jumping, or stretching with the others. Rather, children are included in the group simply by virtue of being in proximity during an activity. At Komatsudani, the three-, four-, and five-year-olds perform their calisthenics in a large circle while the toddlers and infants are assembled in a smaller circlelike constellation in the middle. The nine-month-old babies are bounced about by the teachers to the rhythm of the exercise song, slightly older babies crawl or stumble around on their own with teachers or older children occasionally coming over to manipulate their arms through calisthenic motions, and the two-year-olds, if the spirit moves them and the flesh is willing, attempt to imitate the older children. The few children who choose to use the exercise period as an opportunity to stage a mock-karate battle, to discuss last night's television cartoon show, or just to watch are rarely pressured to do the exercises everyone else is doing. Thus each child in the school is given an opportunity to participate in his or her own fashion. Those who cannot or will not join in the activity are periodically encouraged to join in by teachers and other children, but usually they are allowed to refrain from active participation or, more accurately, to participate in their own way even if that way involves seeming not to participate actively.

By having very liberal, easy-to-satisfy criteria for what constitutes participation in group activities, a Japanese preschool like Komatsudani readily includes children from the youngest to the oldest and from the most easily distracted and badly behaved to the most attuned and energetic in daily group activities.

Classroom activities follow a similar form. During the thirty-minute origami session we taped, most of the children followed Fukui-sensei's step-by-
step instructions and made origami balls, but two boys made paper airplanes
instead, and one did not make anything at all, choosing to while away the
time crumpling up and smoothing out his paper and talking and joking with
his friends. The teacher encouraged all the children in the class to participate,
and she asked the children who chose not to why they were not joining in, but
the tone of voice in which she asked was neutral and inquisitive rather than
supplicating or threatening, and she readily accepted their explanations, and
even any lack of explanation, for not making origami balls with the other
children.

Discipline is handled in much the same manner. Children in Japanese
preschools can commit misdeeds of varying severity without being either
emotionally or physically excluded from the group. We saw in Japan none of
the time-out periods of forced isolation from the group that we so frequently
witnessed in American preschools. By being extremely reluctant to label
children's behavior as bad or beyond the pale, Japanese preschools reduce the
number of situations that could potentially lead to confrontation and thus to
a child's feeling ostracized or in any other way excluded from the group.
Because group participation is so attractive and ubiquitous, the threat of not
being included, when it does arise, is all the more frightening. As group
membership becomes more and more the norm of social interaction and the
primary source of identity for a Japanese preschool youngster, even the
implicit threat of exclusion becomes terrifying, and explicit exclusion (for
example, by *ijime* – scapegoating) a potentially dangerous problem.

Thus Fukui-sensei's gentle warning to a group of recalcitrant cleaner-
uppers that if they did not finish soon the class would begin the next activity
without them proved to be enough to get the children involved in their task.
When this approach fails, the teacher may resort to a stronger and more
dramatic threat, using a form of child management that has long been a
favorite of Japanese mothers: the teacher simply calls, theatrically, over her
shoulder to the children still in the sandbox as she begins to lead the children
in line back inside, "*Ja, sayōnara* (well, then, good-bye)." This usually does
the trick, but if the children in the sandbox are incorrigible offenders, as
occasionally happens, other children in the class will run back to the sandbox
and plead with their wayward classmates to come along quickly. These good
children feel most acutely the misbehaving children's shame, imminent loss
of teacher approval, and the risk they are running of isolation from the group,
so they implore the stragglers to see the error of their ways and come back to
the fold before it's too late. But, of course, it is rarely if ever too late to join or
rejoin the group in the world of the Japanese preschool.
[. . .]

References

Doi, T. (1974). *The anatomy of dependence*. Tokyo: Kodansha International.

Doi, T. (1986). *The anatomy of the self*. Tokyo: Kodansha International.

LeVine, R., and White, M. (1986). *Human conditions: The cultural basis of educational development*. London: Routledge & Kegan Paul.

Lewis, C. (1984). Cooperation and control in Japanese nursery schools. *Comparative Education Review, 28*, 69–84.

Montessori, M. (1912). *The Montessori method*. (3rd ed.). New York: Frederick A. Stokes.

Shigaki, I. (1983). Child care practices in Japan and the United States: How do they reflect cultural values in young children? *Young Children, 38*, 13–24.

White, M. (1987). *The Japanese educational challenge: A commitment to children*. New York: Free Press.

White, M., and LeVine, R. (1986). What is an Ii Ko? In R. Stevenson, H. Azuma, and K. Hakuta (Eds), *Child development and education in Japan*. New York: W. H. Freeman.

Index